ILLUSTRATED HISTORY OF
PRO
FOOTBALL

ILLUSTRATED HISTORY OF
PRO
FOOTBALL

BY ROBERT SMITH

GROSSET & DUNLAP
A FILMWAYS COMPANY
Publishers • New York

REVISED EDITION

For NORA my lovely daughter

PUBLISHED SIMULTANEOUSLY IN CANADA
LIBRARY OF CONGRESS CATALOG CARD NUMBER: 78-120421
ISBN 0-448-14416-6
1977 EDITION
PRINTED IN THE UNITED STATES OF AMERICA

Acknowledgment

For generous and ungrudging help in gathering material and pictures for this book, special thanks are due to Leo V. Lyons, the Official Historian of the National Football League and one of its original franchise-holders; and to Jim Kensil, Joe Blair, Jerry Wilcox, Don Smith, Joe Cahill, and Bill Dudley.

PICTURE CREDITS

VERNON J. BIEVER: 6–7, 150, 153, 161, 172, 200–201, 203, 204, 206, 209, 210, 214, 216, 217, 218, 223, 225, 226, 228, 232 (3,4), 233, 235, 238, 239, 243 (left), 254, 257, 262, 263, 264–265, 266–267, 268, 269, 270–271, 272, 276, 277 (top left, bottom center), 296, 304 (right), 309, 312, 318

AUTHOR'S COLLECTION: 8, 31, 32, 34, 35, 36–37, 38–39, 40, 44–45, 46–47, 52–53, 58–59, 75, 77 (top right), 92

CULVER PICTURES, INC.: 11, 12–13, 14–15, 16–17, 18–19, 21, 22–23, 26–27, 28–29, 48, 50–51

LEO V. LYONS, Pro Football Picture Service: 55, 56, 62–63, 64, 66–67, 70, 72–73, 76, 77 (bottom), 81, 82, 85, 86, 88–89, 91, 93, 94–95, 96–97, 99, 102–103, 108, 116, 138 (left), 144–145

BROWN BROTHERS: 106, 109, 112, 115, 118–119, 121, 130, 132, 135, 137, 139, 175, 186 (bottom), 190, 232, (1,2)

UNITED PRESS INTERNATIONAL: 77 (top left and center), 122, 123, 128–129, 138 (right)

PRO FOOTBALL HALL OF FAME: 69, 156, 183, 186 (top and center), 220

NATE FINE PHOTOS: 159, 162, 166, 167, 170–171, 190, 228, 243 (bottom), 277 (top right)

WIDE WORLD PHOTOS: 289, 298 (left), 304 (left), 308, 317

THOMAS J. CROKE: 277 (bottom left), 283, 313

JOHN E. BIEVER: 290, 298 (right)

DETROIT LIONS FOOTBALL CLUB: 193, 255

CINCINNATI BENGALS (Ron Cochran): 198

ST. LOUIS FOOTBALL CARDINALS: 277 (bottom right)

A classic power sweep by the San Francisco 49ers against the Green Bay Packers. The ball is carried by John David Crow (44), who exhibits the choppy stride favored by pro coaches.

Contents

Tin Cans
and Pigs' Bladders

ANYONE who has ever been prompted to kick an empty can along the road in front of him, or put his foot to an abandoned hat, has savored the ancient beginnings of football. Somebody a thousand years ago or more, idle as ourselves and walking God knows where, sought to keep himself company one day by using his feet to propel some stray object along ahead of him. Then another person, a small boy most likely, undertook to boot it back. So the two of them, using just their feet, played a game of one's trying to kick the object past the other. What elemental urge was satisfied in this way, who knows? Was it origi-

nally a way of bringing some added treasure home while the hands were full? Whatever it was, it has moved boys and young men for uncounted ages, and the game still continues without any real end to it, despite the millions of small victories that have been scored along the way.

When there were more than two boys, each might aim a kick at the prize and drive it off in a private direction. It could not have taken long for the boys to discover that there was more joy in the game if there were only two directions in which the object could be moved. In this way, "sides" of a sort

9

Lawson Fiscus, Princeton's great halfback, is considered the first professional football player. This photograph was taken in 1896 when he was playing for the Greensburg professional football club.

were developed, with each side owning a goal toward which it would combine to drive the talisman—be it ball, bladder, or chunk of wood. Depending on the number involved in the game, the goals might be the two ends of a street, the border dividing town from town, the opposite edges of a broad field. Kids who start this sort of competition hit upon their own rules without much discussion. It would simply have taken the fun out of the game if the stuffed bag or empty purse or bit of random rubbish could have been picked up and thrown or carried to the goal. So the game remained a foot game. When it was planned deliberately, with an object that would roll easily used as the marker, the game became football. And of course in any large gathering of boys, as on the day of a meeting or an election, or at school, there could be a dozen, or three dozen, or even a hundred who might join the push.

"Hustling Over Large Footballs"— an Excuse for Violence

Football at the start was, and remained for many centuries, the simplest game imaginable. It could be played anywhere—in a schoolyard, in a cobbled cloister, over pastures or beaches, through narrow streets, on a plowed field, over hills and across water courses. It belonged to every nation. Even the savage Indians, long before white men settled among them, were playing on the New England beaches a form of football, using as the object to be kicked to the goal a small round pellet not much larger than a modern handball.

In England, and in America until fairly recent times, the most elemental form of football was merely a mass shoving contest, in which a whole school class, or a whole school, might use the ball as nothing but a token to excuse the visiting of all sorts of violence upon the persons of the enemy. Two streets in a city might be chosen as the goals, or one group of young men might merely give themselves the task of kicking the ball into some sanctuary guarded by a rival group. Then the young men would set upon each other with fist, open hand, or foot, and amid yells of triumph, howls of dismay, and screams of pain, the contest would surge back and forth until the ball had been lodged in the goal or the attackers had been hopelessly scattered.

As far back as a man could reach in recorded history—had history ever bothered to make note of all the games boys played—he would probably find some form of football. In the fourteenth century, in England, King Edward II had already been pressed to the point of outlawing the game, in an order that spoke of "the hustling over large footballs, from which many evils arise, which God forbid." In the court of King James I, where all violent physical exercise was banned, there was a special order against football which His Majesty deemed "meeter for lameing than making able the users thereof."

The form of the game in that age was described by one Philip Stickles, a contemporary observer, who argued that "it may rather be called a friendlie kind of fyghte than a play or recreation, a bloody and murthering practice than a fellowly sport. . . . For doeth not everyone lie in waight for his adversary, seeking to overthrowe and picke him on the nose?"

These African natives are playing a form of football, with a tiny ball, in almost the same manner as the American Indians played it on New England beaches before the Pilgrims landed.

A "company of lewd and disordered persons" much like these are what prompted English Kings to outlaw the "hustling over large footballs" in the streets. The sport was also played in this manner in Colonial America.

As for the technique of the game, Stickles analyzed that succinctly. The players, he said, "have the sleights to come one betwixt two, to dash him against the hart with their elbows, to butt him under the short ribs and peck him on the neck, with a hundred other such murthering devices."

These devices remained a part of the game for three centuries. In Manchester, England, in the 1600's, the town fathers, nearly in despair, promulgated a special ordinance against football, with this preamble: "There hath bene heretofore a great disorder in our toune . . . and the inhabitants thereof greatly wronged and charged with the mending of their glasse windows broken yearlye . . . by a company of lewd and disordered persons using that unlawful exercise of playing with the football in ye streets . . . breaking many men's windowes and glasse at their pleasure and other great inormyities. . . ."

The Hog-Slaughtering Season Provided the Ball

When Englishmen moved to America, their sons annually made the town streets in the new cities hideous with the great "inormyties" that went under the name of football. Boys from one end of town might clash with a gang from the other end, and using a pig's bladder for talisman, would shove and kick and fight and surge against one another up and down the narrow streets, swarming

into doorways, luring passersby into the crush, sending frightened ladies scurrying for cover, and bringing frantic shopkeepers out to bellow in dismay as their windows shattered under the sudden press of bodies.

Hustling over large footballs was clearly an annual rite, played usually at that season when other sports could not be enjoyed—when it was not warm enough for playing marbles or bowls, when kites were not easily flown, and when there was too much bite in the air for a lad to spend an afternoon on the bank of a brook. It coincided usually with hog slaughtering season, for the pig's bladder provided an object most boys would be tempted to kick about on

the ground anyway. There must have been more than a dozen different forms of the game, some derived from the size of the ball, the number on a side, or the habits of the neighborhood. Field hockey and hurley, in which sticks rather than feet were used to propel the ball, must have originated from the same diversion, just as "broom-ball," played in these days on the ice in Canada, is clearly descended from the common ancestor. But even while new versions of the game were being developed, the original mass-rush version of the game persisted. In England the game was played only in the secondary schools, for it was deemed too helter-skelter to be anything but a small boys'

The "class rush" version of the game as played in American colleges, with the sophomores opposing the freshmen. The ball was not much more than a sort of chip on the shoulder of the sophomore class. The mere touching of the ball by a freshman would signal a bloody free-for-all.

At Civil War time the game was still disorderly and full of random violence. Here Union soldiers are "playing" it with foot and fist.

game. In America it took hold first in the colleges, where there was always needed some contest to channel the atavistic rivalry between newcomers and the initiate.

At nearly all the big colleges in the United States, throughout the first two centuries of the nation's history, football was always an annual "rush" that set the freshmen against the sophomores, soon after the college year began. The ball, which would be either rubber or leather, was hardly more than a symbol of the challenge, the mere touching of which by some bold freshman would signal the start of the row. Members of both classes then would set upon each other, wrestling, pushing, slugging, clawing, until clothes were shredded and mouths and nostrils set aflow with blood. At some point or other the ball would be pushed clear through the ranks of one class or another and the game would be done. On that instant all enmity would cease, and boys who had been but a few seconds earlier endeavoring to beat each other into unconsciousness would grasp each other by the hand, lay arms across each other's shoulders in friendship, and go share a pint of ale.

At Harvard, football day was known as Bloody Monday, when sophomores and freshmen met on the Delta, where Memorial Hall was built, and lay into each other with the fervor of maddened

15

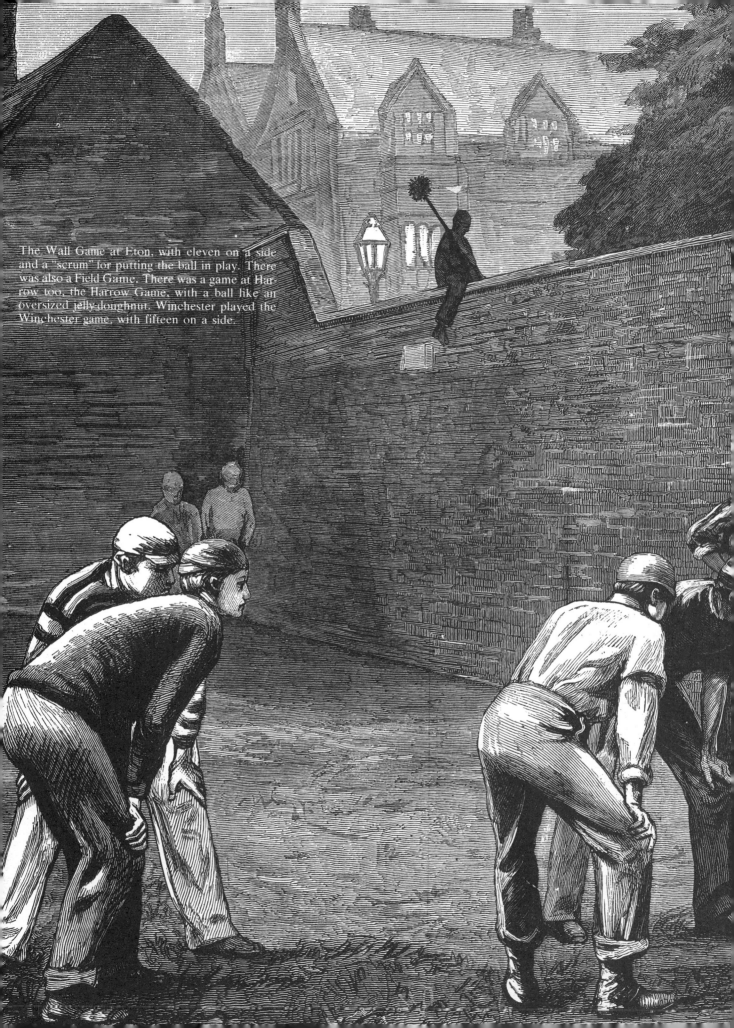

The Wall Game at Eton, with eleven on a side and a "scrum" for putting the ball in play. There was also a Field Game. There was a game at Harrow too, the Harrow Game, with a ball like an oversized jelly-doughnut. Winchester played the Winchester game, with fifteen on a side.

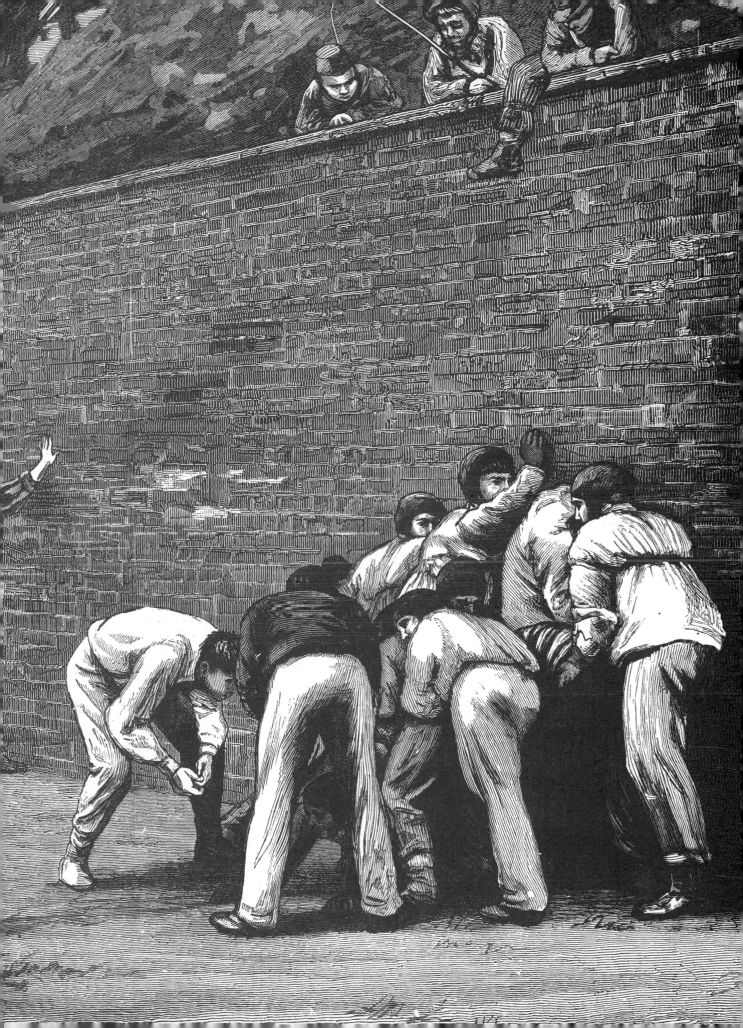

At Rugby, football in the nineteenth century was an almost completely disorganized rush, with no limit on the number of players. Football of this type was not played at the universities but every public school had its own version.

cats. There was always a bone or two broken, many teeth sent wandering, and a certain number each year laid unconscious on the grass. Just before the Civil War began, the college and town authorities, alarmed at the carnage, abolished the rite forever—or for what they thought was forever. The Harvard boys thereupon got together to finance and erect a tombstone to the memory of Football Fightum.

Within a decade and a half, the game of football had taken hold at Harvard. This was a more regulated version, rather like the modern game of soccer, in which a round ball was used and the hands could not be employed in advancing the ball. But this tame version of the class rush did not satisfy all the urges of the younger students and before long Bloody Monday was re-established, only to be abolished one final time, in 1903.

Eleven to a Side—and Let the "Scrummage" Begin

Football developed along several different lines in Old England and was exported to the colonies in various forms. The diverse forms the game took were affected by the space allowed for the game and the number who might decently be involved. It was often suppressed, frequently halted by the police and everlastingly cried out against by the polite folk of whatever community it took root in. When there was really no space to play the game in, a truncated and sometimes bloodier version of the game appeared so it could be fitted into whatever area could be found—as kids on city streets turned baseball into stickball or hockey into shindy. At Westminster Abbey, in the distant centuries, there was no proper place for football at

all, what with all the open area being paved with cobblestones and constricted by solid walls. So football evolved as the Game in Cloister, in which young novice priests cracked their skulls, knees, and elbows on the stones in an endeavor to drive a ball of some sort past a goal. Eventually some buildings were demolished and an area cleared to provide an open green to play in. Then football became the Game in Green. But the boys also kept on playing Game in Cloister.

At Eton, where the open space was bordered by a high brick wall, football became the Wall Game, for it was played right along the wall, on which the goals were marked. Here evolved the putting of the ball in play through a "scrummage," a tight gathering of players against the wall, into which the ball was dropped. The outer boundary of the playing field was marked by a furrow plowed in the turf. Off side play—that is, the use of players to clear the way ahead of the man who "dribbled" the ball along with his feet—was called "sneaking" at Eton and was considered a gross violation of the spirit of the sport. Because of the cramped space, the sides at Eton were limited to eleven, and this was one aspect of its private version of football that Eton exported eventually to America. When extra space was found to play in, and a game known as the Field Game was developed, the Wall Game was still played by some who preferred it, and many of its traditions clung to later versions.

It was at Rugby that the notion of picking up the ball and running with it was supposed to have been born—although surely in other places boys must have found themselves from time to

This is the Yale flying wedge, developed in the 1890's as a weapon against Princeton. There being no scrimmage line or neutral zone, the tackles and guards could surround the ball carrier as he ran down-field. The ball is "snapped" to the quarterback (hands extended) who gives it to the runner.

Football in the 1880's was largely a shoving contest, with the big watermelon-sized ball seldom in view of the spectators, except when the quarterback tossed it back to the runner. "Blocking" meant holding fast against the ball-carrier. Only if the man was in the open was he tackled.

time with the ball or bladder nestled in their arms after it had been bounced or kicked their way. According to the tablet erected at Rugby to memorialize the event, William Webb Ellis, while a student at Rugby in the early years of the nineteenth century, once became impatient in the press of bodies endeavoring to move the football here or there and picked the thing up and ran with it toward the goal. His dastardly deed was not supported by any of his teammates, and they, as well as the opponents, all endeavored to halt his flight. For years afterward this sort of play was deemed illegal, then it was permitted only to players who had made a "fair catch" of the ball after it had been kicked. But of course it eventually became the special feature of the Rugby version of football (in which the ball, incidentally, still retained its bladder shape) and it came in that form first to Canada, and then to the United States.

At Rugby itself the game was not called football or association or any such thing, but merely "Bigside," from its being played on the field known as Old Bigside. Nor was it a weekly or an interscholastic performance. It was an annual, practically free-for-all event in which the Sixth Form, or Schoolhouse, opposed the rest of the School. And it was School vs. Schoolhouse for many seasons, with no thought of ever playing the game once schooldays had been left behind.

In America, Yale and Princeton, as well as Harvard, used football as a sort of initiation ceremony in which the sophomores endeavored to beat some humility and maturity into the freshman class. In fact, history has made note of the fact that, in 1840, the Yale freshmen invented a formation that took the sophomores by surprise and demolished them almost before they could settle themselves into ranks. This was the Flying Wedge, in which the front rank of men formed a tight V, with arms linked and legs churning in unison, while the ball was propelled behind this protection. It smashed the opposition and sent it flying or trampled it underfoot. (This scheme was later re-invented at Princeton for use in the new game of football.)

Every Team Had Its Own Rules

The formal version of the game that was played as an intramural sport or in pick-up style in most of the big colleges was known simply as "association." Each college had its own rules but all used a round ball and all placed a limit on the number of participants. The game that is now recognized as the "first intercollegiate football match" was really a game of association between Rutgers and Princeton (then known as Nassau Hall) played at New Brunswick, under Rutgers rules. Both colleges had been playing the game within their own walls for some years, and Rutgers was moved to challenge Nassau to a go at this game, after Nassau had overwhelmed Rutgers at the New York Game—a form of baseball then just beginning to find favor in the colleges.

The Nassau version of football allowed the ball to be batted with the fist and permitted a "free kick"—where the opponents were required to remain ten yards away from the ball until the kicker had set his foot to it—after a fair catch (a ball signaled for and caught on the fly or first bounce.) As a matter of fact, a free kick is permitted after a fair catch even by today's rules, although the provision is seldom taken advantage of. The Rutgers rules did not permit batting with the fist, although the ball could be butted with the shoulder as well as kicked.

Rutgers Beats Princeton— Drinks and Cigars All Around

In this first game, Rutgers defeated Nassau, then treated all the Princeton boys to a "fine collation," including drinks and cigars, after the game. This celebration perhaps created more excitement than the game, for there had been a small army of followers who had come down from Princeton on a special train to sit on the rail fences and watch the contest. They could not get into the fray, even though the ball, with the sweating players hounding it, several times bounded into the crowd and set spectators sprawling off the fence. The players in this game had no uniforms, or equipment of any sort. They simply wore their old clothes, or peeled off jackets and collars.

Another game was played in Princeton, under Nassau rules, and Nassau won this. The rubber game was never played, for the faculty, alarmed at the intensity of the feelings aroused and fretting lest there be one more diversion to turn students' fancies from the profundities of Horace, Livy, and Euclid, banned the playing of football altogether. It was several more years before the game began to take hold as an intercollegiate competition, and then it began to stir nearly as much fervor as baseball, rowing and cricket.

Each of the big universities seemed to have its own rules for the game and when two colleges met it was necessary always to agree on "accommodation rules," combining features of each

game. There was nothing in any of the games, however, that more than faintly resembled the college game that grew into a peculiarly American sport. The ball was always round, touching it with the hands was never permitted, except when the ball was over the goal or the sidelines (when it was said to be "in touch"), and there were no yard lines or any way to score points except by kicking.

The number of men on a side varied widely. At Yale, a young Englishman named David Schley Schaff brought over from Eton the scheme for the Wall Game, establishing the number of players at eleven. He promptly set the different classes to playing each other under the Eton rules and eventually, despite the earnest efforts of the Yale faculty and the New Haven police to thwart him, fielded a team to represent the college. Harvard too had its own version of association football which it clung to until a team from McGill University in Canada came down to demonstrate the Rugby version of the game, with its oval ball and its rule to permit carrying the ball tucked under the arm. Harvard's athletes were not at first impressed by the McGill version but, after losing to McGill in a Rugby game, they continued to play at it and eventually decided it was far more fun than the version that required a man to "dribble" the ball with his feet.

Before long other universities adopted the Rugby game and for several decades both this version and the old-fashioned association version were played in the same schools, or by "athletic clubs" in the same locality, so that football scores often carried the identification "Rugby" or "Assoc." It did not

Interference in the nineties could be done with arms and hands extended. Because linemen could line up well behind the ball before the snap, the whole team, except for the center-rush, could get a running start and could even hold on to each other as they advanced.

take long then for Americans to corrupt "assoc." into "soccer"—and that is the name under which the game is played in this country today. Overseas, soccer is called plain football, except in England where it may be Rugby or rugger. But in the United States, for the past half century, a boy who went to the store and asked for a football was sure to come home with the Rugby style imitation of an inflated pig's bladder, built of panels of leather with inflatable rubber insides.

Some College "Boys" Who Played Were in Their Thirties

It was not of course only in the col-leges that football of any sort was played. Beginning shortly after the Civil War, about the same time that baseball began to own itself honestly professional, athletic clubs everywhere in the East laid out cash lures to persuade big strong fellows to come play on their football teams. But the clubs were always grimly "amateur" and the athletes usually were awarded some sinecure to serve as justification of their accepting a check every week during the football season. The colleges too did not hesitate to make offers of weekly cash stipends. (One young quarterback

joined a professional team only after his college had skipped a pay day.) One amateur club made a practice of rewarding its football players with fine gold watches, which the players would carry to a designated pawnshop and pawn for twenty dollars. The team manager would then redeem all the watches and use them over again the following week.

There being no eligibility rules to limit the loyalties of young men who played football, a man who carried the ball for Columbia against Yale one week might appear the next week wearing a Pennsylvania scarf around his head, to play against Yale again. And the mere fact that a fellow had graduated a year or two earlier never barred him from

playing with his university team. Indeed faculty members and coaches often lined up with the undergraduates on the football field. Some of the college "boys" who starred in the final decades of the last century were almost in their thirties before they gave up the game.

There were no uniforms either for many seasons. Sometimes a young man on the sidelines, invited to come fill up an empty space in his college line-up, would just peel down to his long-johns and leap into the crush. Players recognized their teammates through the colored scarf usually tied around the forehead as a sweatband. And each club or college had its own umpire, who would carry a scarf with the proper colors tied to his cane and lift it to signal a protest. Differences between the umpires would be settled by a neutral "referee" to whom disputes would be referred. Spectators too began to tie their team's colors to their own canes and wave them wildly in cheering their heroes on. These ultimately became formalized as the pennants that still appear at football games.

Athletic clubs all over the east were playing association football right after the Civil War and undoubtedly were subsidizing most of their players. What was sought usually was speed and size, for despite the rules against "sneaking" or offside play, there were always big fellows running ahead of the dribbler to clear a path for him. The side that carried the most weight often carried the day as well. There was physical contact hard enough to break bones, bloody men's noses, and send players reeling to the sidelines. But there was, in this form of the game, none of the grinding "rush-line" play or flying wedge attack that could maim a man for life or even kill

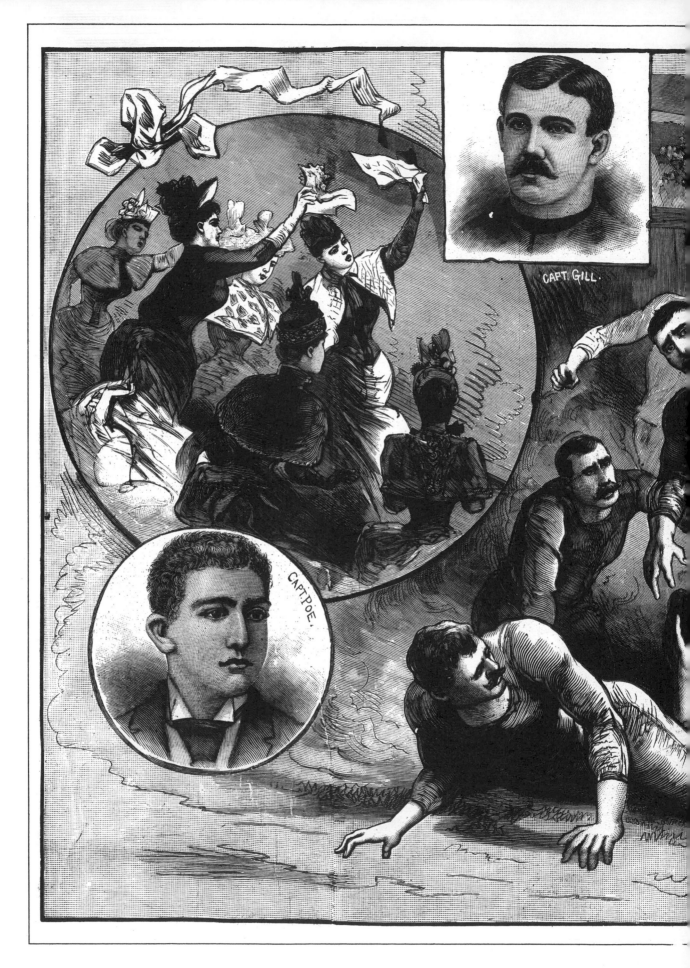

CAPT. GILL.

CAPT. POE.

"SNAKE" AMES.

Intercollegiate football, played with the round ball, was a gentlemanly game, or at least a game for gentlemen. All bodily contact was supposed to be "accidental." But blood did flow occasionally and sometimes bones were broken.

him. Actually any form of "interference" ahead of the ball was illegal. Americans who played the game, however, did not find it in their nature to stay clear of the fray and wait for the ball to come their way. Every man wanted to participate, as in the class-rush form of the game, and so there would invariably be a clot of surging bodies ahead of the man who brought the ball along. At first, in obeisance to the rules, this sort of interference was made to appear accidental. But eventually even the rules makers—who usually had to adjust the rules for each game—began to set forth only that it was wrong to do such blocking "with the extended arms."

Association football, however, never offered the chance for giving and taking a wallop that the Rugby version did. For that reason, the Rugby style of play eventually took over completely in the colleges. The Athletic Clubs, too, although they might still play with a round ball and call their game "association," were given to frequent physical contact. What they were really playing, said some observers, was "demoralized association."

While it is generally believed that Rugby style football took root and grew to maturity first in the eastern colleges, there is some evidence that the game, or a game like it, was played by hundreds of athletic clubs the nation over, just as baseball was played. And while these clubs all maintained that they were strictly amateur, they did field a surprising number of rugged young men who apparently had nothing to do in life but play football. Army posts played the game, and so did western Indians.

Upstate New York and far off California each had a dozen or more topnotch football teams wearing the colors of major athletic clubs. New Jersey, too, harbored some of the best of the professional or semi-professional (or semi-amateur) clubs. Woodrow Wilson is supposed to have coached the club in Orange, New Jersey, before he ever gave a moment's thought to a League of Nations.

The wild west played football of a sort, with teams in Tombstone, Albuquerque and Phoenix. General Leonard Wood, it was said, played in his youth as a semi-pro guard for the Olympic A.C. of San Francisco. Most of the newspaper space, and most of the hero worship and most of the money, however, accrued to the Eastern stars. Full-time professional teams, with no pretense of representing anything but the town they lived in, flourished best in the steel-and-coal areas of Ohio and Pennsylvania.

College stars, of course, decorated the rosters of both the professional and semi-professional clubs. But there were many famous performers in the late nineteenth century whose schooling was limited to what they could acquire free. A number of these were Indians, including Isaac Seneca, who starred with Greensburg, Pennsylvania, and the Pierce brothers, Bemus and Hawey, who played together with the Syracuse, New York, A.C., coached by Pop Warner. All of them learned the game at the Indian School at Carlisle, Pennsylvania.

The Syracuse A.C., the Orange A.C., and the Watertown, New York, Red and Blacks were among the most noted amateur-professional football clubs of the old century. All of them featured several players who had learned their skills at college. One had a "giant guard" (220 pounds) from Columbia by the name of Kingdon, who also played for some of the great semi-professional clubs in Pennsylvania. Watertown had Phil Draper, known for some lost reason as "Shang," who had won fame at Williams by scoring four touchdowns against Yale, and had first appeared in Watertown as a cigar salesman for his father's tobacco company. Around Pittsburgh, there were half a dozen great football clubs, recruited not only from Pennsylvania and Lehigh and the Carlisle Indian School but even from Princeton, Columbia, Harvard and De- pauw. The greatest of the six Poes of Princeton, Arthur Poe, wore the colors at one time or another of several dif- ferent athletic clubs, and appeared on one of the first outright professional clubs — the Pittsburgh entry in the "National Football League" (not the league that was established in 1919 but the one that Connie Mack, W. C. Temple, Dave Berry and some others created in 1902 and that lasted but a season).

Hard Feelings and Local Pride
Cause Bitter Battles

The college game throughout the seventies and eighties had developed or degenerated from a wide-open run- ning and kicking game into a nose-to- nose contest that always drew blood. And this was the type of game most of the coal-and-steel clubs favored. There was always hard feeling aplenty and often a free-for-all row in which spec- tators engaged with fully as much en- thusiasm as the ballplayers. A lad trying out for a village football team, which

Captain Harry Ryan, leader of the La- trobe, Pennsylvania, Professional Foot- ball Club was the most famous tackle in the coal-and-steel area, and the first "All-Pro." After nine seasons with La- trobe, Ryan, in 1902, was hired away by the Pittsburgh Nationals' entry in the short-lived National Football League of that year. The shinguards and pillow britches are all the protective equip- ment Harry wore on the field.

might be captained and coached by a man who had graduated the year before, could expect to be initiated by means of a hard wallop to the jaw the first time the ball was snapped. His reaction to the blow would decide whether he had the sort of stuff good football players were made of. (The ball in those days was actually "snapped" in a manner that helped eliminate the original "scrum" of rugby. Instead of being haphazardly booted out of the scrum to a player in the backfield, it would be stepped on by the "center-rush" in such a manner as to squirt it directly back to the quarterback, who might then toss it off to a halfback.)

Hard feelings were almost always evident in the intertown games in the coal-and-steel circuit—hard feelings and tremendous local pride. There would be bands (the team from Latrobe, Pennsylvania, was proud of its cornet band), female auxiliaries carrying banners and plumes, and a parade of carriages. In the game it was not unheard-of for a man whose end had just been turned to haul off and deal a punch in the nose to the ball-carrier who had done the turning. Phil Draper received such a reward one day when he got around a truculent young man named Stehle, who played end for the New York A.C. Dave Berry, famed football entrepreneur who organized the first pro team in Latrobe, had his jaw broken in a fierce collision with his own captain in a practice game. Lawson Fiscus, one of the first men to admit out loud that he was accepting a weekly check (twenty dollars) for playing football, once took careful aim at the face of a prostrate opponent and broke the man's jaw with his heavy-shod foot.

Some of the bitterest battles involved the teams from Latrobe and Greensburg, who seemed to feel that the winner of their annual contest owned the World Championship and was certainly cock of the Westmoreland County walk. At one game between the clubs, in which the Indian star Isaac Seneca, an earlier version of Jim Thorpe in all-around athletic skill, carried the ball. Seneca was dumped with uncommon viciousness by the enemy quarterback, a New Yorker named Kennedy. Whereupon Seneca rose up and belted Kennedy into momentary oblivion. The Latrobe coach rushed out to keep the fight from spreading but was himself greeted by a clubbed fist en route. Within moments, both squads, the umpires, the spectators and even the refreshment peddlers were embroiled in an aimless uproar that covered the entire field. Peace came finally, when most of the warriors had had their fill of blood, but the Greensburg team refused to go to Latrobe for the Thanksgiving Day return match until the county had assigned twenty deputies to keep the enemies apart. David Berry, manager of the Latrobe club, agreed that "it would be impossible for the people from the two towns to meet without some little trouble." (The previous Thanksgiving a number of Greensburg folk had worn black eyes home from the game.)

The rival newspaper editors joined in ridiculing the claims of the other town and of course residents of both towns wagered heavily on the games, so that something more than local pride went aglimmering when the game was lost. After a victory, the newspaper in the winning town never hesitated to rub in the humiliation. When Latrobe, during

Lawson Fiscus is supposed to have been the first football player to admit he was taking a regular weekly check ($20) for playing football. After starring as halfback at Princeton in 1891 and 1892, Fiscus joined the independent team at Greensburg, Pennsylvania. Despite his gentle appearance, Fiscus was strong and tough. He was known as "The Samson of Princeton" and once deliberately broke a player's jaw by kicking him in the face. In this picture he is wearing the "tiger" uniform of the Princeton eleven, and the one-piece football "smock."

The first admittedly professional football team: Greensburg, Pennsylvania, 1893. This club stopped pretending it was an amateur athletic club and openly paid salary and expenses to its players. Lawson Fiscus was captain of this team, made up mostly of college stars. Lloyd Huff, local businessman, was the angel for this club. A few are wearing the "smocks" invented by Ledou Smock of Princeton.

the Spanish-American War, defeated Greensburg 6 to 0 at football, the Latrobe newspaper ran a story with an imitation "war" headline, in enormous black type: "WIPED OFF THE MAP— GREENSBURG GONE." The story contained such well-reasoned phrases as "Greensburg's . . . boasted 'champions' have been vanquished and the delusive prophesies of the Tribune have all been punctured. . . . The silly twaddle of the Tribune under the guise of a 'comparison' of the two teams . . ." The rejoicing in Latrobe was like the wild scene in Pittsburgh some sixty-two years later, when the Pirates won a

World Series in baseball. Citizens "danced war dances." "Aristocrats embraced miners and thought nothing of it." And young men reeled about the streets singing "Everybody has a score but Greensburg. What the hell do we care! What the hell do we care!" And the Latrobe paper carried a long poem that bragged of the suddenly fattened wallets of the Latrobe backers.

Something of the bitterness that flavored these rivalries may be savored from the fact that once, when Greensburg had a backfield of Best, Barclay, Bray and Walbridge (all from Lafayette), the enemy named them "Bitch, Bastard,

34

The Latrobe Pros of 1896, with Owner David Berry, in chinwhiskers, in the center. The man in the black hat is Dr. Blackburn, the team physician. Harry Ryan, sitting in the front row, coached this club. The only helmet was owned by Marcus Saxman, the bald man in the lower left. The contraption held by Ely, upper left, is a nose-mouth-and-ear guard. His hair provided protection for his skull.

Buggcr and Whore."

Newspapers in that era that reported football scores usually carried the "athletic club" scores right along with the college scores, there being no invidious distinctions at that time, inasmuch as some colleges openly offered pay checks to their stars. Football players were expected to devote their full hearts and energies to the Game. The Pennsylvania squad one year was taken off to Canada for the entire summer, to grow hairy and strong in the wilderness. And football players made no secret of the fact that they would play for the college that offered the fattest stipend for their loyalties.

College Players Join the "Athletic Clubs"

Naturally there were constant efforts to outbid a rival club for a ball-carrier or a quarterback. Players like Fiscus, or the great Doggie Trenchard, from Princeton, or the Pierce brothers, or Phil Draper, would receive offers every week of fat purses and open-handed "expense allowances." Draper played not only for Williams College and the Red and Blacks of Watertown but also for the Cherry A.C. in Chicago, where he was a teammate of a flamboyant half-back named Zane Grey.

The 1896 Greensburg club carried the three Fiscus brothers, easy enough to recognize in this picture. Lawson, the famed "Samson" is seated second from the right, behind the man with the outstretched leg. One brother is second from the right in the next to last row, just in front of the man with the bow tie. The other brother is second from the left in that row. Lawson, who was one of the heavyweights of the club, weighed only 186 pounds. He could run like a deer. Another heavy man, for that day, was Adam Wyant, first man on the left in the very back row, behind the shoulder of the Fiscus brother. Wyant, who was elected to Congress soon afterward, played pro football at about 190 pounds.

Occasionally, as football assumed greater stature at the colleges, rival universities became embroiled in controversies over "professionalism." It wasn't that they objected so much to a man's having taken money. They did not care for the system of enrolling graduates as "students," then permitting them to drop out after the football season. This had been commonplace in the "demoralized association" days but once the football team had become the official representative of the college, more thought was given to maintaining the facade of purity. In 1889 for instance Harvard protested that Princeton's great "Snake" Ames had been playing for various athletic clubs before coming back to Princeton merely to play football. Ames denied the charges, even though affidavits were procured showing he had been in the pay of several football clubs after he had apparently finished his courses at Princeton. Ames continued to play and ultimately the whole controversy was set at rest when all the men on the football squad at Princeton were required to "certify" that they would remain at college throughout the whole term.

But there is no doubt that the amateur-professional "athletic clubs" had as much to do with the popularization of football as the colleges did. The club game usually followed the college rules (sometimes a season behind in the changes) and the bulk of the great club players had become addicted to the game while at college. Nor was the supposedly amateur game played by the colleges one whit less brutal than the

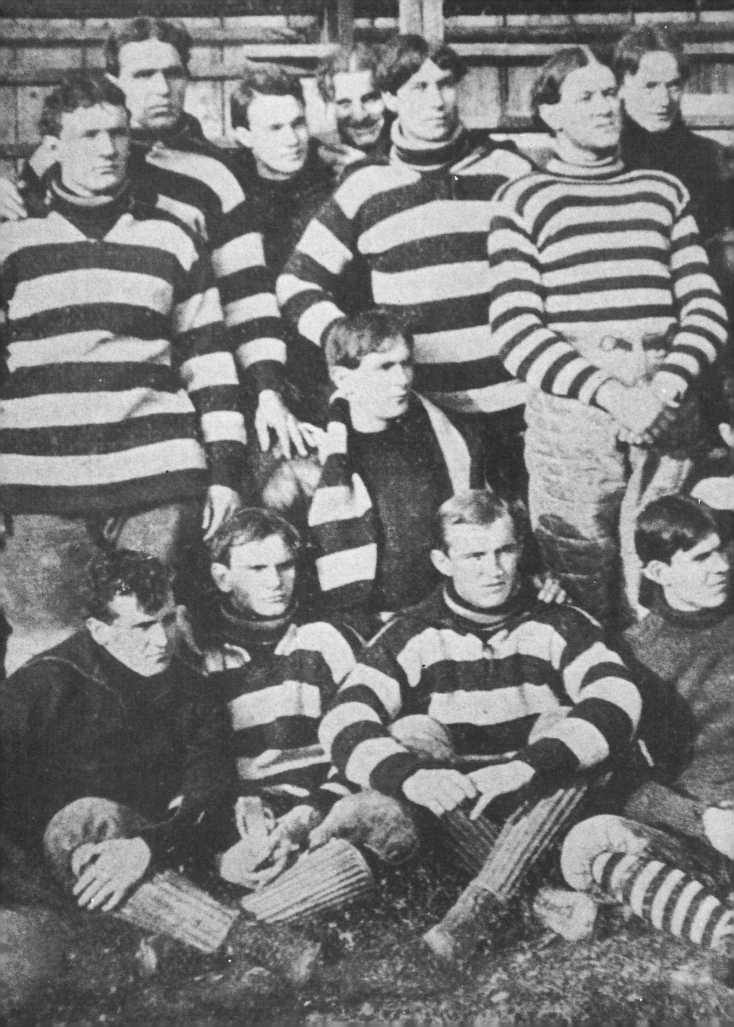

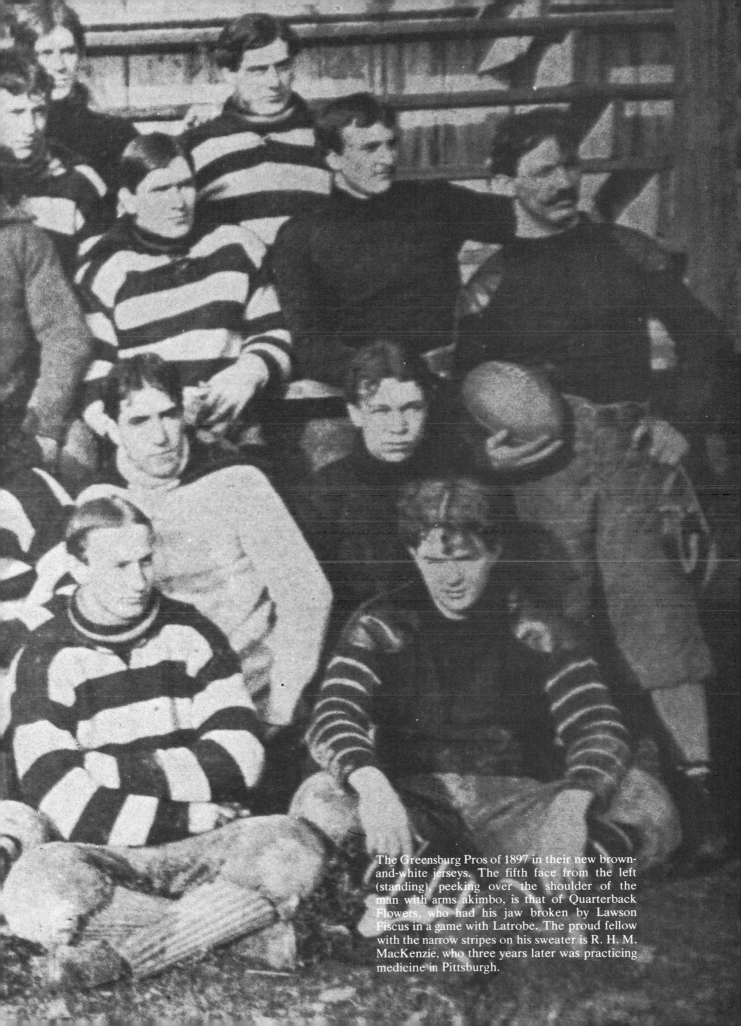

The Greensburg Pros of 1897 in their new brown-and-white jerseys. The fifth face from the left (standing), peeking over the shoulder of the man with arms akimbo, is that of Quarterback Flowers, who had his jaw broken by Lawson Fiscus in a game with Latrobe. The proud fellow with the narrow stripes on his sweater is R. H. M. MacKenzie, who three years later was practicing medicine in Pittsburgh.

Here is the Greenburg team in 1900, posed on their home field with their new sweaters. Seated at the left, with one hand behind the football and the big G on his sweater, is Isaac Seneca, Indian star from Carlisle, who was said to have been faster and stronger than Jim Thorpe. He was the first Indian ever named by Walter Camp to an All-America team.

game the athletic clubs played. In the Harvard-Yale game of 1889 (played at Springfield, Massachusetts) one player was removed from the game for deliberately kicking an opponent and another was sent to the sidelines for slugging the man opposite him. (It was Harvard incidentally that insisted on the rule that a man should be put out of the game the *first* time he used his fist on an enemy. Before Harvard forced the change by staying out of competition until the rule had been adopted, a man was allowed one free punch.)

Young men in that era, like all who had been raised in the culture derived from the warriors who worshiped Woden and Thor, were given to flaunting their manliness and football provided an excellent means of displaying one's ability to withstand physical pain. On that account the game flourished wherever young males gathered together in sufficient quantity. The equipment needed was elementary. While players, when they turned out for the American scrimmage version, no longer took to the field in their underwear, all that was usually required was a pair of shoes, a jersey, long stockings and a "smock"—a singlet overall of padded knee pants and lace-front jumper made in one piece, invented by one Ledou P. Smock (Princeton, '79). It was many years before helmets became commonplace and many more years—right up to the 1940s—before they were made obligatory. Al Nesser of Columbus, Ohio, one of six members of the same family who became famous professionals although they never played in college, never in all his career wore shoulder, thigh or kidney pads, helmet or athletic supporter, and he was famed as one of the roughest and toughest linemen in the early pro game. (Al started playing football as a schoolboy in the 1890's, joined the Rexall Drug Company eleven in the early 1900's, became a professional in 1910, and played until 1931, when he was an end with the Cleveland Indians.)

In New York City and around it throughout the early twentieth century there were dozens of football clubs, all playing for part of the gate receipts as so many baseball clubs did. The game was every bit as popular in Chicago, in Philadelphia, in Columbus, Ohio, in Boston, and along the Pacific Coast. In 1902, a promoter named Tom O'Rourke was even able to stage an indoor football tournament at Madison Square Garden, among athletic clubs from all over the east. It was won by the Syracuse All-Stars, led by the Warner Brothers (not a motion picture company) and featuring the Pierce brothers from the Carlisle Indian School, a ball carrier named Boettger from Princeton, Phil Draper, and a quarrelsome end named Carver who offered vigorous punches in the head to half a dozen different opponents on the night the title was decided.

The game was also played of course by small boys in vacant lot or schoolyard, often with almost no understanding of the rules, with as many on a side as was necessary to get everyone into the play, and with all sorts of grabbing, holding, sparring, slugging, and wrestling. Sometimes it would be merely a game of "pick it up and run," with the lad who grabbed the ball becoming the prey of every other boy in the yard. Or it would be strictly a kicking game, in which the boy who was able to pry the ball loose from all the other hands that clutched it would have a turn to boot the fat ball high into the air.

The violence that contests of this sort engendered undoubtedly had much to do with the gradual dying out of the sandlot game, for mothers in every city must have soon had their fill of patching junior's physiognomy or trying to keep splints on his fractured arm. The game therefore became centered in the schools and colleges, although it was the semi-professionals and the professionals who caused it to flourish in areas where the school most of the neighborhood young attended was the railroad roundhouse or the boiler shop.

Shinguards and Padded Britches

AN important skill for a football player in the eighties and nineties was an ability to drop on the ball, for it often bounded loose and was open to recovery by anyone. Anyone who chose to could kick a loose ball, and possibly on this account most football players wore shinguards, even before anyone thought of putting thick pads on the shoulders. Kicks were dealt out freely, not merely to the ball, but to the opposing players, and not all of them were accidental.

Power was the main feature of the game in the early days, when there were no rules limiting the number of players who might play behind the line. A guards-back or a tackles-back play belonged in every professional team's repertoire. And most teams, in opening the game, formed into a V with the ball carrier protected inside it. There was no real kick-off in old-time American rugby. The rule said the game began when the ball was put in play by being kicked by a member of the team that won the privilege. It did not say how far the ball was to be kicked or who was to touch it. So American players would start on the dead run for the enemy lines and on his way one would lean over and touch the ball to his toe, thus "kicking"

43

The Homestead Team of 1900 never knew defeat. This club, financed by the Carnegie Steel Company, paid enough to lure all the best players in the east to its ranks. The little fellow on the extreme left is "Poe of Princeton"—the great end, Arthur Poe. Fourth from the right in the front row is Hawey Pierce, a Carlisle Indian. On the left in the back row, peering out over the football, is curly haired Gammons, the Red Grange of his day, whose appearance on the field brought everyone to his feet, cheering. Gammons was the quarterback.

it within the meaning of the rule. Promptly the wedge would form around him and the whole club would endeavor to smash its way through the enemy ranks, with the ball carrier holding fast to the belt of the man in front. (In one early form of the game at Yale, one player was charged with the job of playing always close to the enemy goal line, presumably to boot a free ball across it. He was known as the "pea-nutter," which for all I know may have been derived, in those Greek and Latin days, from the word "penultimate.")

The Ball Was Thrown Like a Discus

Despite the fact that the forward pass was supposed to have been "invented" in the 1900's there was passing aplenty in the early game. Most of it was lateral passing in from out-of-bounds, but the ball was also flipped from hand to hand in the field of play. The ball was big, fat, shaped like a stunted watermelon, and did not lend itself to the spiral pass, thrown like a baseball. Instead, one end of the ball was cradled in the throwing hand, while the length of the ball snuggled against the forearm. Then the

ball was hurled away almost like a discus, high over the grasping enemy hands.

The pass was also used to provide a modicum of deception in the usual closely packed scrimmage. Once in a Harvard-Yale game, the wily Yales scored a touchdown by bunching all their players together in the center, with their great ball carrier, McClung, in the middle. It seemed clear that they meant McClung to hold the ball while the whole team united to shove him the final twenty yards to the Harvard goal. But McClung became quarterback in the play and tossed the ball to McBride who then flung it to Wurtenburg, who scampered out to one side of the press and ran the ball almost to the goal line.

One play by McClung was then enough to carry it over.

Pushing the ball carrier or hauling him by means of a harness was an accepted way of advancing the ball. But halfbacks often broke loose and ran long distances and there were many wild pileups when a ball was fumbled, a pass missed its target, or a kick bounded loose. The ball was to be advanced the whole length of the field in four downs or it had to be given up. There were severe penalties for offside play, but in the American game that just meant starting from the rush line before the snap of the ball.

"Blocking" in this early version of the game did not mean wiping out potential tacklers or protecting the passer or the kicker. It meant stopping the enemy's advance, which was usually done by setting every shoulder against the massed rush-line of the attacking team and holding fast. In the very beginning, the ball-carrier was not down until he admitted it, so he might lie buried beneath a pile of sweating bodies for some time, with the breath nearly pressed out of his body, before he gave up and cried "Down!" It perhaps goes without saying that sometimes his surrender was hastened by a judiciously planted foot or fist. This crude feature of the game, rather like the brutal "plugging" that made town-ball so offensive to gentlemen and such a delight to country roughnecks, was relished in the sandlot game, where it persisted long after it had been ruled off every other field.

But it must not be thought that the professional football players were all rowdy by nature, or men who sought out battle scars to improve their standing among their fellows. Many eminent pro-

45

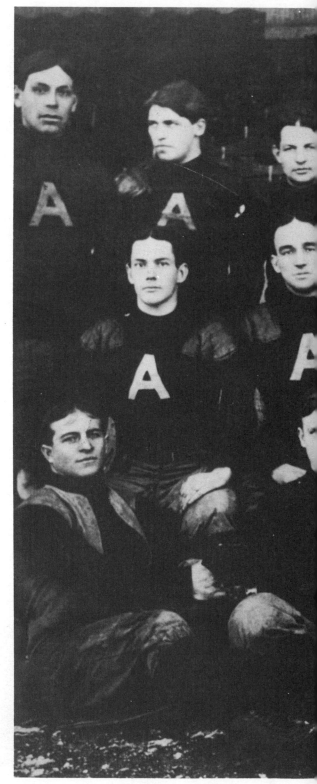

Young Connie Mack (age forty) sits in the middle of his Philadelphia Athletics football team of 1902. This is the club that lost the "World Championship" to the Pittsburgh Pros on November 28 in the game that marked the end of the first National Football League. Seated at Connie's right, holding the football, is Coach Blondy Wallace, who became coach of the Canton Bulldogs and eventually "King of the Bootleggers" in Atlantic City, New Jersey. This club played a night game at Elmira, New York (with searchlights at both ends of the field), and Rube Waddell, Connie Mack's eccentric left-handed pitcher, carried a sandwich sign to advertise the game about town.

46

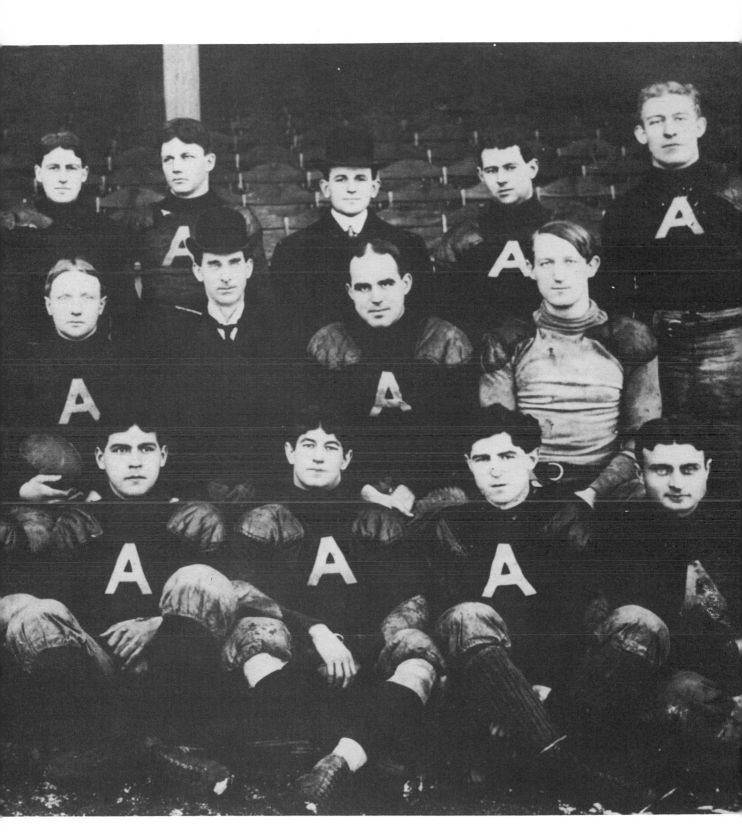

The ball was often passed, even in the nineties. But the technique was rather like that used in heaving a pumpkin. The ball belonged to anyone who could recover it, and a man awaiting the catch could be knocked down before he received the ball.

fessional men and serious scholars sought extra income and pure fun on the football field. There was one, a Dr. Roller, who played for teams around Pittsburgh (although he came from Seattle) who always wore kid gloves in a game, lest he do some injury to the precious hands that were then being trained for surgery. (The good doctor also experimented now and then with a Van Dyke beard.) Lawson Fiscus was a school principal, while playing football for money. Two other doctors, John Geiger and R. H. M. McKenzie, also played on Pittsburgh area football teams. Others went on to become politicians and some to be bootleggers. But, as Mark Twain once said in a similar connection, I repeat myself.

The Game Becomes More Civilized

Before anyone started wearing helmets, players began to sport nose-guards —big ugly appliances that made men look like grampuses. Instead of using helmets, men let their hair grow thick and long, cutting it chrysanthemum style so that it served as a badge of their profession. Indeed the first man to wear a helmet on the professional team in Latrobe, Pennsylvania, Marcus Saxman, of Swarthmore, was nearly bald. His helmet was just a few strips of leather running crisscross and attached to a sweat band that fitted tightly to his head.

Through the early 1900's the game went through many changes, to make it more civilized or to open it up so that the ball might be seen by the spectators (who sometimes numbered ten and twelve thousand). Slugging had long. been done away with and team managers generally agreed it was better to use neutral officials who would not hesitate to eject men who used foot or fist to injure an opponent. The chief aim of the attack, however, was still to generate power. At one time men had been allowed to start moving forward, behind their own rush line, before the ball was put in play. Now rules limited the number who could do that and prevented the stationing of guards behind the line to get a running start with the ball carrier. (It would be a few decades before the architects of the game found a way to get the guards moving ahead of the ball carrier again by having them pull out of the line and form interference on sweeps.)

When the forward pass came in, it was under severe restrictions. It could be thrown only within five yards, laterally, of the point at which the ball was snapped. So the field had to be marked both ways—laterally as well as longitudinally—at five-yard intervals so the officials could enforce this rule. This new marking made the field look like a true gridiron, divided, lattice-style, in five-yard squares to form the grid.

Passers still threw the ball in the standard way, so it rolled end over end as it flew over the heads of the players. A receiver needed a small guard of blockers to stand around him as he awaited the ball, for of course it belonged to anyone who could grab it and there was no rule to prevent an enemy from ambushing a potential receiver and knocking him down before he could lay hold of the ball. If the pass went out of bounds, it went over to the opponents at the point where it crossed the boundary. On that account it was sometimes used instead of a punt to pin the other team into the "coffin corner."

In 1905, the field was marked off in five-yard squares, so the umpires could see that no play crossed the scrimmage line and no forward pass was thrown within five yards of the point where the ball was centered. This was to do away with the fearful mass plays that were blamed for all the injuries.

The pass was almost always thrown from the "short punt formation" with the ends split out to run down the field as potential receivers. When the distance to be gained by the offensive team was increased from five yards to ten yards and the number of downs increased from three to four, then the passing was invariably done on the third down, when the quarterback could afford to "waste" a down while still retaining possession of the football.

There were many commentators who believed that the improvement of sport photography is what led to the ruination of the game, for it was generally supposed that a newspaper photograph of a gory-faced Swarthmore warrior being half carried off the field by his mates is what prompted Theodore Roosevelt, that advocate of the strenuous life, to insist that something had to be done to take the homicide out of the college game. Beginning in the early 1900's, therefore, the rules were given an annual going-over to gentle up the game a little, or at least to loosen up the fearsome crush in which bones were so often broken and so many clandestine punches thrown. The pass and the extra down helped a little. But better still was the rule that limited the number of men in the backfield to four, so bruising characters in nose guards could no longer form a stampeding escort for the ball carrier, with several yards in which to gather momentum. Along with this rule, which was adopted in 1910, the rule makers also made illegal the bodily advancing of the ball carrier by shoving or hauling on the part of his mates. (When the Franklin, Pennsylvania, eleven played the Watertown Red and Blacks in an indoor football game at Madison Square Garden, New York, one night in December 1903, Herman Kirkhoff, a veteran pro who was then playing guard for Franklin, lifted the Franklin ball-carrier up bodily and actually threw him across the goal line. Fortunately the

ball-carrier clung to the fat football during his flight.)

What served best to open up the game, however, and to cut down on the hand-to-hand skirmishing that almost always preceded the snap of the ball, was the establishment of a "neutral zone" that kept the opposing lines separated by the length of the ball. Before that rule was adopted, the jerseyed yeomen used to stand chest to chest, or nose to nose, breathing fire and threat into each other's faces and trying always to encroach another inch or two on the other man's territory. Often fistfights would break out before the ball was snapped, when the defensive team tried to extend its government into land already laid claim to by the opposing rush line. Linesmen were always tightly teamed, each guard with a hand on the snapper-back's back or shoulder and the tackles similarly in contact with the guard. Feet too would be interlocked along the line, to make penetration more difficult. The changes wrought by the Presidential interference, which began in 1905 with a conference at the White House involving representatives from Harvard, Yale, and Princeton, put an end to most of this close-knit and grinding play, although it did not by any

51

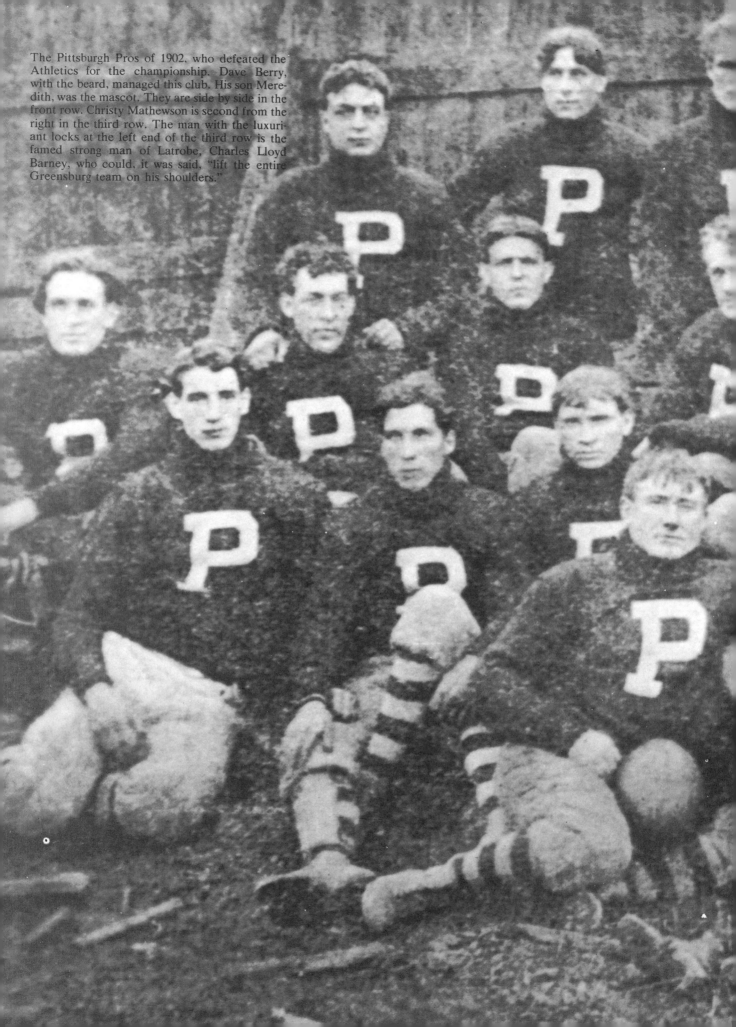

The Pittsburgh Pros of 1902, who defeated the Athletics for the championship. Dave Berry, with the beard, managed this club. His son Meredith, was the mascot. They are side by side in the front row. Christy Mathewson is second from the right in the third row. The man with the luxuriant locks at the left end of the third row is the famed strong man of Latrobe, Charles Lloyd Barney, who could, it was said, "lift the entire Greensburg team on his shoulders."

means take the blood and broken bones out of football. Actually, the carnage of the early days, limited largely to broken noses, split lips, and minor lacerations of cheek and chin, may even have produced less permanent damage than the casualities of the more open and more heavily armored game, in which knees, hit while one sustained the whole weight of the body, might be torn apart, or shoulders separated when an arm was used to grab at a dodging runner, or ribs cracked under the impact of an iron-hard shoulder pad or artificially hardened helmet.

The opening up of the offense resulted in some opening of the defense too. Linemen soon discovered that if a runner managed to pop between them into the open spaces, he could go a long way before meeting a defensive half-back. The defensive backfield usually lined up backwards, with the fullback closest to the line, but still a few strides behind it, the halfback widely separated, a few yards still farther back, and the quarterback far back toward his own goal to play the safety man—the desperation tackler who had to interpose his body between the charging runner and the goal. Very soon, the center, having no ball to snap back on defense, learned that if he played "soft"—held back a few steps and did not charge right into the opposing backfield, or start to struggle with the enemy guards —he might have a better chance to see which way the runner was coming. Then he became a "roving center," shifting about to shore up the line wherever it seemed likely the blow might fall.

On a pass play, the quarterback would do the passing and the other backfield men would stay in the backfield to pro-

tect him, while the two ends hastened downfield to become possible targets for the throw. It was a long time before linemen learned to give ground a little in order to hold the charging opponents off the passer. Many players and coaches clung to the theory that to allow a foreign foot to step into the home backfield was base betrayal and so even on a short punt formation with a pass coming up, the offensive line would charge into the enemy with head and shoulder, and seek to drive him halfway home.

There were not many practitioners of the pass in early twentieth century football, so that a man who knew how to make the ball go where he aimed it, and understood how to put a ball into the arms of a moving receiver, was always sure of a payday wherever he might turn. There were two or three famed forward pass experts who moved from club to club as new club managers sought to add the pass to their plans.

The ball, remember, was big and fat and could become almost round after three quarters of kicking, squeezing and pummeling, so that throwing it with a modicum of accuracy was rather like trying to flip a mince pie to a friend without turning it topside down.

The Offense and Defense Open Up

As a matter of fact, it was 1925 before anyone ever had the courage to suggest that the ball might be replaced after it had become scuffed, misshapen or soggy. The ball, after all, was prize and trophy as well as talisman and one team or another wanted to take it home when the game was over. In December 1902, when Connie Mack's football Athletics played Dave Berry's Pittsburgh club

HOMESTEAD L.& A.C. 1901

H.PIERCE

WEINSTEIN   P.HALE   HUNT

RANDOLPH   MOSSE   M.NULTY   M.CUTCHE

A. POE   B.PIERS   OVERFIELD   SHIRING

CROLIUS   FULTZ   (CAP'T.)

HEIMAN

MONS   SHIELD

MAXWELL   RICHARDSON   MILLER

This 1901 Homestead Team, also undefeated, carried three Indian players: Hawey Pierce, fourth from left in back row; Bemus Pierce, in center of middle row; and Miller, second from right in front row. Many players have begun to wear padding on shoulders as well as knees. But the helmet (on a skeletal lad named Mosse in the back row) looks like a bucket. The great Gammons is at the extreme left in the back row, with Arthur Poe right next to him.

(on which Christy Mathewson played fullback), the game almost ended in frustration when the ball disappeared before the game was over. This was the "championship" game of the brand new "National Football League"—a venture that was doomed to expire after drawing hardly more than a dozen breaths. It was played before a small but frantic crowd of Pittsburgh partisans—but not until canny Connie Mack had sought and received ironclad assurances that the guarantee would be paid. In the final quarter, with the Pittsburghs leading by a score of 6 to 0, a Pittsburgh kick went out of bounds. The referee's whistle blew and Dave Berry hastened to snag the ball. After wrapping it tenderly—for it was soggy with mud and rain—in dry newspapers, he started off home. But the game was not over by any means. There were still ten seconds to play. So Berry was captured, the ball unwrapped, and the game was started once more. Pittsburgh kicked, and Philadelphia's left end, Baeder, dropped the ball. Arthur Poe of Princeton, whose thundering approach may have encouraged Baeder to miss the catch, was coming too fast to fall

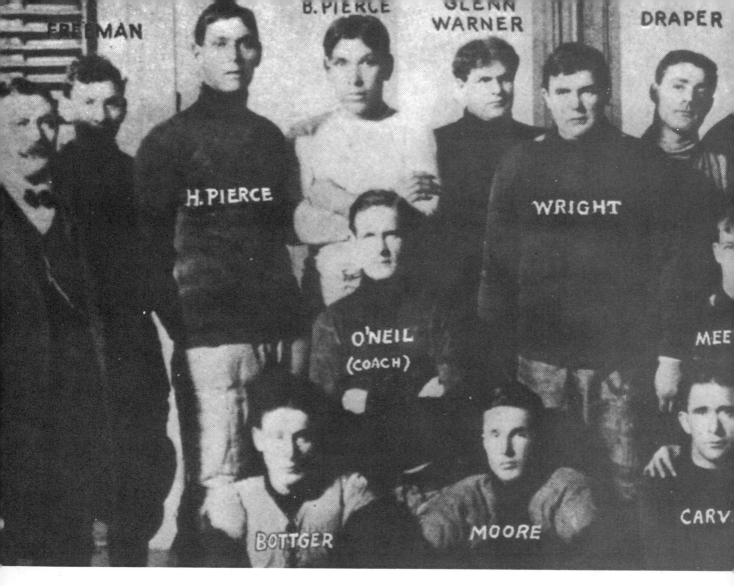

FREEMAN H. PIERCE B. PIERCE GLENN WARNER DRAPER WRIGHT O'NEIL (COACH) MEE BOTTGER MOORE CARV

In 1902 Bemus and Hawey Pierce were playing for the Syracuse All-Stars, along with Glenn (Pop) Warner and his brother, and Phil Draper from Williams, who had also played for other pro clubs. This is the team that won the "indoor championship" in the games staged by Tom O'Rourke at Madison Square Garden, New York.

upon the ball, so he kicked it—there being no rule, remember, against kicking a loose football. The ball flew across the Philadelphia goal line, where Indian Art Miller, playing halfback for Pittsburgh, fell upon the ball for a touchdown. The try for point failed so the final score was 11 to 0, a touchdown in that day being worth only five points.

The game which first saw a new football brought into play when the original one grew too waterlogged and slimy to be either passable or kickable was played in 1925, during the wettest autumn that the nation had ever seen. It rained, in football country, for three weeks without letup. Ohio State played Iowa in the wildest downpour of the whole period, with rain coming down at a rate that set men wondering about how many different kinds of creatures you could fit into an ark. At half time, after two dreary periods in which only six or seven ballplayers and hardly any spectators even saw the football, or could tell it from the mud when they did see it,

NER MASON HAWK STARK

the officials fingered the amorphous and mudcaked object they were supposed to finish the game with and decided to defy the lightning. They called for a brand new ball (worth about ten dollars then). The sportswriters who observed this flouting of laws of our forefathers were, while not precisely at a loss for words, at least momentarily short of them. But one of them did come up with a question he thought would have to be answered before this innovation could be universally accepted. Which ball would the winning team walk home with, for goodness' sake? Or would they take them both? No amount of poring over quaint and curious volumes could

produce a previous instance of an oddity like this.

The pros, although they must have seen how this new extravagance improved the game for the spectators, were slow to adopt it. There were hardly any pro teams, even in that era, who were taking home cash enough to justify their professional standing. Many a game was played for fun, for the take sometimes barely covered the train fare. Dressing rooms were sometimes empty boxcars and many a pro team played two games on a weekend, in order to assure meal money. Paying for extra footballs would have sunk them.

The Game Improves as a Spectacle

The game itself had improved as a spectacle gradually over the years, as techniques improved and rules were altered to knit up the raveled edges. The drop kick, which had been originally a mere evasion of the spirit of the rule for putting a ball in play, became a feature of the game. The big blunt-nosed ball bounced fairly true if it were not dropped from too great a height and men discovered that a strong leg could drive the ball over the crossbar from the middle of the field. The idea of course was to lay the toe into the ball at almost the instant it struck the ground. Originally, when the ball was to be put in play by tossing it into the air, a few sly performers became practiced at kicking it the very instant it touched the earth and it was out of this trick that drop-kicking evolved. (Once between the halves of a game at Michie Stadium, Red Reeder, West Point's mighty drop-kicker, edified both old and young by dropkicking the ball over one goal from midfield, and then turning to drop kick it over the other.)

57

Blocking or "interference" had long been nothing more than plain obstruction in an effort to keep tacklers away from a ball carrier. Originally the hands were used to shove, and even to wallop a fellow who posed an imminent danger, but the rule soon limited the weapons to the arms and shoulders. (There were still of course blows struck in the confines of the scrimmage and even an occasional joint deliberately twisted.) And the Indians from the school at Carlisle, Pennsylvania, demonstrated a new way of wiping a potential tackler right out of a play; by rolling the body into the enemy's legs, like a barrel that had dropped off a brewery wagon. This method was long known as the "Indian roll" or the "Indian block" or simply as Indianizing. Whether it was really originated by an Indian or by that crafty old paleface, Chief Pop Warner, who became the coach at the Indian school, is not known for certain. But it was most likely in use while Warner was still picking up extra wampum by playing football for the Syracuse All-Stars.

In those days fumbles could be recovered out of bounds, so that even if the field were relatively dry, a fumble might result in a scramble for a ball in a nearby mudhole. And one day in Greensburg the kickoff drove the football clear beyond the field and into a creek, from which it had to be recovered (by either side) and run out.

The rush lines had been playing from a sort of crouch, with hands on knees, since 1894. (Before that they stood chest to chest, with fists clenched and chin outthrust.) The quarterback, after the center began placing his hands on the ball (in 1894) used to squat down low enough to peer right into the upside

down face of the center and would receive the ball from the center in that position, almost hidden from the view of the enemy. But even as late as 1905, in some parts of the country, the ball was still occasionally kicked back to the quarterback by the center.

For a long time linemen had been able to run with the ball. In the "guards back" formation it was sometimes a guard who wound up as the ball carrier with a man or two to clear the way and another to shove him along from behind. Rule changes in the early years of the twentieth century required men who carried the ball to line up behind the line of scrimmage, or to run behind the line to receive a hand-off. A "tackle around" play was in almost every playbook right into the 1920's, although authorities warned that too much running by the tackles lessened their

efficiency in the line. The "pulling" guard or tackle—a feature of the modern game—was used in the olden days too, with even the ends sometimes dropping back to "run interference" for the carrier.

Experts of the early days, however, always warned football clubs not to send a light man ahead of a heavy man as an interference, for the ball carrier (running, a la mode, with his head down) might crash into his blocking teammate and "incapacitate" him. So a quarterback, who was often lighter than the ball carrier, was best employed in shoving the bigger fellow along.

"Piling on" the ball carrier after he had been thrown to the ground—a method of persuading him to holler "Down!"—was outlawed in 1894 but it remained a feature of the game for a long time, as men found it impossible to

The Pittsburgh Pros of 1902 are shown here practicing their "guards back" play, preparatory to their Thanksgiving Day game with Connie Mack's Athletics. The first man crouching in the line of scrimmage on the left is an Indian named Hare. Right behind his extended arm is smiling Christy Mathewson, already a twenty-game winner with the New York Giants and renowned as the greatest punter of his day. Mathewson played fullback and carried the ball on this play, which is reputed to have won the Championship for Pittsburgh, in a playoff, after the Thanksgiving Day tie.

resist the temptation to fling themselves bodily into the crush each time the enemy tried to move the ball. And boys who played the game on the sandlots, as we have already observed, clung for several decades to this precious feature of the game, insisting that the runner surrender before the tacklers let up on him.

Hurdling—that is, jumping over the line with both feet together, a fearsome method that had resulted in a good deal of stomped features and cracked bones —was prohibited by the changes of 1905, and the flying tackle was eventually outlawed too, this having resulted in a broken neck or two. But it is difficult to find an instance when such a tackle was actually penalized. By 1925, it was considered that the game had seen all the improvement the mind of man could devise, except for this new notion that more than one ball might be employed in the same game.

The Game Grows and Becomes More Expensive

The professional game meanwhile had known many vicissitudes. It had perhaps drawn the largest crowds and stirred the strongest emotions in the Philadelphia-Pittsburgh area. For the short time that the National Football League (first edition) survived, the two teams in Philadelphia and the one in Pittsburgh were the only ones apparently that could finance the payroll without lapse. The enthusiasm for the game, however, persisted all over the land, from east coast to west, with any number of allegedly amateur clubs in a dozen cities or more. Chicago had a cluster of clubs and Columbus, Ohio, must have owned fifteen or twenty. There were football clubs in Denver, in Los Angeles and in San Francisco,

where men could earn a few dollars every Saturday or Sunday. But the game, with the development of complicated protective equipment, had become increasingly expensive to stage. In the early 1900's it cost over fifty dollars to outfit a football player—and there usually had to be eighteen of them, to provide a few substitutes in case some were injured, fell into the grip of Demon Rum, or just stayed in bed too late. This meant an initial investment of over nine hundred dollars with the payroll and travel expenses, and ground rental on top of that.

Professional football teams therefore almost always needed an angel—as baseball "town teams" usually required the backing of the local grocer or undertaking parlor. The football angel, however, had to dig much more deeply into his pocket and sometimes he had to dig again and again, for the wear and tear on livestock as well as equipment was often severe. The motivation for an angel was usually intense local rivalry, as between Greensburg, Pennsylvania, and Latrobe. But a football rivalry was usually pretty well spent after one or two football matches. These would be well attended (sometimes eight thousand might come out in those days when a crowd of two thousand at a football game was called a jam), but it took more than one or two such gates (at twenty-five cents a head) to recoup all a man might have sunk into the club in a single autumn. And bad weather, which never caused a postponement of a football game, could cut the attendance into a sliver of what had been counted on. The Homestead Pennsylvania club in 1902, sponsored by Carnegie Steel, dropped eight thousand dollars during the season.

Yet teams sprouted everywhere and

pro elevens played against colleges, athletic clubs, and industrial teams, without discrimination. The 1902 schedule of the Pittsburgh pro eleven listed as rivals Bucknell, Pitt, Baltimore Medical College, Indiana Normal, the University of West Virginia, the Orange Athletic Club, the East End Athletics, and the Pennsylvania Railroad Y.M.C.A. Throughout the nineties and early 1900's ex-college heroes from every quarter played on one team after another, sometimes serving two or three clubs in the same season, always stooping of course to the lure of the sweetest check. This sort of competition too added to the expense of operating a club.

There was always heavy wagering on the pro games, although there was seldom a hint of bribery or dumping of games. Wagering was almost a patriotic duty. No red-blooded Latrobe fan for instance would want to admit to his neighbors that he had picked up a dirty dollar by betting on Greensburg. (Much the same sort of bet-my-shirt rivalry existed in the baseball season when towns of every size imported college and prep school heroes, often playing under crude pseudonyms, to come help win away the bankrolls of their dearest enemies.)

Eventually football fever began to flag in the Pittsburgh area, perhaps because men like W. C. Temple, who helped create the first National Football League (he also donated the Temple Cup for which professional baseball clubs competed), and A. C. Dinkey of Carnegie Steel, sponsor of the Homestead eleven, grew tired of picking up the annual tabs. But the players themselves never lost the fever and many of them moved on to newer clubs

in Ohio and farther west.

Players Were Tiny by Modern Standards

The professional football player of that era—1890 to 1910—would look like a high school kid alongside one of today's stars. Several began to play for money while still in prep school, or long before their college work was completed. The 1895 Greensburg pro eleven had two lads of nineteen, neither one of whom weighed more than 160 pounds. But even the older men were small in weight and stature compared to the young monsters who people the pro clubs in the modern day. Richard Laird, the quarterback, a graduate of Grove City College, weighed only 160. The center, R. M. Shearer, was considered a heavyweight at 185 poinds, while the left guard, Adam Wyant, who played four seasons at Bucknell and two at the University of Chicago, was a giant for his day—six feet tall and 196 pounds. (Wyant was elected to Congress while still playing football for Greensburg. He also played professional football for clubs in every quarter of the country, from New England to California.) The right end, Joe Donohue, a star of Fordham, and considered the equal of the great "Poe of Princeton," stood just five feet six inches. He would have disappeared in one of today's huddles or been pounded into the ground by a blocking halfback.

Yet most of these men kept right on playing for one club or another for seven or eight years and some undoubtedly were recruited to strengthen the new teams that sprang up in Oil City, in Franklin, in Massilon, Ohio, and in Canton.

The rivalry between Oil City and Franklin was sharp enough to send both

The first pro team in Massillon, Ohio, had two of the great Nesser brothers on its roster. Seaman, the coach, had played for the Latrobe, Pennsylvania, club in 1896. Salmon (from Notre Dame) was the greatest punter of the day.

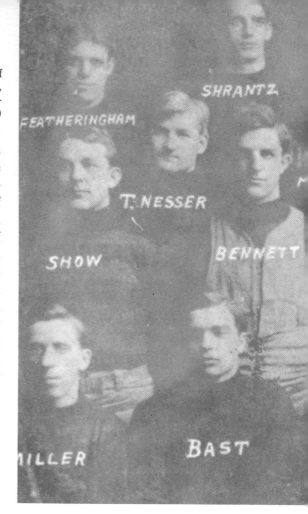

cities bidding after the veteran pros turned loose by the collapse of the National Football League. The competition to sign up the few great players of the coal-and-steel area had always been frantic, with stories of kidnaping, of midnight rides over frozen roads behind lathered horses, and of wild bidding to encourage breaking of agreements. But this time the sponsors of the Franklin club were either better bankrolled or a bit more forehanded. Within weeks they had signed up almost every famous pro in the area, including Blondy Wallace, former captain of Connie Mack's football Athletics, Pop Sweet, reputed master of the forward pass, who had played football in more towns than he could number, big Dr. Roller, the kid-glove surgeon, who had starred for the Philadelphia National Pros, and Bull Smith, who had also played pro football for Connie Mack, after completing his studies at the University of Pennsylvania.

When the Franklin recruiters were finished, the men from Oil City found the shelves bare of all football talent, except for a few creaking veterans—and they dared not risk those ancient bones against the fearsome club that Franklin had put together, so they asked that the projected game be canceled. (There was $20,000 in escrow, representing home town wagers on the game. The Franklin bettors naturally wanted the game declared forfeited. But eventually all the cash was redistributed, and the mighty Franklin club disbanded without ever getting their cleats muddy, and the rivalry sputtered out.)

It must not be imagined that pro football died, or was suspended, in the coal-and-steel country from any lack of popular interest. The crowds were sometimes washed out by the weather and occasionally some important college game would draw too many fans away. But the major games, as between Latrobe and Greensburg (known as "Jail-Town" to the Latrobe fans, because it held the county jail), still promoted as much excitement as ever, even after the new century had begun. Small boys still ran the streets late at night before the game, yelling for victory. And victory was still celebrated with redfire, Roman candles, the organized pounding of kitchen utensils by a "skillet band" and the tireless serenading of the whole town by uniformed musicians. There were still

speeches, toasts and banquets that lasted until midnight. After one game, the victorious rooters even offered to take the rival town apart—and got a good start on the job.

But still it took more and more money to field a football team and the uncertainties of the autumn weather still doubled the risk. So pro football changed its center of gravity at about the time that shinguards disappeared and helmets began to gain more favor. The game became more open, the players more skilled, and the payrolls somewhat larger. And two towns in Ohio—two towns destined to remain forever renowned as seedbeds of football—began to talk about beating each other at this game that offered more downright satisfaction to a man's yearn-ing for physical triumph than any other game ever invented.

The rivalry first took definite form in Massillon, where years later a man named Paul Brown would earn fame as a football innovator. And it was promptly taken up in Canton, the town now marked as the "birthplace" of the professional game. Football had been played in both towns, on a sort of pick-up basis, from time to time, ever since the college game had taken form as modified rugby. But no organized club had ever represented either of the towns, who previously owed their fame to their standing on or near the holy ground that had fathered William McKinley and "General" Jacob Coxey, leader of the first army of jobless men to march on Washington.

Bulldogs, Tigers, and Indians

THERE had been amateur football in Massillon and Canton (as in most other Ohio cities of any size) since the 1890's, with citizens of varying fatness of purse providing the cash that kept the clubs afloat. And, as had happened in Pittsburgh and other neighborhoods, intertown rivalry prompted the occasional bringing in of an out-of-town collegian whose "expenses" would be generously defrayed. When the amateur club from Massillon played Akron for the state championship in 1903, at least four men who helped them win were professional football players imported from Pennsylvania.

Soon after this, as other Ohio clubs began to strengthen themselves by wholesale recruiting of beef from over the Pennsylvania border, Edward Stewart, editor of the Massillon *Independent,* undertook to create a football club that would make no effort to conceal its professionalism—and that would own enough strength to wallop whatever club the neighboring town of Canton could come up with. The very first move Ed Stewart made was the purchase of a collection of football jerseys, possibly left over from one of the earlier amateur elevens. Whether his coming upon this bargain instigated the creation

65

im Thorpe.

ERNST SCHRONTZ THORP CURE WALLACE M

SHELDON LANG REEMSNYDER STEVENSON SWEET

of the team, or the notion for gathering up a team sent him out shopping for the shirts to clothe them, is a point history has failed to record. One thing seems certain, however: the club was named after the jerseys. The garments being of the type that had circular stripes all down each sleeve, the football club was naturally called the Tigers. Eddie Stewart then set about capturing the tigers to fill his jerseys for him. But before he had caged a single one, he sent a challenge to his friend Bill Day, of Canton, who accepted eagerly and joined Stewart in his safari.

Willie Heston Gives His All for Canton

Between the two of them, Stewart and Day rounded up nearly all the great pro football practitioners of that era— 1905. Most of the Philadelphia-Pittsburgh stars who were still ambulatory were brought in and divided up between the two clubs. Blondy Wallace, who had

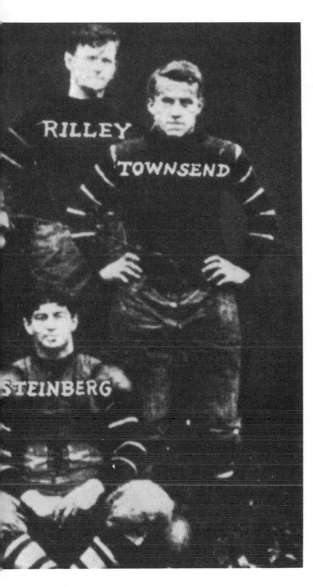

RILLEY

TOWNSEND

STEINBERG

The Bull Dogs of Canton in 1906 had Blondy Wallace for a coach. Steinberg, on the right in front row, had played for Wallace on Connie Mack's Athletics in 1902. The Schrontz in the back row is also Shrantz, who appeared with the Massillon Tigers the year before. Sweet and Cure had also played for Connie Mack. Lang was another who had switched from Massillon. He and Schrontz had been Pittsburgh Pros in 1902.

captained the Connie Mack club (this club had traveled throughout the East in 1902 seeking whom it might destroy and had even at one point fielded the great Rube Waddell in football pants), was named coach of the Canton club, which called itself Bulldogs. To officiate at the upcoming game, Stewart and Day brought in Arthur Poe of Princeton and his one-time Pittsburgh teammate, Christy Mathewson. And Day, in an unexpected coup that he felt guaranteed Canton the victory, offered six hundred dollars to Willie Heston to come play this one game. Willie Heston was Michigan's most famous ball-carrier, but he had played no professional football since graduating in 1904 because he had held out for more than any club was willing to pay. The six hundred dollar fee, however, considering the thousands that were sure to be wagered, seemed moderate enough to the Canton backers.

Eddie Stewart had a trick in his bag too. In working out the agreement for the game, Eddie included a proviso that the game would be played with the ball supplied by the home team. The home team, for this game, would be Massillon. The game was to be played on the grounds of the local insane asylum. And, perhaps to make sure the performance would not seem wholly out of place, Eddie Stewart had bought for the game a little five-and-dime type football, of the sort usually blown up by mouth. It was squishy as a toy balloon and not heavier than a handful of ping pong balls.

The Canton crowd naturally howled murder when they saw the football they were being asked to play with. But Stewart drew out the contract to illustrate that the arrangement was legal, even if a little sneaky, and the Canton boys had to make do with the imitation ball. They never doubted that it was meant to frustrate their kickers, but it would make no difference to Willie Heston, who could carry a loaf of bread for all he cared.

Willie, whose coming had been trumpeted long enough and loud enough to make him the enemy of every boy in Massillon, celebrated his entry into pro football by devoting his first night in Canton to sampling of the local brew and he did not find his bed until after the town clock had rung two—in the morning, that is. He arrived at practice camp at Congress Lake some twenty pounds overweight and still foggy of eye. But he was ready to go and never doubted that he could scamper through and around whatever aggregation of hayseeds and boilermakers Massillon could present.

Willie, with his hangover healed, did hurl himself into the battle with all his heart. But not even he could cope with the disasters that nature had laid in his path. It was generally acknowledged that Willie could run only to his right and the Massillon defense was stacked to meet him. But his first run took him across a spot of glare ice that had been covered over with rice straw. When Willie's feet struck that spot they took off from under him and let poor Willie land upon the deck chin first. The Massillon defenders, in the old-time tradition, all tried to hit him at once and when Willie had scraped himself off the ice he was winded, bruised, and lame. He made no gains at all that day, although he did perform well on defense. (Willie played football for money only once more, in Chicago, where he broke his leg and gave up football forever.)

But Eddie Stewart's boys, either because of the foolish football, the icy ground or superior play, won the game that day and sent the Canton hirelings home with their chins upon their chests. The score was 14 to 4, with Reynolds of Canton, in defiance of all the normal probabilities, having actually booted that ridiculous little balloon over the goal posts for a four-point field goal. The special train that had been hired to haul the football warriors the eight miles between Massillon and Canton was deep in gloom and reeking with arnica when it started back after the game. Then one free soul, a substitute who it was said had not even got into the game, broke into a song. Bull Smith, who was nursing a broken wrist, roared at the young man to be still.

"Nobody sings after losing a game!" he snarled.

The talent gathered for this one test of strength included stars from colleges all over the land: Turner of Dartmouth played guard for Canton (and broke his collarbone); Notre Dame's Salmon, who played for Massillon, was reputed the finest punter of the time; Merriman, who played end for Massillon, had starred at the University of Pennsylvania and had played for Latrobe and for Connie Mack's Football Athletics; Paul Steinberg of Syracuse, who played for Canton, had also played for Connie Mack in 1902; Jack Ernst, also a Bulldog, played at Lafayette; Canton's Harry James came from the University of Michigan.

In 1906, the two towns had at each other again, without Willie Heston, but with some notable shifts in the line-up. Massillon had recruited a famous forward passer, Peggy Parrott of Cleveland, acknowledged master of this new tactic. But Canton had Pop Sweet, the tramp athlete, who had dealt with the pass before. Also playing for Canton

Willie Heston, Michigan's greatest ball-carrier, did not turn pro immediately because his price ($1200) was too high. Canton finally hired him for $600 to play against Massilon. Willie failed to gain a yard in that game.

CARR (GR)   A. KUEHNER   SCHNEIDER   A. NESSER   FRANK NESSER   GRAC

KIRTZINGER   JOHN NESSER   FRED NESSER   TED NESSER   R. KUEHNER   PHIL NESSER

RHU   SNOOTS   1915   DUNN   PICKERAL

COLUMBUS PAN HANDLES - 1911

The Columbus, Ohio, Panhandles in 1915 had all the Nessers aboard. Oldest is Ted, Jr., in the middle. Next to him is his big son Fred. This is the only father-son combination ever known to have played professional football.

were four men who had played in the first game for the Massillon Tigers: Clark Schrontz, Riley, Charley Moran, and John Lang. Lang had played for the Pittsburgh Pros in 1902. P. J. McNulty and Herman Kirkhoff, who played for Massillon, had also been members of David Berry's Pittsburgh Pros and continued to play professional football several more seasons.

The Massillon-Canton Rivalry Ends in Scandal

The 1906 Bulldogs scheduled three games against the Tigers of Massillon. The build-up for this series was like the tension that usually precedes a baseball World Series. Throngs of fans gathered at the railroad terminals at either end of the eight-mile run and frightened the local constables with their wild screaming and reckless dashing back and forth. Betting was heavy. Even the hardboiled pros gathered up a pool to wager on themselves. The first game went to Canton, 5 to 0, and should have brought several hundred dollars extra to the Bulldogs, except that their coach, Blandy Wallace, had, he reported, been unable to get the money off. Fear not, he assured his charges, he would lay all of it and more upon the Bulldogs in the next game, which Canton seemed certain to win.

But Canton came in second in the second game by a score of 6 to 2. Almost immediately afterwards, the Massillon *Independent* accused Coach Blondy Wallace of having bribed one of his own players to throw the game to the Tigers. Blondy, in the face of this accusation, snatched up his clean shirt and military brushes, threw his spare suit helter-skelter into a suitcase, and took a train for far away. Then he wrote back a solemn threat to sue the newspaper for libel. The newspaper editor urged him to come back and take out the summons, but Blondy made no response. He quit the state and quit football, to turn up some fifteen years later as "King of the Bootleggers" in Atlantic City, New Jersey.

This dismal event seemed to dull the taste for professional football in Canton. The Bulldogs, who had doubled all their wagers for the second game, and who had some unacknowledged traitor in their midst, began to lose their own zest for the game. They traveled to Latrobe, Pennsylvania, to meet the crack pro team there, lost the game, could not collect their guarantee, and so disbanded.

After the Bulldogs, there was no full-time pro team in Canton for several years. But the memories of the games with Massillon provided barroom and cigarstore conversation for months to come, as men recalled the lovely header Willie Heston took, or the way Big Bill Edwards, the referee, when he caught the Canton waterboy sneaking information in from the sidelines, picked the lad up by the collar and the slack of his pants and hurled him like a sack of bran clear off the playing field. Oh, those had been the great days—when the "special train" that chugged its way to Massillon and back carried so many extra fans they had to sit on each other, and when there was singing, and drinking, and giving of cheers far into the night. Or when a man who forgot to check his buggy whip (worth ten dollars in that day) at the box office was certain to come back and find some scamp had lifted it out of its socket and made off with it.

The Nessers—They All Enjoyed Their Football

Two stalwarts who played for the first Massillon Tigers were to adorn the rosters of Ohio football clubs for many years more. They were John and Ted Nesser, eldest of the Nesser brothers, around whom the Panhandle A.C. of Columbus, Ohio, would build a football club. The Nessers were boilermakers, employed by the Panhandle Division of the Pennsylvania Railroad, and able, through their employment, to travel far and wide without payment of fare. And because Papa Nesser (an immigrant from Alsace at the turn of the century) helped out as trainer and waterboy, while Mama Nesser kept the socks and jerseys clean, the club was able to function when other clubs sank into bankruptcy.

No redskins among these Akron "Indians" of 1911. At least one of the helmets seems to have been handed down from father to son. The lad on the extreme left in the back row was called "Rabbit," not because he was small but because his name was Maranville.

The Shelby, Ohio, Blues of 1910 were strictly a sandlot organization. This "lockstep" pose was a favorite of professional photographers of that era. Most of the men are dressed in the clothes they played football in.

John Nesser was a quarterback, one of the best in the early game. He had come over on the steamship with Mama and Papa and brothers Ted, Jr., and Phil. Before his football career was over, he had his nephew Fred playing at his side. Perhaps the ablest of all the Nessers was Phil, who was an all-round athlete and, in a later age, would probably have had scholarships from a dozen colleges. But every one of the Nessers was All-America material. Frank, like Jim Thorpe, could punt the old-fashioned football from one end of the field to the other on the fly. Al was a forward passer as well as a ferocious defensive man, who never found an opponent too big or too rough to mix with. None of the Nessers ever attended college but all played football. For, as brother Al said in his later years (when he was not placing the family curse on "cheaters" who did truckmen out of work by sending truck bodies piggyback on flat cars), "Football was made for everybody to enjoy."

This apparently was the theory throughout the whole state of Ohio. Football clubs bloomed in every city, small or large. Ultimately, Ohio State University seemed the focal point for the game, but in the years just before and after the first World War, the amateur, the semi-professional, and the professional games generated practically all the steam. In Dayton, in Cleveland, in Akron, in Columbus, in Massillon, and in Canton football clubs took hold, grew great, and actually prospered, many of them with hardly a college-trained athlete on the roster and all of the members playing for a share of the gate. Some wore the jerseys of various neighborhood athletic clubs which developed almost spontaneously among groups of young men who thought they had as much right to play the game as any college kid had. (When a number of "athletic clubs" played in O'Rourke's indoor tournament in 1903 at Madison Square Garden, New York sportswriters ridiculed the "ribbon clerks" attending the games who tried to sing and cheer like college boys.) Other clubs were created as promotional schemes by various industries. (In Akron, the Goodyear Tire Company, then featuring the fact that their tires hushed the racket a motorcar made, financed a football club called the "Silents.") And a few, like the Columbus Tigers and the Canton Bulldogs, were out to earn money enough to stay afloat by themselves, turn a profit for the promoters, and pay decent fees to the players.

Jim Thorpe Comes to Canton

In 1915, a couple of fellows named McGregor and Clark set out to revive the Canton Bulldogs, hoping to steam up the always simmering rivalry with Massillon. They filled their roster with loyal high school heroes, however, and failed to rally the following they needed. Whereupon another Cantonian, Jack Cusack, brought Jim Thorpe to town and set him to building a real football club. Thorpe, within a few years, had built one that no one in the nation could lick. Some of the opponents in the early years could not even manage a first down against them.

Among the ballplayers Thorpe brought in were Earle "Greasy" Neale, star quarterback from West Virginia Wesleyan, who was destined to become coach of the Philadelphia Eagles; Tuss McLaughry, who would earn later fame as a coach at Dartmouth and Brown,

The Carlisle Indian football team in 1912, the year Jim Thorpe took home nearly every prize in the Olympics, had three future Canton Bulldogs on its roster: Jim Thorpe, holding the football and standing next to coach Glenn Warner; Peter Calac, at extreme left of middle row; and Joe Guyon, second from right in middle row. The Indian Industrial School was situated in Carlisle, Pennsylvania, where the War College now stands.

where he created the Iron Men; Charlie Brickley, most famous drop-kicker in the game; and Fido Kempton from Yale, the smallest man ever known to play professional football. But Thorpe himself was the power source and without him the club lost at least half its strength. When Jim was there the club apparently could not be beat. When he was on the sidelines, they often lost.

Because the real juice that quickened the veins of pro football in that era was provided by the wholesale betting that preceded every game, big Jim Thorpe did not fail to make note of what his presence or absence might do to the

Above: Jim Thorpe, ear-flaps raised as usual, while engaged in a punting exhibition between halves of game with Rochester Jeffs in 1917. Photographer with old-fashioned Graflex has recorded the deed. Jim kicked the ball in the air, from one goal line to the other. Canton won the game, 49–0. *Opposite top left:* Jim Thorpe shaking hands with Charlie Brickley, Harvard drop-kicking star, before start of game between Canton and Massillon, in 1917. Thorpe and Brickley gave kicking exhibitions between halves. Note the hole in Jim's stocking. *Top center:* In 1921, Thorpe was still giving drop-kicking exhibitions. The ball of that day was built for kicking. Jim is better-uniformed and a little fleshier than in earlier pictures. *Top right:* Jim Thorpe's punting form, about 1920. *Opposite bottom:* Jim Thorpe, a fat and jolly Indian, posing at a sports show in 1950 with the greatest woman athlete in the world, Babe Didrickson Zaharias. A few years later both were dead of cancer.

odds. And he was known on occasion to lay many hundreds of dollars on his own club, when the price was right. Sometimes he *made* the price right by acting as if he had been injured or lay sick abed. He did this just before a game with Massillon, sustaining an "injury" on the field and giving out that he would not be able to play against this, their most devoted rival.

Massillon-Canton rivalry in the Thorpe era burned more fiercely than ever. Occasionally when a triumphant enemy departed, or a beaten enemy slunk away, there would be a riot at the rail station, as taunts were swapped for punches in the nose with free will, while howls of victory, like the yells of victorious Indians, drowned all thought. And of course there would be angry challenges to bet this or that, or three times as much, and men would hasten to put down a rival by laying against him more money than they could afford to lose. This time, with Thorpe apparently out of the game, the odds, which usually favored Canton, fell to even money. At that point, sly Jim, the story went, had someone lay $2500 on Canton. And when the game began, out ran Jim, fresh and sound as a two-year-old, and ready to destroy any set of men who stood in his path.

Destroy them is what Jim often did, too. While most of yesterday's heroes would probably find themselves outweighed, outsmarted and outrun by the pro football players of today, Jim Thorpe would still be able to give back more than he received. For Jim was not, like some of his famous hirelings, just a fine football player. He was a great athlete, perhaps the greatest who ever lived. Even though the man who coached

him, Pop Warner, never agreed he was the best (that was Ernie Nevers, at Stanford, said Warner), he did not belittle Jim's ability. It was just that Pop found Jim "sulky and hard to handle"— as perhaps any Indian had a right to be. (Jim was part Sac and Fox Indian and part Irish.) Sometimes, they said, Jim did not try as hard as he could. But he did try hard in the 1912 Olympics and won almost everything except the Swedish crown jewels. (He did win a special trophy—a small golden boat inlaid with pearls—offered by the Shah of Persia for Jim alone.) Then he had to give all his trophies back when some long-nosed trouble-seeker pointed out that Jim was a "professional"—not a professional runner, and jumper and pole-vaulter, but a "professional baseball player," because he had once taken small sums of money for playing baseball in a minor league, just as almost every other college athlete of his day had done.

But Jim was unmatched in speed and strength. He could either run right over a tackler, like a trailer truck disposing of a Volkswagen, or he could offer a quick body fake and dodge into the clear. But those who played with him usually agreed that what Jim liked best to do was play defense, where he had a chance to deal out a fierce wallop that would put an enemy player on the sod to stay for a while. A few who had felt his tackles insisted that Jim wore, for "shoulder pads," chunks of lightly padded steel that were meant not so much to protect Jim's flesh as to deal out deep bruises and lacerations to those who would dare to try to carry the football past him.

One or two close-up observers always

insisted that Jim would sometimes allow a forward pass to be completed in his neighborhood, just so he would not be deprived of the ineffable delight of blindsiding the poor receiver into temporary oblivion. One fellow who felt a tackle of Jim's (it was like being hit with the blunt end of a telephone pole, he averred) recalls Jim's happy and sympathetic countenance looking down upon him, with the words, delivered in a gentle tone: "A man could get hurt playing this game. If he don't take care."

The Competition Begins to Grow

Although the Massillon-Canton rivalry was the sharpest and produced perhaps the largest and loudest turnouts—sometimes 8,000 fans attended and now and then a few hundred of these would take to belting each other at a tense moment in the game—there was competition aplenty for Jim Thorpe's Bulldogs, even before the National League was born. Besides the Akron Silents, sometimes nicknamed the "Mutes," there were the Jeffersons in Rochester, New York, named after the street where the original members of the club had resided; the Buffalo All-Americans; the Maroons in Toledo; the Triangles in Dayton; the Panhandles (who became the Tigers) in Columbus; the Blues in Shelby; and Akron Indians; the Fort Wayne Friars; the Cleveland Indians; the Detroit Heralds; the Zanesville Mark Group; the Pitcairn Quakers, besides teams in Hammond and Rock Island, Illinois. In the effete East, college football, particularly that played at Harvard, Yale, and Princeton, continued to draw the large share of public attention, mostly because Sunday sports

were still outlawed in the big cities. What games were played, among semi-pro "athletic clubs" or industrially sponsored teams were somewhat disorderly spectacles, often played in unfenced parks with the fans crowded close along the sidelines and even moving up behind the offensive team's backfield. In the Midwest and the West however, pro football pulled in crowds of 2,000 and more in a dozen different places. Several cities, notably Chicago, Cleveland, and Columbus, would field clubs of every age and weight, from midget to grown-up, with each drawing clientele enough to keep the hands contented. In Columbus for instance, besides the Panhandles (who played all their games "on the road") there were such clubs as the Ralston Indians, the Beaver Humps, the Linden Whistles, the Bates Pirates, and the Wagner Pirates (who once beat the Jungle Imps for the "city championship" before a screaming crowd of 4,000).

Sometimes it took just a single angel, willing to indulge his fancy in sports for a season or two, to keep one of these clubs solvent. More often, a group of men with money in their pockets, or skill at finding it, would "back" the club and hire a coach from some college. The Dayton Triangles, for instance, were created about the same time as Jim Thorpe's reconstituted Bulldogs, financed by the patent attorney for Delco Products, F. B. McNabb, and by Earl Cromer, another local industrialist, along with several others, including Al Giessler, who sold sporting goods. Bud Talbot, an All-America from Yale, was named coach, and he recruited players from near and far. The real star, however, was a local collegian, Lou Partlow,

The Rochester, New York, Jeffersons in 1907 were made up of young men who live on or near Jefferson Avenue in Rochester. They changed into their uniforms in a windowless attic in Pete Hutchinson's Hotel and walked a mile to West End park. The charged ten cents to see them play. Most of them in this picture are wearing th clothes they played in, with only two helmets and a noseguard among them.

the Dayton University fullback. The home park, Westwood Field, had a set of bleachers but most fans gathered along the sidelines. The club drew an average of 2,000 spectators at home, and then moved to Triangle Park, where more seats meant larger crowds and a better gate. With crowds of 6,000 or more, the club could afford to entertain the "big" teams from Canton, Cleveland, and Detroit.

It was this way with clubs in cities all through the corn belt. College football was thriving but it did not happen often enough to gratify all the local appetites. Nor did it always properly incarnate the sometimes venomous rivalry between town and town, nor offer the ideal vehicle for betting your shirt on the home boys.

Leo Lyons—Promoter and End Extraordinary

The Rochester Jeffersons (there was also a Rochester Clothiers in the 1920s) were born even earlier than Jim Thorpe's Bulldogs, fathered by a man named Leo Lyons, who eventually became the official historian of the National Football League. They were organized, as so many such clubs were, on a neighborhood basis, a bunch of teenagers who wanted a better chance to play the game than they were getting in school. Then they grew into full-time pros as the need for victories sent them reaching farther and farther out to find faster halfbacks and mightier linemen. Leo Lyons joined the Jeffersons in 1910, when he was sixteen years old. He took charge of the club two years later and soon turned it into a team that could even provide opposition for Jim Thorpe's Bulldogs and the assembled Nesser brothers of Columbus.

Pro teams of this type were not really professional in the sense that their members devoted themselves to this calling alone. There was never enough money to pay anyone a wage that would justify his trying to use football to earn a living. The players, except for one or two stars, might get from $25 to $100 a game, and sometimes might have to whistle for that when a "guarantee" failed to materialize or a check proved worthless. Jim Thorpe paid his hearties according to the length of time they worked in a game. The college rules makers had divided the game, in 1910, into four equal quarters, and the pros played in the same way. A man who got into only one quarter of a game for the Bulldogs would take home a small check that day. Or he might get $300 for playing the whole game. Charlie Brickley, after he graduated from Harvard, was paid $3,000 by Jim Thorpe to play just a few games for the Bulldogs. Other big names, who might be expected to bring extra customers in, would enjoy, for a time, fatter paychecks than ordinary.

Of course every club needed a promoter, a man who would arrange the schedule, buy the train tickets, or scrounge for the automobiles, keep the equipment in repair, get the tickets printed, put up the posters and place the ads, hire the stars, appease the workaday players, bind up wounds, pay doctors' bills, make excuses to distraught wives, go drag a forgetful fullback out of a barroom or off the farm, hire the officials, buy lunch and dinner for the hands, recruit a coach (or do the job himself), meet the guarantees, get the team out on the field and bring them all safely home. Leo Lyons managed to do all these things for the Jeffersons and in

addition he played end in a style so ferocious that it took a bold ball carrier indeed to try to dodge past him.

To keep a professional football team afloat in a moderate-sized city takes the sort of energy and ambition that might lead a man to the Presidency. He must always be thinking in larger and larger terms and must be continually concerned with capturing the star that will draw the crowd and beat the enemy. He soon discovers that nothing wins devotion more than victories do, yet he must seek always mightier foes, lest his club find itself cast among the once-were-goods and the second-rate.

Leo made a practice of challenging any football team that dared call itself the champion of anything. And he did not fear to make offers to the greatest stars within a day's travel. He hired Ben Lee Boynton when that devil-may-care young man still carried the glory he had earned at Williams. He even brought in Elmer Q. Oliphant, often called West Point's greatest athlete, to play at the

Bay Street Park for the Jeffersons. Elmer incidentally ripped his fine gray cadet overcoat clear to the neck one day when someone forgot the key to the park and he had to climb over the fence.

Ben Lee Boynton performed some of his mightiest deeds while wearing the colors of the Jeffersons. Men can still recall the day when he "dodged" a tackler by diving head first over the top of the man, landing neatly on his head and shoulders, rolling in a somersault and flipping cleanly to his feet to resume his run like a tumbler. He took the ball seventy yards to a touchdown that day.

Benny with the Jeffersons often exhibited his skills at improvising. He was the sort of man who, despite his diminutive size, might even have held a job on one of today's clubs, for he was cool, alert, quick to size up a defense, and he would react instantaneously to a new alignment. In Benny's day there were no huddles and the quarterback had to call the whole play by signals—giving the "hole" through which the play was go-

ing, the back who would carry the ball, the description of the play, and the snap signal all in the "first set." Benny, barking his code numbers in the voice of a cattle auctioneer, would be quick to cry "Signals off!" and begin all over again with a new play and a new ball-carrier if some shift in the defense tempted him.

By the time Ben Lee began to work for the Jeffersons, Leo Lyons had quit playing and was devoting all his time to rounding up football players and raising the money to feed them. Leo never relied on letters or telegrams or telephone calls to lay hold of a new star. If he did not get an immediate response, he would pick up and take off for whatever hole the man might be hiding in. He signed Ben Lee Boynton right out of a steel mill, where the rugged young Texan was "learning the business." What made this accomplishment particularly sweet is that the man who owned the Pittsburgh open-hearth mill where Ben was working was Eugene Grace, who had been assigned by the Akron club to sign Ben Lee for them. But Mr. Grace, perhaps certain that he had the young man tucked away where no rival foot dared venture, waited too long to get the signature.

Leo very nearly brought Red Grange to Rochester too. Indeed he did actually "sign" Grange through his college-boy manager, who had not been let in on the secret that Red actually had signed with C. C. Pyle before he completed his college season. (Whether Grange had actually signed an agreement with Pyle and accepted money is a moot point. He said he had not. But he certainly had arrived at an agreement with old Cash-and-Carry that made it impossible for him to accept any other offer.) Leo offered Grange's self-styled manager

Leo Lyons, shown here in 1914, joined the Jeffs in 1908 and eventually turned them into a full-time professional club, one of the original franchise holders in the National Football League. Leo, who is now seventy-seven and official historian of the National Football League, played with the Jeffs steadily (at left end) until 1916. But he occasionally got into the line-up after that and kept in condition by running the roads and circling a nearby park.

$5,000 a game—which, as it turned out, would have been a bargain price—and the offer was accepted. But Red never came to Rochester.

Leo, however, did several times go to Chicago. Once he got there and found himself short of a ball-carrier and had to sign a cop off the Chicago mounted force, whose presence on his club brought howls of happy greetings such as "Where's the horse?" from the fans. It also irritated the Chicago Cardinals' management, who accused Leo of bad faith in substituting an unknown for a top college star.

But top college stars did not always keep their commitments. Sometimes weather, and sometimes bootleg gin, and sometimes angry wives or mothers kept young men from getting to the park on time. Leo however was always able to field a full team and sometimes had more men on his roster than he really needed. He was not, however, always able to meet the promised payroll and never really made a dime out of the game. Indeed, had it not been for football, Leo might have established himself as a successful industrialist, or even have run for governor. Football, however, filled his days, kept him up nights, and sent him scampering to and fro about the face of the globe seeking players, money, games, and new worlds to conquer.

Cathartics and Catastrophes Enliven the Game

The world of pro football even then was wide and exciting. It just was not rich. There were long freezing rides in the lumbering Pierce-Arrow that served as team bus. There were drafty dressing rooms and cold showers, or no showers at all. There were rock-strewn playing fields, or fields where runners who dashed out of bounds had to dodge parked automobiles or jump over stretched-out wagon tongues. There were sometimes broken arms or legs that needed splinting, even long hospital stays for an injured star. There were also minor feuds and flare-ups among the players to bedevil Leo's waking hours.

Leo was bewildered one day, when his club was playing at Atlantic City, to see Lou Smythe, his big fullback from Texas, start for the sidelines. The enemy hastened to "cover" this unexpected man-in-motion but Lou kept right on going, across the sidelines, into the locker room, far beyond the end zone. Leo immediately had to stop play to put in a substitute and his club was penalized. Ten minutes later, Smythe reappeared, amid hoots and laughter from the fans, and sat down on the bench beside Leo. For heaven's sake! Leo inquired (or perhaps he used some other exclamation), what kind of a stunt was that? "Oh, Ah'll kill that Gah dam Sheard!" Lou Smythe replied. "He must have found out Ah drunk his gin! You know them chiclets he give me on the train? Take two, he says! They were Feenamints! Ah swear, Ah'll kill him!" (Shag Sheard was Lou's star halfback from St. Lawrence. In Providence he had bought a pint of bootleg gin and the backfield boys had finished it for him and filled the bottle with water.)

But there were worse catastrophes than sudden doses of cathartics in Leo's path. At a time when his finances were at their shallowest, with all salaries paid and games against the Providence Steamrollers and the New York Giants completed without so much as a broken fingernail, Leo was invited to play on election day in Orange, New Jersey, where, his players agreed, Leo should get the whole guarantee to enable him to finish the season somewhere short of bankruptcy. The guarantee was $1200. At the final moment, in the lobby of the Astor Hotel in New York, a group of Leo's best players, for whom he had all but emptied his veins to keep the pay envelopes full, met and decided they would have to have an extra twenty-five dollars apiece. After stilling that rebellion, Leo led his charges off to the train. And in the game one man after another cracked a bone. First Frank Matteo, the tackle from Syracuse, broke an elbow. Then Charlie Strack, the Colgate guard, split his collarbone. Then Leo's prize end, Gene Bedford, who had starred for Southern Methodist, had his thighbone broken in a crush. Bedford had to be wheeled off the field and fed into a Pullman car through a window. He lay six months after that in a Rochester hospital (at Leo's expense). Leo collected his guarantee before he took his wounded troops home. There was $500 in cash and a check for $700. The check, having been issued of course under the same evil star, was returned without honor by the bank.

But promoters were not the only ones who knew lean days in the early years of the organized game. Paychecks as well as guarantees sometimes turn sour. Injured players were not always taken home and cared for. And occasionally a ball-carrier who had lost a little speed could find himself abandoned far from daddy's rooftree. Ex-college stars who had grown used to being courted, winked at, and made allowances for by the college coach were sometimes alarmed to discover that the profes-

sional coach hardly had time to snarl in their direction. There would be no free tickets for the ballplayers, either. Rather, they were often expected to help unload a few box seats in their spare time. And the headline stars sometimes spent a good part of their guarantee buying tickets for their own admirers.

There were often club owners whose knowledge of the game was two yards lower than rudimentary who still would not hesitate to come roaring into a locker room after a game had been lost, to lecture the men on how they should have executed this play or that.

Johnny Blood and the "Gimme-the-Ball" Attitude

Obviously a man had to be in pro football for more than the money. And there *was* much more for a young, unattached man with an appetite for violent play and reckless wandering. Practice sessions in the old days were not much more violent than some playground games, and often consisted of little more than running through signals. Travel was not often first class but it was usually merry and always in good company. In the strange new cities there were girls for the taking, no curfew hour, and dim-lit speakeasies to prowl in.

There was an air of abandon about the game, with some players using assumed names so they might play out their college eligibility without penalty, then hanging on to the false names as handy *noms-de-joie* in case there might be tattletales afoot.

There was a player once, from St. John's in Minneapolis, who, seeing the name "Blood and Sand" on a theater marquee, decided that he and his foot-

The Jeffs of 1911 were still slightly ragamuffin in appearance but they had begun to reach out for better ballplayers. In this picture, Leo is sitting with the football in his lap in the front row. Fourth from the right in the back row is Henry McDonald, who may have been the very first black man to play pro football. In 1970, at the age of eighty, McDonald was umpiring baseball games in Geneva, New York.

ball partner should borrow those names to use, in the accepted fashion, so as not to flaunt unduly the fact that they were taking money for playing games. So John McNally became Johnny Blood and he built himself a reputation that well became his borrowed name, which stuck to him long past the time when he no longer needed to pretend to amateurism. These were the triple-threat days, when a truly great football player was expected to execute with high skill every feature of the game—to run fast and elusively, to pass strongly and accurately, to kick the ball long distances and with deadly aim. And of course every ball player had to be able to play a fierce defensive game, regardless of his size. Johnny Blood was a triple threat. At least he was ready to try almost anything, on the field or off.

Typical of Johnny's attitude was his sudden decision one day to take over a job he had never tried before. He arrived at a game with Brooklyn (Johnny being then captain and assistant coach of the Pittsburgh Steelers) after having been cloistered all week with bottles and poker chips, just in time to refresh himself with a hot shower and get into uniform to find his own club back on the four-yard line, at fourth down. The team punter hopped up from the bench and affixed his helmet. "I guess this is for me," said he.

"Naah!" said Johnny Blood. "I can do it better!" Whereupon he trotted in, never having punted in pro ball before, took the pass from center deep in his end zone and booted the ball out to the Brooklyn twenty-yard line, seventy-six yards from the line of scrimmage.

It was this "gimme-the-ball" quality that provided the pro game its special flavor then, despite short pay and rough travel, with games sometimes piling upon one another on Saturday, then on Sunday, until a man might crawl into his bunk aching too much to eat his supper.

The Paper League

WHEN the National League began it was called the American League and it had so little substance that not everyone is sure exactly when It was born. If we are to believe one of the few men who actually assisted at the delivery, the league was created in 1919 in Canton, Ohio, on a steamy afternoon in the big showroom of Ralph Hay's Hupmobile Sales Agency, where several football "managers" had gathered. Ralph Hay was himself General Manager of the Bulldogs, and Jim Thorpe, who really ran the club, sat there that day on the running board of a brand new touring car. The only chairs in the place were already occupied by Hay, Leo Lyons of Rochester, Joe Carr of the Columbus Panhandles, Frank Neid of the Akron Indians, and Carl Storck of the Dayton Triangles. Each of them, representing the original five cities in the league—Rochester, Canton, Columbus, Dayton, and Akron—chipped in twenty-five dollars each to finance the league. This was not much more than enough to enable them to print stationery, listing Jim Thorpe as president.

About all the business, besides the assessment and the election of Jim Thorpe, that was completed that day was the adoption of a code of ethics con-

87

Elmer Q. Oliphant of West Point, who played pro football for the Rochester Jeffersons and the Buffalo All-Americans, earned letters in so many different sports at the Military Academy that a special order of the War Department was required to create a new letter "A" to go on his sweater. He called it his "Act of Congress A."

This picture of the Youngstown (Ohio) Patricians, taken in 1914, looks more like a team photo of a school club. But they played for money. And this may be the only picture of a pro team that includes the public relations man, far right in the second row, wearing a hard collar. The objects at the players' feet are not footballs but helmets. The only football is the large squash-size one with the lettering on it.

sisting chiefly of an agreement not to recruit college players until after they had completed their studies. (This agreement, as the league spread out and competition for talent grew fiercer, was earnestly ignored by new franchise-holders.) Next year, there were too many applicants to find seats even in Ralph Hay's big showroom, and the franchise fee was jumped to one hundred dollars. Joining the league this year, 1920, which is still the "official" birth date of the league according to the keepers of its archives, were the Massillon Tigers, the Cleveland Indians, the Chicago Cardinals, the Decatur Blues (sponsored by the Staley Starch Company of Decatur, Illinois), and teams from Rock Island, Muncie, and Hammond. The Decatur club, which became known as the Staleys, moved to Chicago eventually and became the Bears. On board the starch company club at the time was a young baseball player who had missed his chance with the New York Yankees and hadn't been making enough money in St. Paul. This was George Halas, a hard-fisted end from Illinois who had played some football at the Great Lakes Naval Training Station during World War I. George had first tried for a job in Rochester but Leo Lyons had no more room for another end (if he had, he might have taken the job himself). Whereupon George accepted an offer from Hammond, Indiana, where he played end. He came to the starch company the following season. George, in putting together a club made up largely of men he had seen in action at Illinois or at the Training Station, chose as his quarterback a voluble little fellow who just bubbled self-confidence—Chuck Dressen.

(The Staley Starch Company also fielded a baseball team, managed by Iron Man Joe McGinnity.)

The New League Has Its Troubles From the Start

The new league proved unwieldy right from the start. It was impossible for every club to face every other an even number of times. Some clubs had hardly any place to play at home, or had to share the space with a college team. Some could not keep their roster filled without slipping in a high school player or two. But in a few places—mostly around Columbus, Ohio, and Chicago—the thirst for football could never be slaked. In Chicago on a single weekend, in addition to whatever games might be scheduled by the colleges, there were semi-pro and amateur football clubs in action by the score. The Kelly Roamers, the Pullman Panthers, the White Stars, the Mike Igoe Boosters, the Mohawks, the Badgers, the Pirates, the Titans, the Teddy Bears, and, for heaven's sake, the Livingston Tiger Lilies, were all fielding football elevens in the twenties.

The game being played then had, according to those who knew all about it, attained a state of "perfection." The rule that kept seven men in the scrimmage line had wiped out the last vestige of the old flying-wedge-type attack. The forward pass could be thrown more freely now and the pros used it far more often than the college boys dared. For now the dropped pass was not a free ball, nor did it go over to the enemy if it sailed out of bounds. The potential receiver of a pass now was protected by the rules so he could not be assaulted before he laid a hand on the ball. The neutral zone kept the scrimmage lines rigidly separated so that a modern spectator,

Henry McDonald, who played ten years for the Rochester Jeffersons (1911–1920), w reputed to be the fastest professional football player of his day. But this get-up v borrowed from Hobart College, where Henry, at the age of seventy-two, was still wo ing as trainer in 1962. At age eighty, he was umpiring baseball in Central New Yor

Charter member of the National Football League was the Dayton Triangles (they played at Triangle Park). Star of the club was the spindle-shanked young man standing next to the coach at the far right in the back row—Eugene Partlow of Dayton University.

had he been transported back to that golden time, would at least have recognized that the clubs were playing football. The lines crouched lower then, undertaking to plow a pathway through the opposing flesh. And the defense concentrated largely on punishing the enemy about the head and neck—a feature of the game accepted as legitimate "use of hands." The hands, however, were often taped into clubs and the destroying of the opposing guard or tackle was sometimes attended to with such devotion that the defense forgot the runner.

The center snapped the ball with his head down, looking back between his legs at the waiting hands of the quarterback, and trusting in his advance knowledge of the snap-count to allow him to get his head up and moving forward be-

fore some blunted guillotine fell upon his neck.

Forward passing was done from five yards behind the scrimmage line, with the ends split out and dodging about in tag football fashion to get out where the quarterback could find them uncovered. The standard offensive formation was what would be called today the "tight T" except that the fullback was about a stride farther back than the two halfbacks. Now and then some coach would offer a spread formation in which one of the halfbacks took his position several yards to the right or left of the rest of the company and he might even have a lineman out there in front of him. The center usually had to pass the ball directly to the man who was going to run with it, timing his pass so as to meet the run-

92

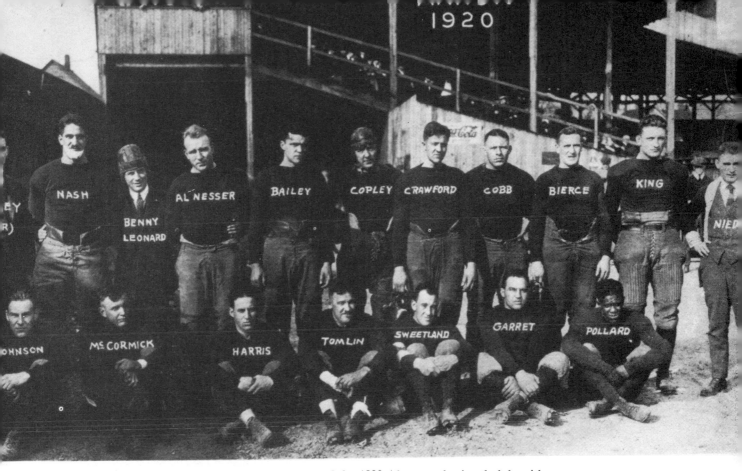

1920

NASH   BENNY LEONARD   AL NESSER   BAILEY   COPLEY   CRAWFORD   COBB   BIERCE   KING   NIE...

EY (R)   NIE...

JOHNSON   McCORMICK   HARRIS   TOMLIN   SWEETLAND   GARRET   POLLARD

Benny Leonard, shown in the back row in this picture of the 1920 Akron professional club, with one arm around big Al Nesser, was no football player. He was lightweight boxing champion of the world. Far right in the front row is one of pro football's earliest black stars, Fritz Pollard of Brown.

ner en route. This required such intense concentration that the center's effectiveness as a blocker was greatly reduced. (Now and then a coach might have his center line up with his back to the enemy, squatting over the ball like an Indian fakir about to open a pot of snakes, and flipping it up to the proper man on the sounding of the signal. In this position he was, of course, not really a blocker but merely an obstacle.)

Momentum Was Difficult to Develop

Momentum plays were hard to evolve out of this tight formation and backs did not have much room to find daylight. But if the carriers could slip through between tackle and end, they had a good chance of making handsome gains, provided they knew how to change direc-

tion swiftly once the scrimmage line had been passed. A solid block on the opposing end, with the tackle being dealt with by the offensive guard, would mean that the halfback, if he owned any speed, had just a few widely scattered opponents to deal with, and some of them already behind him. There would be the defensive halfbacks several yards away and a safety man farther back still, with a fullback and "roving center" chasing after the runner. Sometimes a really fast halfback could simply outrun the defensive end, with the help of some interference; then he might travel a long long way without an unfriendly hand being set upon him.

But momentum had to come from "end around" plays, in which the end turned, after a short delay, and came

93

Left: Baby Bear before he became Papa Bear. George Halas of the Staleys in 1921. *Right:* A good idea of the size and shape of the old-fashioned football is offered in this pose of lithe Fritz Pollard, one of the hardest men to tackle in pro football. Passing in Fritz' day was like putting the shot.

Ben Lee Boynton, shown in his Williams College uniform about 1920. The felt padding, known as kidney pads, was favored by carriers who might be hit from behind. But hardly anyone could ever run fast enough to hit Bennie from behind. Bennie quarterbacked the Rochester Jeffersons in 1921 and 1922.

back through the backfield to take a hand-off from a back traveling in the opposite direction. When this play worked well (and of course it depended on a good bit of play-acting by the back to persuade the enemy that he still had the ball), about the only man that had to be blocked out was the "waiting end" on the side toward which the play was aimed. And occasionally even he was sucked in by the original flow of the play and would be far out of position when the ultimate ball carrier came hammering past. There was also a Statue of Liberty play in which the presumptive passer in the "short punt formation" would hold the ball back as if to heave it, and instead would allow the circling end to pluck it out of his hand, to continue around the end opposite to the one from which he started.

Sometimes a "tackle around" play provided a bit of surprise, along with an extra-heavy ball carrier. But most deception was accomplished by "cross-bucks" in which the halfbacks traveled in a criss-cross path and the quarterback offered the ball to one before giving it to the other. The quarterback in this old-fashioned formation had to be a ball carrier as well as field general, for passing was still used sparingly. He often had to be a punter too for an "onside kick," in which the quarterback booted the ball with two or three backs behind him—all "onside" and thus eligible to recover the ball—was not uncommon. Because substitutions were severely limited (a player once removed could not be re-

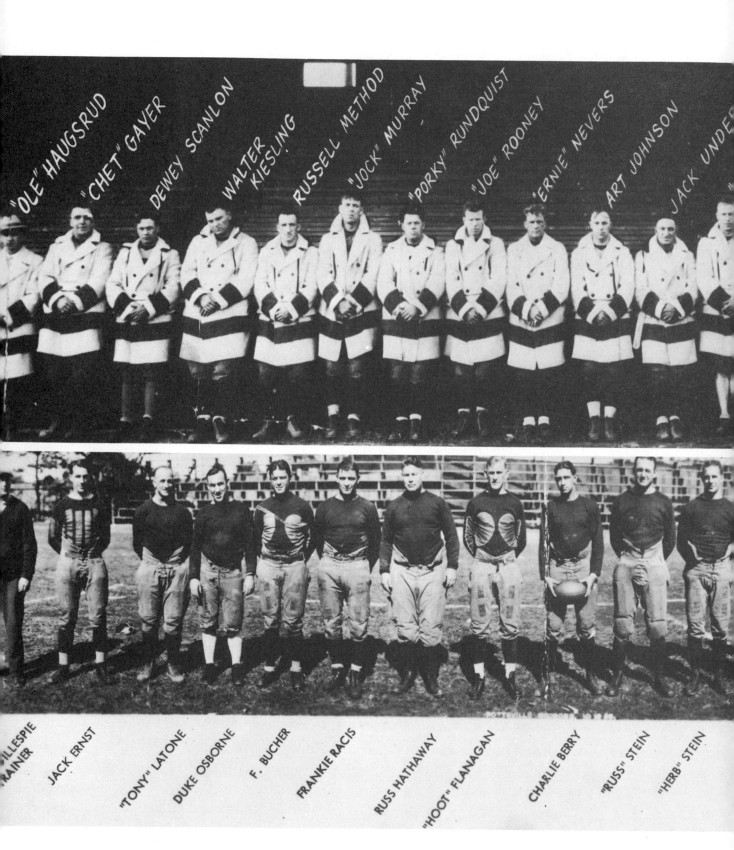

"OLE" HAUGSRUD   "CHET" GAYER   DEWEY SCANLON   WALTER KIESLING   RUSSELL METHOD   "JOCK" MURRAY   "PORKY" RUNDQUIST   "JOE" ROONEY   "ERNIE" NEVERS   ART JOHNSON   JACK UNDER

GILLESPIE TRAINER   JACK ERNST   "TONY" LATONE   DUKE OSBORNE   F. BUCHER   FRANKIE RACIS   RUSS HATHAWAY   "HOOT" FLANAGAN   CHARLIE BERRY   "RUSS" STEIN   "HERB" STEIN

STEIN · JOHNNY "BLOOD" MCNAL... · JAMES MANION · "OKIE" CARLSON · PAUL FITZGIBBONS

Best dressed club in the National League in 1926 was the Duluth Eskimos, led by Ernie Nevers. Johnny Blood is fourth from the right. Ernie Nevers is right in the middle.

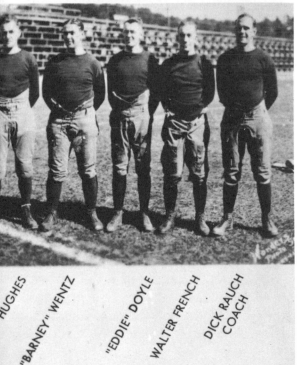

HUGHES · "BARNEY" WENTZ · "EDDIE" DOYLE · WALTER FRENCH · DICK RAUCH COACH

The Pottsville Maroons of 1925 featured Charlie Berry, who was destined to become a major league baseball umpire, and the Stein brothers, Herb and Russ, tackles from Washington & Jefferson and Pittsburgh, who played with the Jacksonville All-Stars against Red Grange.

turned in the same half), there had to be a punter in the line-up at all times. Usually he was the triple-threat back, but occasionally a club not blessed with such a virtuoso would have the punting done by a lineman.

While the goal-from-the-field by drop-kick or placement had long since (1909) been devalued to three points, with the touchdown now at six and the converted goal after touchdown only one, in the twenties drop-kickers were still indispensable hands, and the pros signed them eagerly. Jim Thorpe could score goals from far out on the tundra. But men like Paddy Driscoll of Northwestern (who directed the Chicago Cardinals), Frank Nesser, who graduated from a railroad roundhouse, and Charlie Brickley, who won many a game for Harvard with his toe, could equal Jim in this department and could always find a paycheck with the pros.

One oddity of the game had been eradicated in 1920 (the year that the rules committee decided the game could not be improved except in minor degrees). That was the punt-out. Before that, the point from which a goal after touchdown was to be tried for was determined by having the scoring team punt the ball out from the goal line. Another player on the scoring team was out in the field to catch the ball and wherever he caught it was the point from which the goal was to be kicked. But even after this change, the conversion attempt was not made from scrimmage. The kicker instead stood out before the goal posts while the enemy troops lined up along the goal line. At a signal the opponents would rush out with hands upraised to try to block the kick. The kicker, who had no blockers in front of him, still had plenty of time to get the ball away and was much more likely to be thrown off by the vision of this army of attackers bearing down than he was to have the kick blocked by an upraised hand.

Lineplay Was the Most Obvious Feature

Lineplay, however, was the feature of the game that made football of the twenties so different from the game of today. The offensive line all crouched close to the ground, in a three- or four-point stance, each man prepared to launch himself head first into the body of the foe, to unbalance him with a fierce below-the-belt attack and to carry him backward as far as need be. The defenders crouched almost equally close to the ground, with the weight low, bodies bent forward and hands in sparring position to catch the attack of the opposite linemen and hold them off or shove them aside. The result of this low-center-of-gravity give-and-take was usually a general sprawling upon the ground of both lines, with only the backfield men and the defensive ends still erect and moving. (Of course, as we have observed, the linemen sometimes gave so much attention to the mayhem they worked upon each other—pounding the head and neck, butting the solar plexus, riding the enemy on one's shoulder—that the movement of the man with the ball was sometimes overlooked.)

The football of that day, plump as an oversize Christmas pudding, was meant for kicking rather than passing. Yet there were many long, long passes in the game and a number of practitioners—including two great Indians, Jim Thorpe and John Levi of the Haskell Indians—could send the ball in a spinning accurate spiral for a hundred yards. (Levi

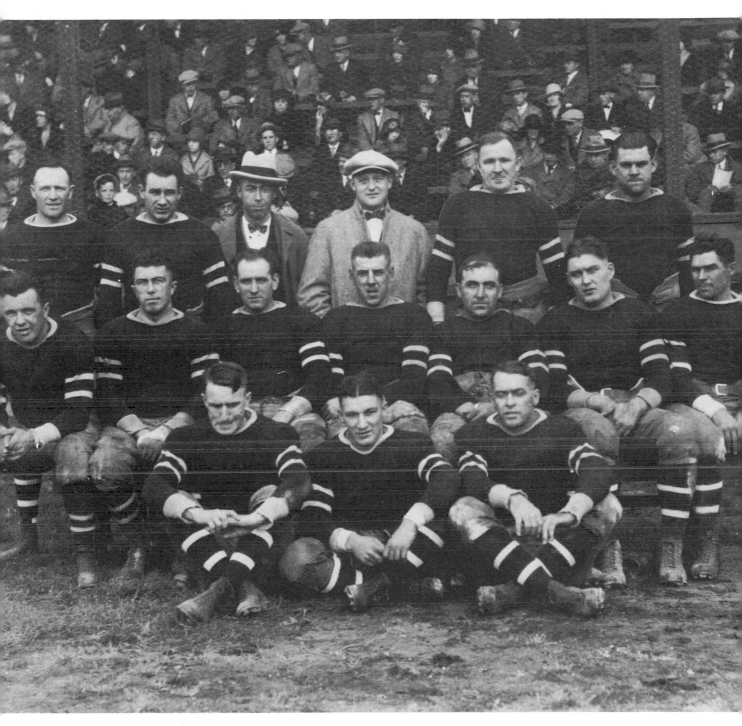

The Rochester Jeffs in 1925 were a well-uniformed and well-trained club. Well-coached too, by veteran Leo Lyons, who is sporting the pearl-gray fedora in the back row. At the extreme left in the middle row is Eddie Lynch, the "quarrelsome character" noted by Westbrook Pegler for almost ruining Red Grange's appearance in Washington. D.C. In the center of the middle row is Hank Smith, named on the first "All-Pro" eleven selected by the Cleveland *Plain Dealer*.

threw the big ball underhand.) It took a large hand and plenty of time to get the fingers placed on the ball to perform such feats, however, and most forward passes were short indeed.

Knute Rockne and Gus Dorais, who performed in Canton before Jim Thorpe made his debut there, were supposed to have popularized the pass by first showing how much could be accomplished by it. But it took daring innovators like Curly Lambeau of Green Bay and George Halas of Chicago (his Staleys moved into the big city in 1921) to turn the pass into the major offensive weapon in the game. For many years the colleges shunned the pass, except as a sort of desperation measure, to be used only on third down and never to be thrown inside your own twenty-yard line, regardless of the down. College coaches and other sourpusses decried the flamboyant use of the pass as a freakish feature of the pro game that was turning football into something it was never meant to be. (Basketball with bruises, one commentator called it.)

The Championship Adds Interest to the Game

The pros had to make the game worth watching as a show, and keeping the ball in view of the spectators was one way. Another way, of course, was to fight for the championship of the league, presumably of the world, inasmuch as the league from the start allowed that there were no better teams anywhere.

When there were just five teams in the league the championship had little substance. But the Canton Bulldogs, who won it, were certainly the best team in the corn belt, or any contiguous region. Next year, with eleven teams in the league, the champions were the Akron

club who beat the Canton Bulldogs in the rain on Thanksgiving before 6,000 paying customers. "A freak accident!" the Canton followers proclaimed. Their quarterback, Cecil Griggs from Texas, trying to catch the slimy ball when Akron kicked it, dropped the ball three times and each time Akron recovered. Quarterbacks always played safety man in that day and consequently were charged with catching and returning kicks. But Akron had something more than a wet ball to help them. They had Fritz Pollard, of Brown University, one of the first of many black stars in the game. And Fritz could run in any sort of going. He kept his body so low as he scooted along, it was said, that tacklers just shot over his head. Rain did not slow Fritz. It just made him harder to hold on to.

The Staleys, soon to become the Chicago Bears, won the championship next time, but did not play *every* team in the league (*nobody* played Cincinnati) and so left some questions about their right to the crown. By this time Jim Thorpe, perhaps weary of eating the white man's bread, or perhaps having worn out a portion of his welcome, had departed from Canton, where he sometimes missed games altogether and once removed himself from a game against Buffalo—in driving rain—thinking a score was impossible, only to have sureshot Al Feeney of Buffalo kick an "impossible" field goal and win.

Jim vowed he was going to put together a whole team of Indians who would lay all the paleface aggregations low. In Canton he had had two redskins on his side—halfback Joe Guyon, who lasted just short of forever in the game, and end Peter Calac. Jim took both

Indians with him when he left Canton to organize his "Oorang Indians." (They were named after a dog kennel but entered the league as representing Marion, Ohio.) Despite Jim's coaching and mighty arm and foot, the Oorang Indians proved something less than invincible. But they did provide a good show for the spectators, sometimes appearing on the field with full sets of feathers and occasionally wearing Indian costume over their football togs.

It proved impossible to find enough Indian ballplayers to provide the basic eighteen that most rosters required, so Jim Thorpe made honorary Indians out of a number of braves whose tribal homes lay in reservations like Galway, Bavaria, or Brest-Litovsk. But just to read Jim's roster provided a certain delight, for it contained names of such ripe renown as Eagle Feather, Gray Horse, Tomahawk, Deadeye, and Running Deer; Big Bear, Black Bear, Red Fang, Red Fox, and Little Twig; Buffalo and Wrinkle Meat. When Thorpe played with this tribe they were a mediocre outfit. When he was absent they were a sorry lot of redskins indeed. One day Akron massacred them 66–0.

While the league, with its annual struggle for a championship of sorts, did add interest to the game, and provided a certain stability, it did not better the lot of the ballplayer in any considerable degree. Players now signed "contracts," but they were still paid by the game and seventy-five dollars a game was a pretty fair wage for any player whose name did not ring far beyond his home confines. As a matter of fact, that is the wage that George Halas accepted from Dr. Young of the Hammond, Indiana, club, after he had been turned down by the Rochester

Jeffersons, and before he took the job as Athletic Director with the Staley Starch Company.

When a club was well financed (usually in the first year or two before the sponsor began to feel the bite), it might establish a pre-season camp at which the players, or most of them, would undergo a certain amount of conditioning and practice basic plays so that they might work together more efficiently. (When the Rochester Jeffersons first went to Canton to play Jim Thorpe's Bulldogs, in 1919, they ran through their practice in their stocking feet in the hotel ballroom. A practice pass went sailing out an open window and practice had to be held up while the ball was retrieved.) Squads were often just barely big enough to permit substitution in case of serious injury, and in more than one club the coach himself had to pull his football suit on over his aging bones to fill out the line-up, or to get someone on the field who at least knew the signals.

Huddles and Freak Formations Come Along

The football huddle came into regular use in the 1920s. There had been occasional huddles in football—usually called for with a cry from the quarterback: "Team back!"—but they had been used only when some complex play was to be explained or when there was suspicion that the other club knew the signals. After "team back" the players would line up in standard formation, and the quarterback would give voice signals in the usual manner except that he would announce "First set called!" and go into the second set of numerals, which would include the signal for the snap.

Now and then a coach would come up with a freak formation, always called by the quarterback aloud. He might, for instance, experiment with "backs in line" —like the current "Power I," except that both halfbacks, the fullback and the quarterback would take places in the single file that formed behind the center, and the back who was to receive the direct pass would hop out of the line at the proper moment. The rest of the crew would then run interference for him. When a kick formation was called, it was also announced by the quarterback, with the name of the player who was to do the kicking: "Kick formation! Jones back!" Sometimes a coach would station a back or two out wide, behind

the end, to take a lateral pass, in hopes of thus finding the running easier. But such variations were never standardized and the blocking assignments that went with them were not often worked out.

The defense against this old-fashioned tight T was unimaginative—just a sort of reverse of the attack formation. There would be linemen playing head and

head on other linemen, except that the offensive center would have no one crouched directly in front of him, his blocking capability being so crippled by his need to peer back between his legs that he was not an immediate danger. Behind the six-man defensive line would be two close-up linebackers —the fullback and the "roving center." The halfbacks would be on either wing, several yards behind the line, and the quarterback, unless a kick was looked for, played "safety" some fifteen yards behind the center of the line. If a kick was expected, the quarterback would drop as far back as need be to get the kick on the fly.

When a pass was expected—as when the enemy formed into a short punt formation—the defensive halfbacks would move out to be ready to pick up the two receivers as they hurried downfield. Otherwise the defense remained just about in the same position at all times, with only the fullback and roving center shifting about trying to anticipate the direction of the attack.

Place kicks were used often for the point after touchdown as well as for kick-off. The ball-holder, on a place kick, would lie flat on his belly with one arm outstretched to get a finger atop the ball and hold it straight. His chief concern often seemed to be to snatch his finger away just in time to avoid having it mangled by the kicker's cleated shoe.

The champion New York Giants of 1927 owned a playing coach, half-back Earl Potteigger from Ursinus, kneeling in the center of the front row. The Nesser in the back row was the indestructible Al, who played professional football for twenty-two years. Kneeling in front of him is the Indian star, Joe Guyon, Jim Thorpe's teammate in Canton. Steve Owen, who was to become the coach, is holding the football. Century Milstead of Yale and Cal Hubbard stand in the back row.

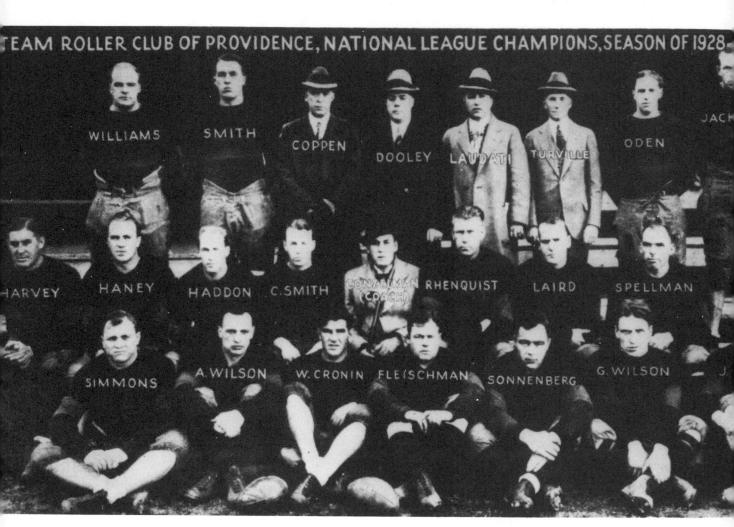

WILLIAMS SMITH COPPEN DOOLEY LAUDATI TURVILLE ODEN JACK

HARVEY HANEY HADDON C. SMITH CONZELMAN (COACH) RHENQUIST LAIRD SPELLMAN

SIMMONS A. WILSON W. CRONIN FLEISCHMAN SONNENBERG G. WILSON J.

The Providence Steamrollers in the 1920's featured several Eastern College Stars. Curly Oden, second from right in back row, was a reckless triple-threat man in the old tradition at Brown University. Orland Smith, second from left in that row, was one of Brown's 1926 Iron Men. John Spellman, far right in the middle row, was a wrestling champion at Brown, an All-America tackle, and captain of the Brown football team. Gus Sonnenberg, third from right in the front row, starred at Dartmouth and became a professional wrestler. Tony Laudati, in fancy clothes in the back row, was voted best-dressed man at Brown. He did not play football.

Pro clubs, concerned with keeping the customers entertained, probably used more experimental formations than the colleges did, although even high school coaches in this era liked to invent new ways of surprising the opposition (and too often their own boys) with freak splits and spreads. There was even a play illustrated once that had the center and quarterback isolated on the flank, with the whole team a few yards off, to be activated when the quarterback flipped a lateral over to one of the waiting halfbacks.

Scheming and Conniving to Spring the Ball-carrier

Glenn "Pop" Warner, who had played professional ball with the Syracuse club and had coached the Indian School at Carlisle before signing as coach at Stanford University, is given credit for most of the early innovations in the game. But in his day there were men scheming all the time either to conceal the football (one club had patches of football-shaped leather sewn on every jersey and one had a jersey fitted with a pocket to hide the ball in), or to take the defense unawares, or to recover some of the backfield momentum lost when the massing of interference in the backfield was outlawed.

Warner was supposed to have invented the "dead man" play that almost enabled Stanford to beat Harvard in the Rose Bowl one year. This was a bit of pure fakery that would earn (and deserve) the name "bush" if anything like it were permitted today. The halfback, having carried the ball, and having been downed, would not get up from his spot on the sod but would remain flat on his back with the ball clutched to his belly. The rest of the team would line up but poor Bill would not move. Then a teammate would approach him and inquire, "Are you all right, Bill?" whereupon Bill, having been maneuvered into legitimate center position by his teammates, would flip the ball up to the man who bent over him and that man would take off for the goal. The referee of course would have to be told in advance to watch for this play, so he would not cancel it out of plain bewilderment. It gained eighteen yards against Harvard, which hardly seemed to repay all the deep thought and conniving that must have gone into it.

Every club in the twenties would have a "shoestring" or "sleeper" play, which would try to get a man (sometimes pretending to tie a shoestring) "hidden" on the sideline, uncovered, where he would be free to get a quick pass from the quarterback. And coaches everywhere tried stunts that would make tackles or other linemen eligible for passes, through a sudden shift that would turn the lineman into an end.

But in all this time there was never any stunt or maneuver that could equal the thrill of a long run through a broken field by a ball carrier who had got free by sheer speed and elusiveness. And until professional football managed to capture the greatest broken field runner of his day, it remained the stepbrother if not the chosen enemy of college football. Some college coaches even viewed it as a menace to the noble game that would have to be destroyed through closing it out of the stadiums and depriving it of fans. The fans however wanted to see great runners carry the ball, and so they tended to gather where the best, or at least the most famous, runners could be found.

Twelve Thousand
Dollars and a Black Eye

NO runner in football ever achieved greater national fame than did Red Grange of Illinois. And when Red Grange, whose real name was Harold, first went to the University he did not want to play football at all. He had starred in high school but he was concerned now with preparing himself to earn a decent living, and no one, Red knew, ever got rich out of football.

Red's fraternity brothers, however, through judicious application of a large wooden paddle (such as upperclassmen were authorized by college tradition to use to make freshmen welcome), persuaded Red that his viewpoint was self-ish, that he loved the dear University too much to fail her this way, and that he owed it to them all to glorify the name of Illinois. Red was no pampered athlete nor make-believe scholar. He worked hard at his studies (he was majoring in economics) and he worked hard every summer, delivering ice to his neighbors, to help finance his board and tuition—which his father, a deputy sheriff in Wheaton, was helping him with. But he became a campus hero almost with his first appearance. And by the time young Harold reached his final season at the University, in the fall of 1925, his name was known in every town

Red Grange as a pro seldom broke away for the long runs he was famous for in college. But here he is carrying the ball for a long gain for his own New York Yankees against Wilson's Wildcats at Yankee Stadium.

big enough to harbor a theater. Views of Grange in action, recorded in the recently perfected newsreels, set boys and men to cheering in every movie house from coast to coast.

It took no special shrewdness then to figure out that the addition of Red Grange to a pro team's roster might happily influence the gate receipts. It did take, however, a certain amount of aggressiveness to lay hold of Red before any of the dozens of other hungering entrepreneurs had entrapped him. And not many schemers of that day could outdo theatrical promoter C. C. Pyle in aggressiveness. Just how C. C. managed to throw a halter on Red, or what form their agreement took, was never made entirely clear. But the rumors of Red's turning professional began to gather around the Illinois campus long before Red's final game was even close at hand.

Then the campus at the University filled with clamor. Students who hardly knew Red's real name vowed to help defend his amateur standing, or to see to it that he never sullied his reputation by trading it in for cash. (Cash-and-Carry Pyle was the name a Chicago sports writer had assigned to the mustached dandy who was said even now to be stalking the young athlete, with the avowed intent of then auctioning him off to the princes of pro football.)

Red Grange Continued to Give His All for Illinois

Red, apparently never heeding a word, went on scoring touchdowns for Illinois, usually at the end of long, long runs that saw opponents clutching vainly at his britches, and dropping off as if they had been bewitched. In October, at Franklin Field in Philadelphia, with mud thick as beef stew underfoot, Red carried the

football thirty-six times against the University of Pennsylvania, gained 363 yards, and scored three touchdowns. Wet field or dry and no matter how mighty the foe, Red seemed to own some mystical power that enabled him to shake himself free from tacklers or just to cast a spell upon them that kept them from even laying a finger on his hide.

Actually what Red had was a surprisingly fast take-off and an ability to run at "controlled speed" until the opening showed itself, then to accelerate so fast the men who had been closing in on him found themselves grasping air. He also had some first-rate blocking by his teammates, to whom he never failed to give credit. But it took far more than blocking to accomplish the feats Red performed in college. Against Michigan in 1924, for instance, he took the opening kick-off on his five-yard line and ran all the way to the other end zone. From scrimmage, Red scored three more times before the quarter was ended, on runs of forty-five, fifty-five, and sixty-seven yards. Altogether that day he passed or ran for five touchdowns. And this was the sort of performance fans in every city were ready to pay large money to see.

By the time Red's final game was near, the campus uproar was unending. Newspaper writers and photographers had moved right into the dormitory with Grange and permitted him no rest. Men he had never heard of gave testimony to the papers that Red had already signed himself away to Pyle. (Not so, said Red. I never signed even a *scrap* of paper.) C. C. Pyle himself was quoted as having strongly hinted that Red was already securely tied to him on a contract. Young

Red Grange, during his college days at Illinois, was no coddled athlete. Here he pose in his torn pants and worn jersey.

men who wrote editorials for the college paper were outraged. Pro football was a dirty business, they declared, to lure their hero off the path of virtue for something so cheap as money. Why, Red Grange was a holy name in the University and the sacred jersey he wore, with the great number 77 on the back, was destined to be enshrined forever in glass and in the hearts of the alumni! (They'll forget all that by next year, said Red. Would they lend me a dollar then?)

One day before the Ohio State game Red Grange missed practice. What was this? The act of a prima donna? A symptom of infection by professionalism, which as all men knew robbed young men of their College Spirit and turned the Game into a trade? The president of the university, who apparently had never even noted the presence of those newsreel men and what-not in Grange's dormitory, promptly allowed that if Red cut any classes he would find himself suspended. Coach Bob Zuppke and Director of Athletics Huff called Red into a private conference, from which not a whisper leaked out. Nevertheless, rumors, originating practically at the coach's keyhole, spread word across the campus that Red had been directed to turn in his suit if he had *really* signed a pro contract.

After the conference, Red offered interviewers a rueful comment: "I'm all mixed up. And I'm worried. But I don't intend to sign anything until I play my last game for Illinois." With that, Red took off for Wheaton, presumably to take counsel with his father, who had been declaring to the newspapers that he too agreed that Red should abstain from pro football and leave his contri-

butions to the Noble Game untarnished. Write a book, yes, even though Red had exhibited no skill at writing. Or act in a movie, even though he had never shown any talent as an actor. But sell his football skill? Never! (To be an imitation writer, offered Westbrook Pegler, then a Chicago sportswriter, or a fake movie actor, would surely be less virtuous than becoming a real football player.)

At home Red continued to meet his interviewers and fend them off with complete good nature. Would he *really* sign a contract with the Chicago Bears? Well, that remained to be seen. As for Red's father, he now agreed that this matter of "commercialized football" was "all up to Red." Well, would Red then become a salesman, as some had hinted? No, said Red. I might go into manufacturing or some such thing. But never a salesman. "I wouldn't have the nerve," Red explained.

Major Griffiths, director of the Western Conference, now publicly declared that, if all these rumors of signing with the Bears and agreeing to make a movie with Chaplin were true, as they seemed to be, then Red was already ineligible to compete with athletes who had always taken care to use assumed names when playing ball for money and had never accepted checks. Bob Zuppke angrily dissented. Red was not ineligible unless he had actually taken money. And, Red vowed, he had never accepted a single dime—not from Pyle, not from the Bears, not from the movies. And he fully intended to play against Ohio State.

Red Grange Signs as a Pro with the Chicago Bears

Meanwhile, in a Chicago hotel room, Red's future was being bargained for by four weary men: George Halas and Ed Sternaman, owners of the Bears; and Charles C. Pyle and Frank Zambreno, Red Grange's "managers." (Pyle and Zambreno were both in the theatrical business—Pyle in Champaign and Zambreno in Chicago.) The give and take lasted all one day and night and part of the following day before the men agreed on a deal: $3000 a game, or 30 percent of the gate. (Pyle and Grange had already agreed, presumably in a verbal deal, to split the take fifty-fifty, with Pyle assuming all promotional expenses.)

Grange's actual signing with the Bears was still, presumably, a secret when Red took the field against Ohio State at Columbus. Coach Zuppke, by this time, was in open despair at the attitude of his club. They had become "carefree," he mourned, and exhibited far more interest in Red's pending deal with the Bears than in the game with the ancient enemy from Ohio. Besides, Red's missing practice had "demoralized" them all. But they were not so demoralized that they could not beat Ohio. With Grange performing in sturdy, if unspectacular, fashion, Illinois won the game 14 to 9. Red got away for a typical loping, twisting run of thirty-seven yards with an intercepted pass and made one twenty-five-yard gain from scrimmage that had his fans on their feet. But there were no long scoring carries. In twenty-one tries Red gained better than a hundred yards.

Once the game was over, Pyle gave the news to the world. Red would indeed sign a contract with the Bears and would play for them on Thanksgiving Day against the Chicago Cardinals. Well then, the sportswriters persisted, hadn't Grange *already* signed. "No," said Red.

"I'll be sitting on their bench tomorrow, but I haven't yet signed."

But hadn't he even *talked* to the Bears? Well, just once, with Sternaman. And what was said? Why, he wished Red luck and hung up "without saying good-bye." There was really no need to say good-bye, for Red, the night after the game in Columbus, turned up the collar of his coat, pulled his hat brim down over his eyes, and stole down the fire escape of his hotel, into a waiting taxi. He climbed aboard the Chicago train in the railroad yard, temporarily safe from further questioning.

The next day, Sunday, Red Grange appeared on the Chicago bench, his spare frame (he weighed only 175 pounds) handsomely bulked out with the current status symbol, a brand new raccoon coat. While the Bears were handily trimming the Green Bay Packers 21 to 0, the crowd kept craning for a look at Grange and shouting his name. Red had avoided autograph seekers before the game by sneaking into a hotel well apart from the one usually frequented by the Bears. At half time during the game, Red remained in the dressing room. Five minutes after action resumed, he decided it would be safe to proceed to the Bears' bench. But he had mistaken his fans, who were far more interested in Red Grange than they were in the ball game. Hundreds of them still lined the ramp when Red emerged from the locker room and he needed help from the police to get back to the bench with his fur coat and his dignity intact.

There had been 7500 fans out in the bitter cold to watch the Packers play the Bears, with Grange on the bench. For the game in which Grange was to make

his first appearance, the call for tickets began almost at once. Halas and Sternaman could undoubtedly have doubled the ticket price and sold just as many tickets but they were old-fashioned businessmen who still believed that there was profit to be had through playing fair with the steady customers, so tickets for the Grange game were offered at the standard admission—$1.75 for grandstand reserved seats.

Grange Has a Disappointing Debut

When the tickets were first put on sale at Spalding's store on State Street, the ticket line extended outside the door, up the block, around a corner, down the next alley, and around to the store again. No one had foreseen any such rush as this and the printer had simply not made enough tickets. When only half of those waiting had been served, the tickets were gone and the rest had to come back a few days later, when the tickets were devoured within an hour.

Of course there were speculators who had been first in line and had bought tickets by the fistful, which they then offered to the late comers at five and ten dollars apiece. At this point, a Chicago alderman, Jacob Arvey, charged out upon the field and vowed to see justice done. Speculators, he averred, had secured blocks of five to fifteen hundred seats and he was now going to put a stop to the whole business! The Bears, he noted ominously, have no license to stage a performance on Thanksgiving. It turned out, however, that the Bears needed no license, their performance being covered by the license already held by the Cubs at Wrigley Field. As for the speculators, if any of them had fifteen hundred tickets, he had no rea-

son to rejoice, for the Bears put 2000 standing room tickets on sale on the day of the game and left many speculators holding bouquets of tickets outside the park.

Altogether some 36,000 people crowded in to see the game, which some said would be a put-up job, for there were still many of the football fancy who held that all professional football was mere hippodroming, with the victor chosen in advance. For games with such as the Rock Island Rockets (even with aging Jim Thorpe aboard) and the Duluth Eskimos, crowds of 5000 were deemed healthy, and that was about the measure of interest in the pro game. All the added customers had obviously been drawn to the park by Red Grange.

Whatever such fans may have told each other during the game or afterward, the appearance of the mighty man on the pro gridiron was a frost. Paddy Driscoll, captain of the Cardinals and the greatest punter of his era, took special care that Grange would never catch a punt to run back. He angled every kick far away from Red, no matter what the cost in yardage. Somebody, he said afterward, was going to look bad—either Grange or Driscoll. "I wanted to be sure it wouldn't be Driscoll."

But Grange did not look good in runs from scrimmage either. The weather was miserable. There was snow in the air and on the ground and the mud was up over Red's cleats, so he was badly handicapped. Altogether he gained thirty-six yards. His longest run was a seven-yard gain over tackle.

Even the fans who had come to the ballpark muttering "fix," convinced that the whole affair would be rigged to give Red a chance to run with the ball, booed

Red Grange exhibits his drop-kicking form as well as the holes in his college jersey and the rip in his pants. Illinois, apparently, had no equipment fund.

wildly at Paddy Driscoll each time he carefully aimed a kick at the sideline, where Red could not reach it. The game ended without a score by either side. Still, in that day, merely making the scene when some publicity laden personality was on hand was accomplishment enough and the fans went home to paste their ticket stubs into scrapbooks. The Chicago Cardinals, after the game—Paddy Driscoll and all—lined up to shake Red Grange's hand.

The Bears, to cash in on Grange's presence, had scheduled games on into the following January, in almost every major city in the land. The next game was played in Chicago against the Columbus Tigers, and it ended in victory for the Bears, with Grange gaining 138 yards, despite the fact that he was playing with only two days' rest. But most of the cheers from the crowd of 28,000 went that day to a little fellow from Columbus, a ball-carrier who had never been to college, had never even received any coaching at all in the game, who weighed about twenty-five pounds less than Grange, yet outgained and outscored the Great Man by a wide margin.

This little fellow was Bob Rapp, the best halfback in Columbus, who had been playing football for money since before Red Grange got into the university. Rapp, who could run a hundred yards in ten seconds, gained 203 yards in the game, scored a touchdown at the end of a sixty-one-yard run (Grange's longest gain was a twenty-eight-yard kick-off return) and returned one punt forty-two yards. Bob Rapp had never been anything but a sandlot football player, but he was captain of the team and, had he and Frank Nesser been able to pull off the victory instead of just

missing (14 to 13), he would have been the headline hero of the week.

Bob started playing football for sheer fun with a team of youngsters who called themselves the Outlaws—perhaps because they were not playing for their high school team. Then Bob joined a team of grown-up amateurs known as the Westerns. His success with them prompted him to sign with a semi-pro team called the Jungle Imps. Here little Bob (he was five foot eight) proved himself as tough as any man they could set against him, and ready to accept or hand out whatever rough treatment the bigger men dealt in. Finally a local cattle dealer who was sponsoring a team named the Linden A.C. persuaded Bob to play for him at five dollars a touchdown. Usually that meant ten or fifteen dollars a game. But one day Bob found the footing especially favorable and cut loose on run after run. With ten minutes still to go in the game, Bob had scored nine touchdowns and the cattle-dealer angel decided he had peeled off all the five-spots he could spare.

After that, Bob was offered a good per-game fee to play with the West Side A.C., and from there he graduated to the Panhandles, who were at that time, 1922, members of the National League. The Panhandles became the Tigers and Bob, after winning the worship of all the local fans with his speed and elusiveness, became captain. In summers, Bob played minor league baseball. His fame however never spread far beyond Ohio, although he put in six seasons with the National Football League, winding up with Buffalo. Had Bob played today, he would have commanded a comfortable salary and might have retired with a pension in the offing, for Bob Rapp always drew the customers in and kept them yelling. Like many of the players of his era, who dared not own up to an injury lest they find the job pulled out from under them, Bob played on despite bruises and lacerations. (He played part of the Grange game with a broken rib.) And he let no man, not even big Steve Owen of the New York Giants, intimidate him. Bob found Steve in his way one day when Steve was playing left tackle for New York. With Steve weighing 265 to his own 148, Bob doubted his ability to bowl him over. So he quickly dealt Steve a fierce blow in the solar plexus with his fist and, as the big man stood gasping, scampered past. It took Steve but a second or two to recover himself and to let out a roar of rage. But by that time Bob was twenty-five yards away and gaining.

Bob was no doubt as fast as Grange and could probably do other things as well. But Red's extra pounds and his college reputation gave him the edge, so that eventually the Columbus game was recalled only as one in which Grange "made a good showing." But good showing or not there was still a to-do in and around the university over Red's turning pro and he still felt some urge to apologize for it, as if he had violated an oath. He would certainly come back to college, Red promised, and get his degree. Oh yes, Bob Zuppke commented sourly, about as soon as the Kaiser gets his job back in Germany.

Zuppke, as long as the subject had been opened, offered some long-distance advice to Grange, urging him to forget about a career in pro football and concentrate instead on the exploitation of his name through newpaper articles and motion pictures. Red had already

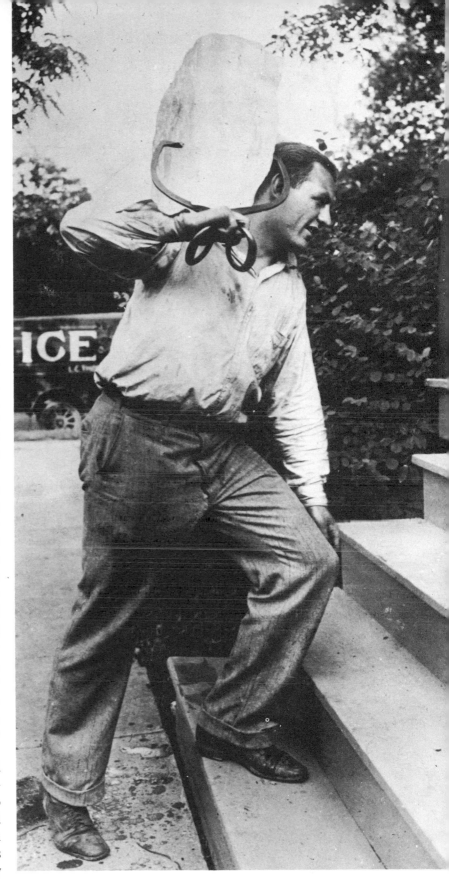

This was a publicity shot taken while Red Grange was in college. But he really did have a job delivering ice in Wheaton, Illinois.

WARD STERNAMAN   GEORGE HALAS   HAROLD "RED" GRANGE   C.C. PYLE

"RED" SIGNS HIS FIRST PRO CONTRACT, NOVEMBER 1925.

This posed picture of the "signing" of Red Grange to a pro football contract gives no hint of the all-day-all-night bargaining between Halas, C.C. ("Cash-and-Carry") Pyle, and their associates that went on while Grange was still playing football for Illinois.

signed to do a motion picture, and money was coming in from endorsements of one sort or another. Still, he seemed to agree with Westbrook Pegler that the honest way to use his fame was on the football field, where he had earned it.

Grange and the Bears Go Barnstorming

Altogether the Bears had scheduled eight games in twelve days to squeeze the value out of Grange while he lasted. He very nearly did not last. But he never complained and he threw himself into the chore with his whole heart. Pegler traveled with the Bears and reported the adventures in often painful detail.

The first out-of-town game was played in St. Louis against a collection of sand-lotters, semi-pros, and plain stiffs gathered together by a local undertaker who was suspected of having filled the bench with a few of his recent customers. They were called "Donnelley's Stars" but the only man among them who deserved the rating was Big Jim Conzelman, himself a graduate of the Staleys, who had also carried the ball for Rock Island, Milwaukee, and Detroit. The Bears beat the Stars 39 to 6, with Grange scoring four of the touchdowns on long break-away runs. Bitter cold cut the attendance to 8000 but all those went home happy, for they had seen just what they had paid to see—the great Galloping Ghost of newsreel fame dodging and slithering away from tackler after tackler.

The St. Louis game was played on Wednesday. The next meeting was scheduled for Saturday against the Frankford Yellowjackets in Philadelphia, a long, long sleeper jump away. The very next day a game had been

scheduled against the Giants in New York. The weather, in that worst and wettest of autumns, was consistently miserable, but still there were 35,000 football fans in Philadelphia mad enough to come out and sit through the cold drizzle in hopes of seeing Grange break away as he had a few weeks earlier, in going just as muddy, against the University of Pennsylvania. (Football fans, Pegler commented, were obviously goofier than baseball fans, who at least had sense enough to come in out of the wet.)

The mud was as deep as ever and Grange made no long runs at all. He scored both touchdowns in the 14 to 7 victory but he averaged only three yards a carry. He completed two forward passes and caught one. When he dragged himself off the field, he carried several pounds of mud distributed haphazardly over britches, shoes, jersey, and face. One Chicago man, after the battle, threw his gear jockey-fashion on a scale and noted that, mud and all, it weighed forty-five pounds.

The publicity uproar had been gathering strength in New York City, where Grange had never been seen in action. Tickets to his debut sold faster and in greater quantity than they had in Chicago. Pegler expressed scant admiration for the ability of the ballplayers who were to face Grange and even less for the good sense of the 73,000 fans who fought to see him. (At least five hundred got into the park without paying.) The New York club, in Pegler's eyes, were the "alleged Giants." But Pegler was expressing only the standard sportswriter attitude toward the professional game, which was supposed to be lacking in spirit and basically a fraud, according

RED GRANGE
BY ARRANGEMENT WITH C.C. PYLE AND W.E. SHALLENBERGER
"ONE MINUTE TO PLAY"
WORLD PREMIER
A SAM WOOD PRODUCTION
DISTRIBUTED BY GREATER F.B.O.
STRAUSS & CO.
Clicquot Club
GINGER ALE
COLONY
GRANGE ONE
NUTE TO PLAY
RED GRANGE
IN PERSON
B.S. MOSS' COLONY
RADIO
TARR PHOTOGRAP
GOWNS

RED GRANGE

ONE MINUTE TO PLAY

Red Grange's movie debut drew a mob to the theatre on 42nd Street, New York City.

to those brought up on the sort of football played by alleged amateurs in the big universities.

There was nothing fraudulent about the efforts of the Bears or Giants that day. To make the jump to New York on time to manage a workout before the game, the Bears had to jam their slimy uniforms into handbags or even wear them onto the train and change in the Pullman. What they went through as they suited up at the Polo Grounds may be imagined by anyone who has ever squirmed into a wet, cold bathing suit on a chilly day.

But the Bears were full of fight, and they needed to be, for the Giants acted as if they had made a pledge to themselves not to let Grange leave the field alive. According to Pegler, the officials permitted the Giants to do everything to Grange except actually remove his head from the upper end of his neck. One backfield man (Pegler reported), angered when he missed connections with a pass, hauled off on Grange and sent him staggering with a blow to the back of his head. Another Giant, said Peg, kicked Grange deliberately, and still another, after tackling Grange around the neck, sat down upon his captive and actually *did* try to twist his head free from its moorings. Grange by this time was in visibly bad shape anyway, his face drawn and deeply lined, his body covered with bruises and his eyes red from lack of sleep, for newsreel men, reporters, and autograph bugs trailed him everywhere and left him no chance to rest.

The Bears beat the Giants 19 to 7. Grange made none of his ghostly runs. But he did intercept a pass to trot unimpeded for a touchdown, with the joyous

screams of the spectators rattling the Polo Ground rafters.

The Bears, after a night of revelry in New York, which saw some of them fumbling their way out of a speakeasy at dawn, traveled next to Washington to play before a weekday crowd of only 8000, against a hastily gathered group of college all-stars, many of them from the local universities. If this group, Pegler noted, had had even fifteen minutes in which to run off some plays together, they might have murdered the Bears. Instead the Bears, weary and wet, trimmed the stars 19 to 0, with Grange contributing only a six-yard run and a single point after touchdown, by drop kick. The longest run of the game was made by Chicago's John Bryan, who carried sixty-five yards to a score. Pegler however was more impressed by "a quarrelsome bare-legged party named Lynch," a Holy Cross lad who had been playing end for the Rochester Jeffersons. It was he, said Pegler, who largely spoiled Grange's afternoon. Grange left the field with a badly wrenched arm, a bruised mouth, and a battered nose—and he had but a few days to rest before meeting the Providence Steamrollers in Boston. By all common sense, Grange should have ended the tour right there. But he was a man who believed in living up to his commitments, and he was obsessed with the notion that his fame would not endure more than a season. He did not know what the "secret" was of his ability to escape tacklers, if it were not the blocking his teammates provided, and he felt that all this might be snatched away from him before he had time to lay up the security he needed. So he suited up over his bandaged body,

Red Grange on his barnstorming trip with the Bears in 1925 clearly shows the strain.

Red Grange on his only run from scrimmage in the game between the Bears and the Pittsburgh Pros in December 1925. He gained three yards. Soon afterward his arm muscle was torn by a kick.

and played on despite overpowering weariness and pain.

The Excitement Over Grange Begins to Fade

In Boston, the Bears met the Steamrollers on the coldest day of the year. Still, there were 25,000 people there to see Red run. Grange on the field this day was a listless figure, obviously needing a chance to lie down in quiet. But the fans had no patience with him, for they had been lured to the park by visions of a man moving by magic through a sea of opponents. What they saw was a man looking a good ten years older than his twenty-two years, unable to make even a good start on a long run, unable to complete a pass or deliver a sound kick. Grange made but a few short gains, knocked down two passes, and made three tackles. At one point, he picked up the football and tossed it to the referee to be put in play, where-

upon the stands broke into sarcastic applause to see him "complete" a pass.

At the end of the third quarter, Grange withdrew from the game, to the loud dismay of the fans, some of whom set out to follow him to the ramp that led to the locker room, hooting at him, reviling him and his female ancestors, ridiculing his appearance, and proclaiming him a fraud. Eventually one of Red's teammates turned and provided a hearty punch in the face to the nearest tormentor. Then the whole crowd boiled over and clawed each other to get at the Bears and dismember them. Only vigorous persuasion by the police won the fans to peace and let Red Grange, drooping in body and spirit, seek the lonely comfort of the locker room.

Next stop was Pittsburgh, and here they found the poorest crowd of the whole trip—a mere 5000 fans, a good turnout for an ordinary pro football

122

This game, between the Chicago Bears and the Los Angeles Tigers in January, 1926, finally gave Red Grange a chance to show his great skills. He loses his helmet as he makes a touchdown.

game but a near disaster in the face of Grange's fat guarantee. The Bears won this game, against a clot of semi-pros gathered up on a few days' notice by Barney Dreyfuss, owner of the Pittsburgh Baseball Club and one-time manager of the Pittsburgh Football Pros. The fans cheered Red Grange heartily, for all they really wanted was to set eyes on him and go tell their friends they had done so. The final score was 24 to 0 in favor of the Dreyfuss semi-pros and Grange's contributions were of no account. He made a three-yard gain through the line, caught a pass for four yards, then received a blow on the arm that tore a muscle and he had to be helped to the sidelines.

In Boston, Red Grange had met Babe Ruth, who had urged him to "get the money while the getting's good" but not to be afraid to say no. In New York, he said no to his autograph seekers by changing his raccoon coat for the cloth coat of a teammate and by keeping a wide-brimmed hat pulled low over his face. Now with his arm puffing out like a cobra, he said no to the Bears. He was not going to take the field again in this condition. The rest of the club had its own collection of bangs and bruises (George Halas had a boil on his neck). But no one had been damaged as Grange had been and no one tried to persuade him to play. The club took the field in Detroit for the next scheduled game but, when it was announced that Grange would not play, thousands of dollars had to be refunded. Only 6000 fans remained to watch the game.

The club returned for the final game of this tour to Wrigley Field, Chicago, where more than 15,000 had bought tickets to see them play the New York Giants. Grange, unwilling to see another long disgruntled line at the refund window, took the field in spite of his inability to use his injured arm. The Giants won the game 9 to 0 and after the game Red's hometown fans chased after him, not to call him names, but to pat his back, shake his hand, and announce their joy at his return. It took a dozen policemen to work him free from the mob.

Red now had a chance to draw his breath and rest his damaged carcass. But the Bears were not through exploiting him. Coming up was a long trip through the South and West, with somewhat better advance work and some additional human flesh to fill out the roster. As for Grange, his arm got well and his spirits were mended by counting over the wealth that had accrued to him through his movie contract and his myriad endorsements—$300,000 from the motion picture that was yet to be made, and $40,500 for putting his name on various products.

First stop on the new tour was Jacksonville, where a group of hot-eyed promoters had recruited still another group of all-stars, built around Stanford's blond Ernie Nevers, the player who (to poor Jim Thorpe's dismay) had been named by Pop Warner as the greatest football player he ever coached. Nevers, fullback on the football team, forward at basketball, sprinter on the track team, and a strong-armed pitcher for the baseball club at college, had been guaranteed $50,000 to come play football against the Bears—and against a few other pro football clubs not yet named.

By this time, Grange's exploits, and particularly the golden gates he had drawn, had set half the football stars in the nation to fancying themselves professionals. The Four Horsemen of Notre Dame, given their nickname by Grantland Rice, hastened eastward to enroll themselves under the storied banners of the Hartford Blues (who had but a short time before been known as the Waterbury Blues). It was reported by some semi-professional tattle-tale that one of this quartet had previously signed to play with a team in the National League and league members were solemnly warned to shun the apostate and all his kin. (The Pottsville Maroons ignored the warning and played the Blues anyway, even violating the territorial rights of the Frankford Yellowjackets to do it.)

The "Red Grange of the East" was supposed to be Eddie Tryon of Colgate, a relatively small and speedy young man who had registered many long gains. (There were some who said Eddie had no real elusiveness at all but merely speed, which he used to outrun the opposition to the sidelines.) Eddie, who was probably a better drop-kicker than Grange, or at least kicked goals more often, announced that he too was going to lap up some of this wealth by signing a pro contract with the New York Giants, and play that winter in Florida. His mother, hearing the story, promptly said no such thing, Eddie was not going to play professional football at all. It took Eddie two years to talk Mama into permitting him to play. Then he played one season with Red Grange's New York Yankees, who folded up quickly themselves.

Grange and Pyle Form Their Own League

To make ready for their swing through the south and west the Chicago Bears outfitted their squad in a new off-gridiron uniform, consisting of baggy golf knickers—the "plus fours" that were then *de rigueur* in the colleges—with V-neck sweaters and matching woolen hose. The sweaters carried the lettering "Bears" on the bosom and each man wore his own number on his back.

Despite many yards of throaty publicity and an air of forced gladness, Florida that season was a sorry place to be. Real estate values, which just a few months earlier were rocketing upward with every breath the governor drew, had begun to sink faster than some of the new structures were settling into the swampland. The promoters of the football games, however, never dared doubt that there were still hundreds of thousands of "sportsmen" abroad looking for places to rid themselves of ten-dollar bills. Ticket prices were set at $8.50 and $5.50, or about what a man might expect to pay for seats at a Broadway hit musical. Local newswriters spotted a harbinger of success in the presence of One-Eyed Connelly, the most famous gate-crasher in the world, who would never have wasted his skills on an event of ordinary stature. Temporary seats were hastily erected to accommodate the expected overflow (after all, there had been over 70,000 in New York) and the city engineer was prevailed upon to assure the herds of spectators that were presumably impatiently pawing the ground somewhere outside the gates, that the new stands would not give way under their combined heft.

When the gates opened, however, there was no stampede for the seats. The game's promoters therefore undertook to play up the high quality of the select few who did attend. In box seats at midfield were George Ade, whose *Fables in Slang* still put old folks into stitches, and two of Broadway's most glittering names: actor Raymond Hitchcock, who was still trailing the glory he had earned for his performance in *Hitchy-Koo,* and that most solvent of all producers, John Golden. And wandering about the field, looking as thoroughly disreputable as was his wont, there, sure enough, was One-Eyed Connelly, who had honored the park by somehow sneaking in without a ticket.

Red Grange did not stir any blood, although he was roundly applauded. Ernie Nevers played almost as good a game as Grange, and received the bulk of the newspaper space, inasmuch as the local editors were intent on demonstrating that the local all-stars (who owned only two experienced pros, the Stein Brothers of Pottsville) were in every way the equal of the Bears. The Bears, however, won the game 19 to 7. Grange's longest gallop was nine yards, which did not seem particularly ghostly. In writing up that run, the local sportswriters made note of how "fiercely" Ernie Nevers drove Grange out of bounds. Grange did complete seven passes and one of them scored a touchdown. His greatest play was a defensive one: He overhauled Bowser of the All-Stars on the one-yard line and stopped him short of the score.

Between the halves of the game, the clubs gathered, sandlot fashion, right on the field, in a war council formation, to hold their half-time meetings. A thousand fans thereupon climbed out of the stands to eavesdrop on the discussions and to absorb some of the aura the great men gave off.

In the final quarter the fans were finally provided with a deep-down thrill when Russ Stein of the All-Stars and Jim McMillen of the Bears squared off in a fist-fight that drew hundreds of people out of the seats to stand for the glory of Jacksonville. The police were able to get the two players off the field with dispatch but then they found themselves engaged with the fans who resented this abrupt suppression of a sporting event and who may have harbored a few lingering gripes at the treatment they had received at the gate. The conflict between police and customers surged back and forth on the field for several minutes, while the fans who had held their seats screamed encouragement to their embattled fellows.

The promoters of the game did manage to come up with the $5000 guarantee Pyle had demanded and were left to contemplate the $50,000 still owing to Ernie Nevers. They all set about earnestly whistling up their courage by counting over the value of all the publicity that Jacksonville had earned, despite the feeble draw. There was a game coming up between Nevers' All-Stars and the New York Giants (who played the Bears at Coral Gables to a gate that did not even cover the guarantee) and they counted on a reduction in the ticket price to double or triple the gate for that. But, even with a general admission charge of only fifty cents, most fans still stayed home, and just a few wilful folk sat and watched the All-Stars have at the Giants, 7 to 0. The rest, the local editorial writers mourned, had been persuaded by "unthinking people" that professional football was not worth watching. The All-Stars promptly called off their remaining games to cut their losses, paid off Ernie Nevers, who immediately signed a contract with the St. Louis Browns baseball club for a "four-figure" bonus, and then announced that he was going to join up with some of the New York Giants to

play basketball for money. Apparently there was no money to be had in that field, however, and Ernie played no basketball at all. His next football job was as a ball-carrier with the Duluth Eskimos. Later he became a coach with the Chicago Cardinals. (His baseball career, too, was brief. In three seasons he pitched in thirty-two games for the St. Louis Browns, and won six, while losing twelve.)

Red Grange left Jacksonville without any mob of autograph seekers to dog his heels. His final "appearance" was a picture of his glowing countenance in a Jacksonville newspaper along with an announcement, to any who might be moved by the news, that he owed his stamina to the dutiful daily ingestion of Yeast Foam Malted Milk.

The Bears had played to scanty gates at both Coral Gables and Tampa and now they pushed on to New Orleans, where still another convocation of "all-stars" of doubtful magnitude awaited them. There were only 6000 people there to watch the Bears win the game by a score of 14 to 0. And at least some of them must have gone home feeling they had got their money's worth, for Grange did get away in this game for a fifty-one-yard punt return. It was partially offset by a clipping penalty but while it lasted it was as good as the motion pictures. Red also took off on a twenty-yard run from scrimmage that caused men and women to stand and shout. And the day before the game, there had been a Red Grange Handicap at the local racetrack, which was won by a redheaded jockey on a nag named Prickly Heat. Red Grange himself presented to the wide-eyed jockey a large floral football.

After this the Bears entrained for

California to meet a crowd of ex-collegians led by Brick Muller, the University of California's greatest end. There were actually only sixteen players on Brick Muller's club, which called itself the Buccaneers, but there were forty imitation ballplayers sitting on the bench to dress up the scene. These "extras" were bartenders, college kids, a cook, and other males of assorted backgrounds. In the stands, to the delight of C. C. Pyle, there were 65,000 fans. And to *their* delight, the Buccaneers beat the Bears 30 to 6.

There was one final game on the coast—a meeting at Portland, Oregon, with a somewhat sorry collection of semi-pros, whom the Bears really destroyed, 60 to 3. Then Red went to Hollywood to make his movie, in which he proved to be a pleasant, curly-haired, and diffident young man with eyebrows that seemed in a state of constant alarm and without a trace of acting talent.

Red and C. C. Pyle had profited of course just as handsomely as Pyle had promised, and money still trickled in from royalties and endorsements. But Red had scars and bruises to prove he had earned the money. His reputation had dimmed somewhat from his failure to break loose consistently on those ghostly runs for the goal line. It was said by more than a few that what Red missed was the expert blocking he had received in college—and *that* was missing because of the wide disparity in the pay scale: $3000 for Red Grange and a couple of hundred dollars or less for a lineman. No one ever could point to a time when Red's teammates actually played him false. But it cannot be denied that incentive was in short supply. There was in that day no Super Bowl or League Championship prize on the horizon to stir a man to the frantic efforts sometimes required to wipe a tackler out of the runner's path. Even the glory went to Grange, unless a man on the opposite team did a particularly good job of chopping Grange down; then the chopper-down got the headlines.

The real moving spirit of course was C. C. Pyle, and he did not run the ball club. Indeed, he was not always in the finest odor with Halas and Sternaman. But *he* might have developed some of the *esprit de corps* a winning team requires had he just distributed a few $500 incentives along the scrimmage line. And he might thus have spared Grange some of the physical beating that slowed him down and kept him, from time to time, out of action. Observers who chanced to see Red making ready for games on this trip used to marvel at the yards and yards of bandage and adhesive tape that were needed to swathe his body before he could drag it out for one more effort on the gridiron.

In 1927, Grange and Pyle broke with the Bears and started their own league, no less, with Grange starring for the New York entry, named the Yankees, and with a Chicago franchise named the Bulls—the Bulls being the opposite, in stock market jargon, of the Bears. There was a brief and bitter war with the National League, with each league trying to snatch stars from the other. It was over after a season and Grange went back to the Bears, where he became a solid, workaday defensive man for seven seasons. There were not many players of his day who had studied the game more earnestly than Grange had, nor any who could explain it more lucidly. Thanks to this skill, Red was able to find a place for himself in, or near, football again, after he had gone broke, like so many

Red Grange is off on a fifty-five-yard run to a touchdown in a game between C.C. Pyle's New York Yankees and the Boston Bulldogs. Sparsely peopled stands spell the doom of Pyle's venture.

other of the newly rich, in the depression of the thirties. Red pulled himself back to solvency first of all by his own efforts, as an insurance salesman. Somewhere he had found the "nerve" to succeed in the very vocation he had shied away from in the long ago. It always gave him a special satisfaction to know that he made good at this job without benefit of newsreels, sports page publicity, or C. C. Pyle. Indeed he frequently found himself dealing with men who had no notion of who Harold Grange might be and had never seen his features in print.

His football job was as television commentator. He still lacked any flair for acting and his eyebrows still took flight at the end of almost every sentence. But he was articulate, knowledgeable, and quick to find illustrations or forecast plays. So, until some of the younger movie-star-cum-Madison-Avenue types began to move in, Red remained one of the sharpest of the paid tellers of football stories.

Red's entrance into the game is supposed to have marked the beginning of respectability for professional football. Yet there were many hard times ahead, as there were for Red himself. There were franchises that were abandoned, some that were sold and shifted, clubs that went broke without playing a single league game. But it was Red Grange, after all, who first demonstrated to the college football player, who often found himself friendless after his scoring days were done, that the professional game was not all bruises and haphazard paydays, and that a man could walk home after the game was over with something more than a black eye. Red got the black eye, all right, in his first game with the Bears. He also took home $12,000 for his efforts on that one autumn afternoon.

Wings on the Football

PRO football teams, through the 1920s and into the 1930s continued to use variations of the tight-T formation or the Notre Dame "box," which set one back in front of another in an open square, so that any one of them might take the pass from center and take off with three others to blast open a pathway for him. The short punt formation however had proved exceptionally flexible in the hands of some coaches and it was out of this, in all probability, that Pop Warner of Stanford developed the single-wing formation that was going to turn football into a far better game to watch.

Defenses against the tight-T, which offered the ball carrier so little room to maneuver, had grown so sophisticated in the early thirties that scoreless tie games or games in which drop kicks provided the only scores became common. Brutal and fruitless struggles of this kind (as between Fordham and Pittsburgh) may have enthralled college boys and worked wonders of character building among the participants, but they made poor spectacles.

It took but a minor change in the short punt formation (which had the backs lined up in a triangle, with the passer-kicker at the apex, and with two

131

Bronko Nagurski during his college days as tackle for Minnesota. The football was still shaped like a watermelon, making it perfect for drop-kicking.

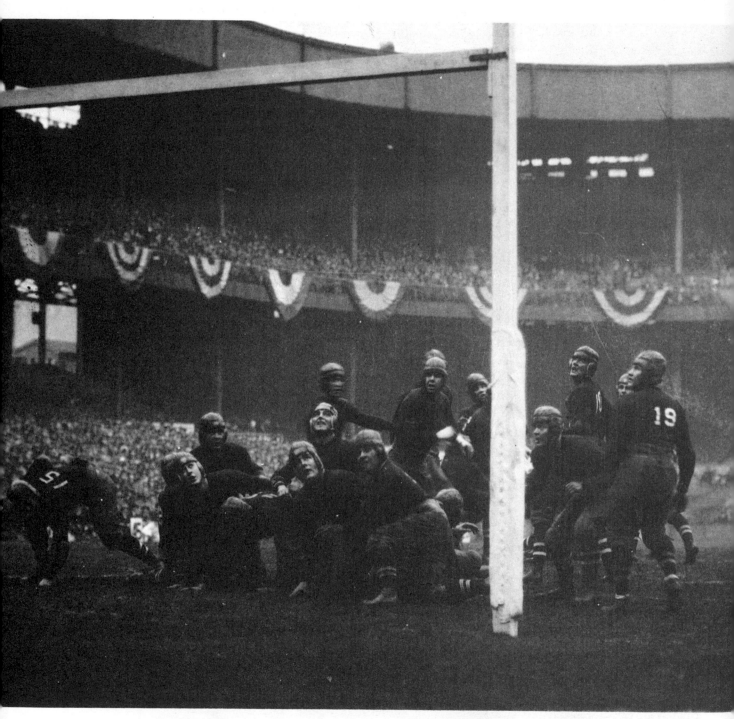

Nearly everyone watches enraptured as the ball is kicked over the bar. But the right end looks as if he is still waiting for the play to begin. New York Giants at Polo Grounds, 1926.

backs on the kicking-foot side and one back on the other side) to develop the single wing. By shifting the single back to put three on one side, Pop Warner came up with the wing back, who played outside the offensive tackle. And then, with a lopsided backfield, Warner provided a lopsided line, putting two guards on the same side of the center. From this formation it was possible to develop some really frightening momentum. It enabled one guard to pull out of the line and add his own weight to that of the blocking backs, providing a whole herd of beef to hammer around the end, or off the tackle, ahead of the ball carrier.

It also made possible a "reverse" run, in which the wing back circled behind the tail back to take a quick hand-off, then continued around the short or weak end of the line with a pack of blockers ahead of him. Out of this, of course, could come a double reverse, or a "naked" reverse, in which the end on the weak side would turn and take a hand-off from the wing back and go back around the strong side without a blocker to bless himself with. When this play was worked with sufficient skill and deftness, the ball carrier would pop out suddenly all by himself, with all twenty-one other players moving in the opposite direction, to scamper unattended, and momentarily unnoticed except by the spectators, toward the enemy goal.

The Single Wing Frees the Runner At Last

Plays of this sort could set spectators' hearts to pounding even though they owned no special loyalty to either side. Getting the ball carrier out around the end where he could run had long been the aim of football coaches and this new formation seemed to have brought the dream to fruition. It also made possible a quick kick with the tailback suddenly retreating a few steps to give himself room to boot the ball, and a new "spinner" play, in which the tailback (still called the fullback by many die-hards) would turn completely around, pretending to hand the ball to the circling wingback, but keeping it himself and plunging straight into the line with two blockers ahead of him. Any of the other backs of course could receive direct passes from center and dive off-tackle, plunge up the middle, or try to circle the end.

This was an ideal passing formation too, with the protection already set up and the tailback in a position to get rid of the ball promptly.

Naturally the pros fell upon this formation hungrily, for they were intent on improving the game as a spectacle. But these were still hard times, for other people besides football promoters, and the league did not immediately prosper. The American League had died and Pyle's franchise had gone to Staten Island, New York, where it became the Stapleton Giants. Milwaukee had been tossed right out of the league for hiring, in their desperation, four high school players, to fill out the roster. The franchise holders solemnly agreed, not once but several times, not to hire football players before they had completed their college courses (observance of this rule would have barred Red Grange, of course), but there was always someone trying to chisel on his agreement. College coaches banded together to fight the "threat" of professional football, and Knute Rockne, a former star with the Canton Bulldogs and the Fort Wayne Friars, and now, as coach of Notre Dame, one of the most famous personalities in the land, vowed that he could gather together a group of good college players who could clobber any professional team in the land, for fun, money, or marbles.

Many a college hero discovered none-theless that the elusiveness that kept him from harm or the speed that carried him far from the hands that would de-stroy him were of very little account in the pro game, where linemen were not so easily faked out of position, and where years of dealing with fancy ball-carriers had made defensive men wary. One of the greatest names in football, Albie Booth of Yale, who had seemed to own a magic akin to that of Red Grange, himself, could not spin a single thread in the professional game, being so small and so easily batted down. Even a performer as ferocious as Red Cagle of West Point—a man who would twist a bandage around his head after a scalp injury to keep the blood out of his eyes and get right back into the fray and a speedster who had stopped, on his way to the Rose Bowl, to race jackrabbits—was only briefly successful among the pros.

The professionals now were really professionals, not men who changed from overalls or aprons to football togs in time for the game, but strong, well-conditioned lads who were able to de-vote to football the time a college boy would have to divide between football and studies. And because they were recruited from far and wide, not just pulled together from the confines of a single campus, they were nearly equal in skills, in agility, and in size, so there was no finding a weak spot and working

on it for the length of a game. They were also men trained in the giving and re-ceiving of physical punishment and they could be counted on to treat any opposing ball carrier with utter disre-spect, aiming for his bad leg if he had one and rejoicing if they put him down to stay for a while. This is the manner in which they expected to be treated and they respected a man who could hand them back the same coin they were paying out. (Once Al Nesser, the hard-as-nails ironmonger from Ohio, offered to kill an opponent who was feeding him a closed fist whenever he could manage it. But after the game Al shook the man's hand and told him he'd played a hell of a game.)

Not that college football in this era was not rough. (Said Century Milstead, mighty tackle from Yale who played for the New York Giants: "I was slugged in high school, I was slugged in prep school, I was slugged at Yale. But I was never slugged in pro.") Many colleges now were recruiting their beef from the coal-and-iron areas. (One tree-trunk type who was working in building construction won himself a college edu-cation by single-handedly putting three hold-up men to rout who had pointed a gun at a wealthy Dartmouth alumnus in a Chicago alley.) And because most games were played with but three of-ficials, a good deal of dirty work along the scrimmage line was bound to go unnoticed.

Knute Rockne Challenges the Pros

All the same, the pros were tougher. They played more football. They played it under more rugged conditions against teams that were consistently their equals. And professional players usually spent the off-season in some muscle-

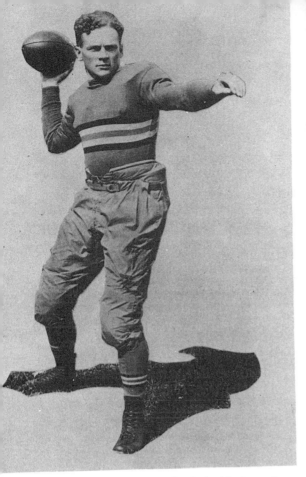

Christian Keener (Red) Cagle in his Army football togs, holding the fat football. Cagle used to improvise reverses and pass plays from the short punt formation. He would sometimes drop back fifteen yards while reversing the field.

Handsome Benny Friedman practices place-kicking. He was also an elusive ball-carrier who made a practice of driving into the line with the ball held high, as if to pass, thus freezing the secondary for a crucial moment.

toughening pursuit, such as hard-rock mining, steel puddling, or professional wrestling, so they were ready for hard physical contact, without any warm-up games, such as the big colleges usually scheduled early in the season.

Still, Knute Rockne (who may have been the greatest college coach who ever lived) would not grant that the professionals played real football. Having himself recruited a good many hard-muscled young Poles and Italians to come play for the "Irish" in South Bend, Rockne was convinced that he had put together at least three combinations that could trim any pro club in the land. He just could not imagine a professional player's being motivated as a college lad was, by something very

akin to patriotism, or the blind loyalty that sometimes made soldiers face death without flinching. Mere hope of cash reward, Rockne argued, was not enough to prompt a man to play over his head. A professional player, as Rockne knew well, was sometimes motivated by a brief pep-talk from the coach that consisted of a single sentence: "Win this one or get yourself another job." And pro football players were often at the mercy of a cranky coach who could bench a man for failure to address the coach with proper respect, or for questioning his strategy, or just in order to persuade the owners that the blame for failure belonged to one or two players rather than to the coach himself. (One coach used to "motivate" his players by promising them free beer after the game if they won—or a $100 fine for drinking if he caught them taking beer after a loss.)

Rockne told so many different people that he had clubs that could beat "any professional team" that one day, in 1930, someone decided to call him on it. A game was planned, for the benefit of "the unemployed" (who were more numerous then than "disabled veterans"), to be played between the New York Giants and a group of Notre Dame All-Stars, including the matchless Frank Carideo.

Leader of the New York Giants at this time was a solid and handsome young man, not much given to bragging, named Benny Friedman. The son of a Cleveland tailor, Benny had moved from one high school to another in Cleveland when the coach at the first high school solemnly sized Benny up and told him he would never be a football player. At the second high school, however, Benny became more interested in basketball and would not have bothered with football at all had the coach not refused to let him play basketball unless he played football too. He had, said the coach, "the perfect halfback build"—he was not overly tall but was solid, loose-limbed, and square-shouldered. Benny was also deeply interested in his studies. But the coach insisted he was not going to do without Benny on the football team, so Benny played football. He did not possess, the coach decided, the "leadership quality" required in a quarterback, so that job was handed to a boy of Japanese ancestry named Arthur Matsu (who looked every inch an American). Matsu, who went to William and Mary College,

eventually played quarterback for a season with the Dayton Triangles. (The Triangles also carried for a time a husky Chinese-Hawaiian lad named Walter Achui and called "Sneeze.")

Benny Friedman went on to the University of Michigan, where he starred as runner, passer, and kicker on the freshman football team. He also earned high grades in his studies, as well as the hearty dislike of many of the young monsters he shared the campus with, who found Benny more full of self-confidence than they thought any Jew had a right to be. Benny for a time, unable to understand perhaps that what was self-confidence in a Gentile was deemed conceit in a Jew, considered transferring to Dartmouth. But after a summer of hard work (no one in Benny's family was permitted to loaf), Benny came back with some of the rough edges rubbed off, or at least with enough newly developed wariness to avoid laying himself open to some of the less refined ridicule that college boys of that era went in for. He almost immediately became a college hero—through sheer ability on gridiron and in classroom, combined with a carefully cultivated modesty.

By the time Benny had graduated from Michigan he was a seasoned football player, ready in every way to become a pro. One of the brainiest men ever to play the game, Benny was also a reckless, knock-them-down type ballcarrier such as never fails to excite a crowd. He was a man who played every second with his whole heart, savagely fighting to advance the ball even when he was already snowed under by tacklers. Benny played one season of pro football in his home town of Cleveland,

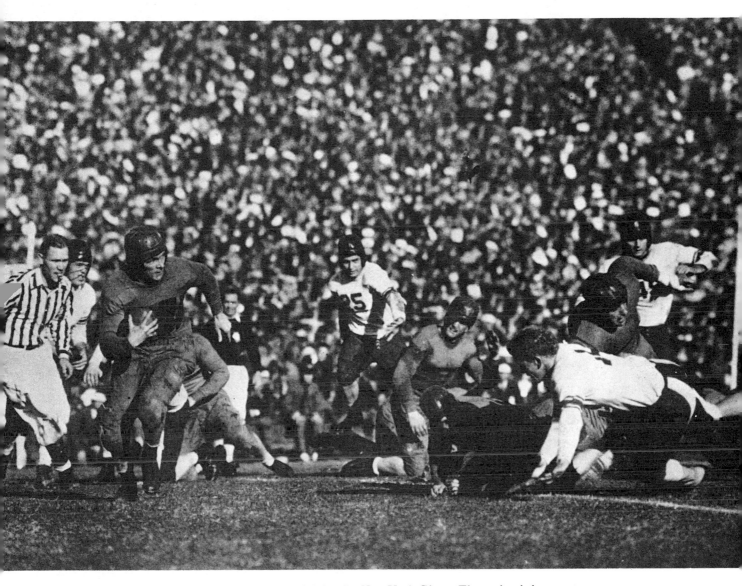

Red Cagle playing his last game for Army before joining the New York Giants. The action is in a post-season game against Stanford at Palo Alto, December 31, 1929. On the way out to the game, when the train stopped in the desert, Cagle got off to race jackrabbits. The race was a tie.

This posed action shot shows a two-man football club—ball-carrier Joe Sternaman of the Chicago Bears led by his teammate, Bronko Nagurski, who could block out a half-dozen ordinary ballplayers on one play.

Bronko Nagurski (Bronko was his real name and not a nickname) demonstrates for a photographer the ferocity of his play. Bronko could have been All-Pro either as lineman or ball-carrier. No one ever hit harder than Bronko did.

spent one year with the Detroit Wolverines, then came to New York to play five seasons, first with the New York Giants, then with the Brooklyn Dodgers.

It is an oddity of football statistics that Benny Friedman's name is hard to find listed therein, for his accomplishments did not lend themselves to cataloguing. He was not a high scorer, and played his best years before anyone started naming "all-pro" selections. He broke no distance records with his kicks, runs, or passes, because no one was keeping records in the league when Benny began. Yet when he was in charge of the New York offense, it was Benny that the fans came crowding to see and a club owner would have been

a prospect for prompt psychiatric attention who offered to trade Benny off for less than a complete football team.

Benny was never seriously hurt at football and to this day he cannot understand why quarterbacks cannot avoid getting their knees hashed up. (Benny never threw with a stiff leg planted in front of him but always with knees flexed so they would give without harm under any sudden irresistible pressure. Of course Benny did not have any gang of six-foot-six pass rushers to cope with.)

Benny was an innovator, an improviser, an inspired field leader, and a man who played with such fiery enthusiasm that hardly anyone wanted to leave the park, no matter what the

One of the greatest kickers in the game, Ken Strong, practices his place-kicking. Both Strong and his holder, Ed Danowski, have studiously kept their eyes on the ball, Danowski to the point of mesmerizing himself.

score, when Benny was still driving his horses down the field. Whether Benny was the first quarterback to use the "flea flicker" type play (in which the quarterback passes the ball forward to a receiver, the receiver passes it back to someone else and the third man heaves it way down field), who can say? But he did employ it more than once to add sudden life to a slogging offense and bring fans hopping to their feet.

When Rockne chose to toss his challenge at him, Benny was the coach as well as the quarterback of the Giants. (Leroy Andrews held the title but Benny ran the club.) Benny flung out no thundering defiance, but there is no doubt that he and his charges were panting to

set the anti-professional-football clique (of which Rockne was a leader) abruptly on their tails. The game was ideally suited to the place and the time, for New York at this era was filled with subway alumni who had rooted for the Irish of Notre Dame for so many years they sometimes were not sure but what they *had* attended the blessed institution themselves. They never failed to talk of the Notre Dame team as "we"—just as Brooklyn Dodger fans always seemed to include themselves in the lineup at any game. And they were still glowing (and bragging) of the glorious day, just a year before, when Jack Elder of Notre Dame had run ninety yards to make the touchdown that was needed to beat the favored Army team.

These were hard times too in New York, as many people may have forgotten and most never knew. So a football game offered a chance for a short surcease from the frets of scanty wages and piling debts or provided an opportunity to work off some of the nameless venom any man in those days was bound to store.

The Pros Demolish the All-Stars

Before the game Rockne told his charges just how to proceed. "These Giants," he said, "are big but slow." (This was not a fact, for lumbering bigness was no longer tolerated in the pro ranks.) "Score two or three touchdowns in a hurry and then just hold them." But no one, least of all a collection of slightly gone-by ball-carriers who had not taken the trouble to get into top condition, was scoring "two or three touchdowns" on Benny Friedman's Giants. The great Four Horsemen of the decade before—Miller, Crowley, Lay-

139

den, and Stuhldreher, who had themselves played as professionals—quickly discovered that they were not knocking down any defenders with their reputations. They retired very early for a younger group, led by Frank Carideo, whom Rockne named the best quarterback alive. But Carideo was soon grateful just to be alive, for he was never able to move his crew against the aroused Giants, and he made the mistake of trying to get in Benny Friedman's way when Benny got ready to go.

The total yardage amassed by the Notre Dame All-Stars that day was minus thirty. They accomplished just one first down, completed by means of a forward pass—a weapon that Rockne felt was overrated by the pros. On the first series of downs, the Four Horsemen and their stablemates were shoved steadily backward, although they had the football. Stuhldreher was finally nailed in the end zone for a safety. In the third period, after three successive running plays, the All-Stars found themselves with thirty-two yards to go on fourth down.

The final score was 22 to 0. It might just as well have been 70 to 0, except that Benny Friedman showed mercy toward the end. He took himself out of the game (he had bruised a knee) and allowed Red Cagle to steer the ship the rest of the way. Benny had savored his big moment near the end of the second period, when he ran twenty-five yards for a touchdown. Benny burst off tackle, knocking linemen aside, then veered head-on into the Notre Dame secondary, never varying an inch from his course, no matter who stood in his way. When he crossed the goal-line his pathway was marked with stretched-out

bodies, including that of Frank Carideo. One by one he had met them all and bowled them all over. Benny scored thirteen points himself that day, as he fought with a ferocity none of the fans had ever seen surpassed. There was no money in the game for anybody—it being a benefit for Jimmy Walker's Fund for the jobless—but Benny played it for blood and seemed bound he was going to rub the noses of the All-Stars in the mud and make them say they relished it.

Red Cagle too enjoyed an especially sweet moment. Having been himself a member of the Army team that Notre Dame had humiliated the year before, he was out to square matters if he could. His opportunity came when Jack Elder, hero of the previous year's victory, set out around the end with the ball under his arm and his eye on the distant goal. Cagle came roaring up then and halted Elder in mid-course with a tackle so shattering even the spectators' teeth rattled. Run ninety yards, would he?

It was this game, perhaps as much as the game with Red Grange in it, that sold professional football to enough New Yorkers to keep it alive through the depression. After Grange had appeared with the Bears and even C. C. Pyle had been rendered half-speechless at the size of the gate, there had been a rush to grab or create pro football franchises. Pyle and Grange had established their New York Yankees—and then had given away a reservoir full of coffee and a couple fathoms of hot dogs to any newspaperman or any friend or distant cousin of a newspaperman who would agree to come sit and act as decoy in the perennially vacant stands. The Yankees lasted two seasons.

After the All-Star defeat, Knute Rockne remained unconvinced. It had been just a contest between a team of well-trained "ex-collegians" and "twenty-five men who had not practiced." Of course Knute was right. His All-Stars had at least learned the bitter lesson that you just could not run through a few plays together out in your backyard and then take on conditioned athletes who played the game for a living. Later groups of All-Stars did practice long and hard together and they managed to stage some fierce battles with the pros and frequently beat them. But these were stars gathered from a hundred colleges, all men who were ready to play professional ball themselves. Even though Rockne insisted he could still "take last year's Notre Dame team and beat the Giants if we had time to practice," this was still a pipedream. You just could not recruit that much top football talent from one campus in one season. And there were some who thought these animadversions would have come with better grace if they had preceded the game.

While keeping the football team alive was hardly the chief concern of most citizens of the city in that dismal day, Benny and his boys did succeed in the struggle. Benny's combativeness and the warmth of his sporting blood attracted both rich and poor. As a matter of fact, it cost less in that day to attend a professional football game than it did to go to one of the big college features. The crowds too were of a different cut. While, even in these bedraggled years, raccoon coats were plentiful in the stands at a college game, they were seldom seen, except in the very front boxes, at the games the pros played. It had long been a tradition to carry pocket flasks to football games in the colleges and this tradition was honored to some extent among the pro fans, although, because the pro fans were older, there was less flamboyant drunkenness and fewer young men stumbling about in a state of semi-consciousness when the game was over.

Benny Friedman's Giants consistently pulled in crowds of five to ten thousand. And he pulled in even more one day when he agreed to meet the Stapleton Giants on a winner-take-all basis—the sort of old-fashioned sporting event that would make a league official in this carefully "structured" day turn pale.

The Stapletons were led by another New York darling, Ken Strong, who had starred at N.Y.U. when coach Chick Meehan used to have his minions march out of the huddle like cadets at drill, and would cause a cannon to be fired to celebrate every score. Ken, a square-built fellow with a shock of black hair that would have looked almost natural on a football player of the 1890s, had the speed and power of a Red Grange. He was also the greatest kicker of his day.

Ken Strong might have been a famous forward passer, except that an operation on his right hand had made it impossible for him to close his fingers on a football. But, in those days of power sweeps around end, Ken made many a long gain, for he had great speed as well as an ability to cut, dodge and break tackles. When his Stapleton club played the New York Giants in the winner-take-all game, the Stapletons took it all, partly because Benny Friedman was able to play only a few minutes and largely because Ken Strong took the opening Giant kick-off and ran it back ninety yards for a touchdown.

There were of course other great performers in this day, a few of whom found themselves jumping from city to city as the franchises were sold, shifted, or abandoned. Red Cagle put in three seasons with the Giants, playing often without a helmet, exposing his flaming hair. He moved then to Brooklyn where he and John "Shipwreck" Kelly tried to keep a club in operation, with attendance so scanty that sometimes the game was held up to permit five or six more spectators to buy tickets. (The franchise was sold finally to a wealthy young man named Dan Topping, who was destined to become part owner of the New York Yankee baseball club.)

There had been of course a Yankee football club, belonging to Grange and C. C. Pyle. Here a sticky-fingered pass receiver named Steve Badgro earned a small but fanatic following, then joined the Giants when Pyle sold the Yankee franchise to Stapleton. Badgro ended his playing days with Brooklyn.

Mel Hein, a center from Washington State, joined the New York Giants in this era and stayed there fifteen seasons, with hardly ever time out for more than a few deep breaths.

George Halas and Bronko Nagurski Add Excitement

Most of the excitement in this era originated in Chicago where George Halas was cooking up new football formations and his Bears were winning league championships. In Chicago there were two full-time pro teams—the Bears and the Cardinals, and uncounted semi-pro and amateur clubs that played wherever they could find room. The greatest football player in Chicago at this time was not George Halas but Bronko Nagurski, the one-man team who could play every position on the field well enough to win it and who was said to "run his own interference." Bronko (this was his real name and not a nickname) was surely the most destructive blocker and runner since the days when Jim Thorpe was destroying tacklers with his steel shoulder guards. Indeed, no one, or almost no one, ever really "tackled" Nagurski because one man could not stop this fearsome lad that way. The only way for a single tackler to bring the Bronko down was to take the big man's feet from under him with a perfect "Indian" block. And like as not, before the block could be thrown, Bronko would set his own shoulder into the foeman and flip him into short orbit.

Bronko was himself a great defensive man, the equal or the superior of any lineman on the club. And when he ran interference for such as Red Grange or Laurie Walquist, it took a mighty man indeed to stand fast against him. Bronko, in those days when such shifting about was permissible, would sometimes start a game at tackle and move into the backfield before it was over.

Bronko had a special way of running that turned his body almost into a projectile, for he kept his head down and his trunk nearly horizontal as he pounded along. (Fritz Pollard too had run that way.) His pumping knees would rise almost to his chest and there was very little of him for a tackler to wrap his arms around. Bronko's effectiveness was doubled by a rule change that the professionals adopted in 1933. This season the pros permitted a back to pass the football forward from anywhere behind the line of scrimmage. (Before that he always had to be five yards behind the line.) This rule allowed the Big Bronk to come charging at the line (where terrified defensive men would hastily stack up to meet him) then stop in his tracks and flip a pass to a receiver just a few yards beyond. Bronko used to jump into the air as he tossed his short passes, enabling him to get the ball over the heads and hands of the crowding defensive players.

Another rule change in 1933, the year that the pros finally declared their independence of the intercollegiate rules committee, was the moving of the goal posts back to the goal line. (The college rules committees had pushed them to the end of the end zone to cut down on injury and prevent the use of the goal posts as extra linemen on defense.) This prompted a revival of field goal kicking all through the pro ranks and, along with the change in the passing rule, assured a spectator at a pro game that he would at least catch an occasional glimpse of the football. The changes also began to cut down extensively on the number of scoreless or near-scoreless ties.

The Bears Return to the T Formation

The Bears about this time promoted another innovation that was to have a sweeping effect on all of football: they returned to the T formation. The man who brought it back is supposed to have been Ralph Jones, former assistant to Bob Zuppke at Illinois, where he had dealt with both Halas and Sternaman, now co-owners of the Bears. When Jones returned the Bears to the T, the opposition used to laugh out loud at the sight. But after Jones and Halas, over

a few seasons, had added the quirks and refinements that made it the "modern" T— the man in motion, the quick, brush blocks in the line, the quarterback in contact with the center, so the center could play heads up—every club in pro football had to adopt it and it swept through the colleges and high schools as well.

Jones was hired as coach because Halas and Sternaman simply could not run the club together. ("We had two offenses," one player complained. "A Halas offense and a Sternaman offense.") And he soon turned the Bears into the best club in pro football. They went all through the 1934 season without losing a game. But when they came to New York to play the Giants in the post-season playoff for the championship, they ran into an innovation that neither Jones, nor Halas, nor Sternaman had ever thought of. And with it the Giants won the championship.

The game was played, as so many of pro football's playoff games have been, in sub-zero weather. The surface at the Polo Grounds had frozen as hard as a dance floor but the two clubs played in the standard shoes, with cleats built to cut into the turf. On the unyielding surface, the cleats offered no more purchase than ball-bearings. Runners trying to cut went sprawling. Linemen trying to charge felt their legs shoot out from under them. Passers slid to one knee.

Between the halves, coach Steve Owen of the Giants undertook to deal with this problem. Abe Cohen, the tailor who kept the Giant uniforms in repair, volunteered to chase up to Manhattan College to try to borrow basketball shoes. He came back with nine pairs, enough to provide good traction

The offense in this 1935 picture of the Detroit Lions defending against the Chicago Bears seems to be leaning the wrong way, and a few players are apparently engaged in some other pursuit. Players in that day were still permitted to play without helmets.

for all the key players. When the second half began, the Bears were leading 10 to 3. The Giants, getting their feet under them at last, were able to stop Nagurski's charges, while their own carriers moved about as easily as goats on a rocky hillside. In the fourth quarter, after the Bears had managed to squeeze in one more field goal, the Giant offense broke loose. In the final quarter they scored twenty-seven points, galloping and passing, while the frantic Bears were sliding and grabbing like men on roller skates. Ken Strong ran forty-two yards for one touchdown and then scored again on seven short rushes that averaged better than seven yards each. The Giants' most inspiring deed however was stopping the unstoppable Nagurski when he tried for an "easy" first down on the Giant forty-eight-yard line. After that, the Bears were no longer in the game. And after that, not only the Bears but most other clubs kept rubber-soled shoes on hand for use on hard-frozen ground.

Another bright light of the thirties was Earl "Dutch" Clark of Portsmouth, Ohio (later coach of the Detroit Lions). Clark was one of the great dropkickers of the era and he was perhaps the last one to give up that method of putting a football over the goalposts. The football authorities, having observed what some simple changes could do to improve the game as a spectacle set out to make the ball easier to pass by changing it from a pumpkin into a cucumber. As it grew narrower and more pointed at

the end, it grew more difficult to drop kick, for if it landed anywhere but right on its sharp little nose, it tipped off at a sharp angle and could not be kicked with accuracy. But Dutch Clark continued to kick long goals by drop kick regardless of the shape of the ball. Dutch was also one of the most exciting of broken field runners, who could dodge, fake, shift, start and stop with the agility of a jackrabbit. He came out of a small school, Colorado College, and while he was an All-America, he did not come into pro football trailing any long cloud of newspaper publicity. He worked for $144 a game, far less than some lesser runners commanded who had been bid for by half a dozen different clubs. As quarterback at Portsmouth, Dutch brought his club in right behind the Bears in 1931 and pressed the Bears again in 1934 when he was with Detroit. In 1935 he led Detroit to a championship (matching the baseball championship the Tigers had won the year before).

While defensive men everywhere in the league agreed that there was no harder man to bring down than Dutch Clark, Dutch never made much newspaper copy. Dutch Clark never sought the spotlight, never staged any tantrums on the field or off, and never went in for eccentric activities in public. He just kept running the football long distances and when his day was done he slid uncomplaining into obscurity.

There were of course other great men still drawing in their own devoted fans to the football field, in weather sometimes that would have driven timber wolves into hiding. (Once a Chicago man, playing in Green Bay, Wisconsin, stood knee deep in snow to get off a punt from his end zone.) Ernie Nevers, who led the Duluth Eskimos one season, when his Eskimos played twenty-nine games, missed only twenty-seven minutes altogether, or about a minute a game. The Eskimos, who started out in life as the Duluth Kelleys, were one of the best accoutred football clubs in the league and one of the first to establish a regular pre-season training camp out of town. But it eventually became impossible to draw cold-weather customers out of their igloos.

In Boston there were the Redskins—named the Redskins so that some fans might imagine they were kin to the baseball Braves. And to keep *their* customers yelling, there was a rock-hard runner from West Virginia Wesleyan named Cliff Battles. Cliff was a high-dollar man in the thirties, playing for $250 a game (and collecting his pay after every game, with a percentage held out to make sure he completed the season). Cliff was a big man for a halfback of that era. He weighed 195 pounds, ten to twenty pounds more than Grange, and he ran with speed and elusiveness very nearly equal to that of the Illinois ghost. Cliff, however, brought no championship to Boston, although he and his mates got into the playoff with Green Bay in 1935. Then Cliff got himself hurt when the battle was barely five minutes old, and could play no more. The Redskins lost 21 to 6.

Throughout these Roosevelt years, as the country tried to whistle itself back to prosperity, pro football was just coming to recognize the fact that it was going to live or die as an entertainment. And, urged on by a number of imaginative showmen, it undertook to improve its entertainment value. The most important move it made was the establishment of a real rather than an imaginary championship. By dividing the league into Eastern and Western divisions, and then scheduling each club so that it played home-and-home with every other club in its own division, and played as many games as every other team in the league, the authorities made it possible to come up with two divisional champions, whose right to the title could not be questioned. Then it provided a genuine championship play-off that had more meaning than a rough comparison of two unequal schedules. It laid the groundwork for a good-sized gate that would provide payoff enough to charge up the incentive of the clubs involved.

The Pro Game Becomes a Better Show

The rule changes that opened up the game also greatly improved its entertainment value. But still some further touches of showmanship were needed. For too long the players had been permitted to go on the field looking like a bunch of overgrown sandlotters, with stockings or without, helmetless if it suited them, and often wearing their own private notions of what they needed for protection. (Players on many clubs had to provide their own uniforms and they were not inclined to buy more than what they required to get them through the game. The league decreed at last that players would wear helmets whether they wanted to or not and uniforms became decidedly uniform.)

One of the first to show concern for the visual quality of the performance was G. A. Richards, the owner of the Detroit Lions, who first owned the club when it played in Portsmouth, Ohio,

under the name of the Spartans. When Richards landed them in Detroit he outfitted his players in anything but a Spartan manner. He provided them with helmets of blue and silver. (He called the shade "Honolulu Blue.") He put bright, visible numbers on every jersey and provided "uniforms" for off-the-field wear, as the Chicago Bears had when they took Red Grange to Jacksonville. Richards also offered, in every game, well-planned half-time entertainment and put all his home games on radio. (Other clubs had tried from time to time to ignite a sort of collegiate spirit, by hiring grown-up girls to come act as cheerleaders and by putting bands on the field. But the girls drew only whistles and the bands were sometimes no more smartly outfitted than the scrubs on the bench.)

George Halas and George Preston Marshall, the wet-wash king who owned the Redskins, were perhaps the two men who did most, however, to make the pro game a better show. They pressed for the rule-changes that made the game more open and kicks for goals more frequent. They eliminated the old wasteful way of "running the ball out" on a side-line play so as to have it brought far enough in bounds to provide room. And they worked to have the league lay out the schedules instead of letting each club arrange its own. Marshall also provided a big band, all beautifully attired with feathered headdresses and all, that became a standard attraction at home games. (There was a band in Green Bay too—the Lumberjack Band —but that often carried horn players who could not tootle a note and became "musicians" just as a means of getting into the out of town games for free.)

What Do the Packers Pack?

WHEN Curly Lambeau, in Green Bay, Wisconsin, wanted to start a new football team, he walked straight into the office of the president of the company he worked for—the Indian Packing Company (which packed processed meat rather than Indians)—and sweet-talked that kindly gentleman into promising $500 to pay for jerseys, pads, footballs, and pants. The club thereupon became the Packers, but before the club had worked out for more than a season or two at the plant's athletic field, the Indian Packing Company was no more. They had grown suddenly rich supplying canned meats to the fighting armies in Italy and they grew suddenly poor when the government contracts all dried up.

Perhaps they should have put the promoters of the football club to work promoting the canned meats. For the Packers soon far outgrew their canned-meat origin and became more famous than the town that spawned them. When the National Football League grew up Green Bay was the only city of its size that still held a franchise therein. It was against all common sense that such a town should support a club that could win championships from the likes of Chicago, Los Angeles, and New York.

149

Curly Lambeau, in his later years, still expressed himself with his usual lucidity. Having left the Packers, he came back to Green Bay in August 1950 as coach of the Chicago Cardinals, to play the Packers in an exhibition game. *Everything* went wrong.

(Charles Bredell—Green Bay)

Green Bay, Wisconsin, the smallest town to hold a pro football franchise. Many players decide to settle in the town after their playing days are over. Here are two new boys in town: Jim Grabowski (left) and Donny Anderson. (1966.)

But by this time even nice old ladies who thought the Chicago Bears lived in the zoo and who might have imagined that the Cardinals flew out of a birdhouse knew that the Green Bay Packers played football. No one could even think of Green Bay without thinking of the Packers, not even those who never dreamed that the bay itself was an arm of Lake Michigan.

The club was started as a sandlot aggregation, to take the place of one that had folded up the year before. It was not Curly Lambeau's notion that anyone would ever be able to make a living just playing for this club. He, like many another ex-college athlete (he played one year at Notre Dame), just could not bear to give up the game in which he had won so much local fame. A newspaper reporter met Curly on the street one day and the two of them, while mourning the disappearance of the local sandlot club, began to wonder out loud why *they* could not start another football team.

There were enough fellows in town, including the alumni of that earlier club, to put a team on the field that would match anything some other promoter might gather out of the backyards of Appleton, Oshkosh, or Menominee. (George Calhoun, the reporter, may have had a brighter vision, for he would never allow that the Packers could not match any club in the nation.) Calhoun and Curly, and a few others, met in the editorial rooms of the Green Bay *Press-Gazette* at just about the same time that Jim Thorpe and the men from Rochester, Akron, Massillon and Dayton were putting together in that Canton auto showroom the beginnings of a football league—a league that would one day be dominated by the lineal descendants of the club being organized in these cold reaches of another state.

The Packers Are in Business to Stay

The first Packer games were played at Hagemeister Park, a playground where there were no seats, nor any board fence to hold out the non-paying spectators. All that kept the scattered fans from wandering on the field was a wire fence strung around the playing area. The players dressed at home and rode to the park carrying their cleated shoes, or even trotted in stocking-footed. Kids scampered across the field during the play and sometimes fans would dodge under the fence and stand close to the scrimmage line. The gate receipts were gathered in George Calhoun's hat, passed about in the first half by George himself who could impale a non-contributor with a glance so fierce that the boldest gatecrasher in the crowd would go digging into his pants after a quarter.

There being no locker room, the teams between the halves would hold their meetings in the open air at opposite ends of the field with the Packers surrounded by a dozen volunteer coaches, in addition to kibitzers and eavesdroppers. (The real coach at the start was the local high school coach, who gave his services without pay.) During time-outs, a devoted young lad named Jack Rudolph, who became an editor of the local paper when he grew up, used to rush in and out with a water bucket and a long-handled dipper. And the only "entertainment" the Packers offered between halves was the sight of most of the kids in town scrambling after a single football in a game of "pick-it-up-and-run," in which Sunday pants were often torn and innocent little noses bloodied.

The Packer style of football was played all over the land and had been played in Green Bay too since the 1890s. Large cities bred dozens of such clubs and promoters in small cities were going broke throughout this era, trying to hold together just such aggregations of local heroes. The sandlot club Green Bay had owned just the year before had not lost a single game out of seven they played. Originally called the South Side Ski-doos, the club after one game changed its name to the Whales, probably so it might broaden its recruiting area. What with stars leaving for college before the season was well under way, and the influenza epidemic forcing cancellation of a playoff for the imaginary "professional" championship of the state, the Whales had more than their share of heavy weather. But George Calhoun, who had worked hard to promote their cause, was still convinced, even after the Whales had foundered, that a champion club could be gathered together in his home town.

George Calhoun Keeps the Packers' Image Bright

When the packing company sponsor of the club would contribute no more it was George Calhoun who ferreted out new contributors. He also wrote reams of publicity that was printed all over the state and talked creditors into holding off yet a little longer before coming down to take the water bucket or the footballs away. (The club started with twenty jerseys, a dozen footballs, and not enough shoulder pads to go all the way around.) George, who was always called Cal, was one of those selfless individuals everyone has met in his lifetime—crusty on the exterior, apparently begrudging every penny he let go of, ready to snarl at any man who tried to soft-soap him—yet carrying about in his chest "as warm a heart as ever beat, 'Twixt this and the judgment Seat."

But George had no warmth, or even mercy, for those who would try to sneak past him to see the game free, once there was a turnstile and a fence. It was easy to imagine his following a gate-crasher clear to the man's home kitchen to pry the ticket price out of him. The only ones who ever successfully penetrated George's lines were the make-believe musicians who carried instrument cases into the park as if they meant to take part in the mackinawed and bearded Lumberjack Band that helped enliven the major games. And eventually Cal closed down on them.

It was Cal, almost alone, with his stacks of lively copy and his weekly newsletter, mailed to friend and foe alike, who kept the Packers' glory bright. No one who ever received Cal's newsletter was likely to forget it, for he seemed to spend his idle hours sedulously mixing metaphors. A tackler, he might write, "collared the runner around the ankles." Or he was perfectly capable of describing a man as "having both feet on the ground and not rocking the boat." A final score might "break the camel's straws" in Cal's columns, and once he predicted that the Packers would have "a tough row to hoe in the Loop swim if they want to walk off with the league flag." And when Cal seized old Time by the forelock he allowed that he was "taking the bull by the hands." Those close to Cal insisted that he thus did violence to the tongue just

so his readers would be sure to hand the newsletter about. (In recent years, a racetrack won top-page pictures in a dozen papers by having the sign-erector misplace the Y in Raceway.)

Whether he intended it that way or not, Cal did win special attention for his newsletter and the name of the Packers therefore was, if not "on the tip of every ear," at least not "born to blush on the desert air." And Cal did nearly everything else that was required off the field too. He missed only one game in all his active career with the club—and that was a game played in Hawaii when he was ill. Yet he liked to brag that he never saw a kick-off. He was always right there at the turnstile to see that no village One-Eyed Connolley got by and that the dollars counted equaled the tickets sold. He also booked hotel rooms, bought bus and rail tickets, assigned roommates, paid for meals, and kept the books.

The Packers Wallop the Beloit Fairies

In their first season, the Packers were still just a bunch of local strong boys but they had trouble finding a club they could not lick. They put in ten days of practice together (ten afternoons, that is) and then began to play. They beat the Racine Legion 76 to 6 and the Maple Leaf club of Milwaukee 53 to 0. But they were beaten in Beloit through the combined efforts of the Beloit football club, the spectators, and the officials. After calling offside on four successive touchdown plays by Green Bay, the officials stretched the first half by just enough seconds for the Beloit club to score. Later in the game, as spectators swarmed close to every play, a local partisan stuck out his foot and tripped Ray

The incredible Green Bay fans, most of whom own a share of the team. Here is a section of the stands during the 1967 championship playoff with the Dallas Cowboys. It was thirteen degrees below zero that day, and even some of the spectators admitted it was chilly.

McLean of Green Bay as he headed for the goal line after taking a pass out in the open. (Green Bay sought prompt revenge on Beloit for a $2000 side bet in a game to be played on neutral ground with a neutral referee. But Beloit backed out. Two years later, when Green Bay came to Beloit to play, the Beloit club called itself, unblushingly, "The Fairies." What Lambeau or George Calhoun made of that was never written down. Green Bay walloped the Fairies.)

After surging up and down the state of Wisconsin for two seasons seeking teams to dismember, and after dismembering such clubs as Sheboygan Company C (87 to 0), Oshkosh (85 to 0), Marinette (61 to 0), Kaukauna (56 to 0), and De Pere (62 to 0), Curly Lambeau borrowed $150 from a friend and bought a franchise in the new National Football League. Here he hoped to meet the kind of big-time competition he hungered

for. And to prepare for that day, Curly began to prowl the outer reaches of the state to find better football players.

Among the first that Curly persuaded to come make believe he had been born in Green Bay was the University of Wisconsin's mightiest tackle, the great Cub Buck, who had served one season with Jim Thorpe's Canton Bulldogs before there was any league. Cub, whose first name was Howard, did the kicking for the Packers his first season and boomed some Thorpe-style punts to keep the foe at his distance. Green Bay's greatest punter, however, was Vern Lewellen, captured in Nebraska in 1924 and brought to Green Bay to stay. Vern helped Curly turn the punt into an offensive weapon, by booting long, long kicks into the enemy's "coffin corner" (the five-yard line or thereabouts) again and again. Curly also used the forward pass with what coaches of that era would have called utter recklessness. In an age in which college coaches were warning their charges *never* to throw a pass while inside their own twenty-yard line, Curly was throwing passes from behind his own goal line. When the defense managed to cover his receivers, Curly never hesitated to toss the ball right over the sideline—a commonplace maneuver in this day but one that not many passers resorted to before Curly did it. According to Curly, it was his own reckless, or seemingly reckless, use of the pass that drove the pro defenses out of the seven-man line and set them to putting more men into the backfield to make ready for passes to start falling. Whether this is exactly accurate or not, Curly did help popularize the pass among the pros. His clubs used the forward pass, by his own reckoning, some 75 percent of the time. In one early game, Curly threw forty-eight passes and completed thirty-seven.

The Packers Offer Fringe Benefits

But Curly actually sponsored a brand new feature that has had a lasting impact on the game. He was undoubtedly the first to offer "fringe benefits" to lure the choicest of the college ball players up to his icy little part of the continent. His first move was to provide—at a time when some clubs were still offering "per game" stipends—year-round employment with a guaranteed salary. Of course in this he had to have the hearty cooperation of local businessmen. But they were quick to see what the success of the Packers was likely to do for their businesses. So, many of Curly's imports became real hometown boys through this simple device of planting them in steady jobs. A number of them are still there, old residents now, who still feel that their hearts belong to the Packers. Curly also sweetened his offers to college prospects by providing them insurance against injury, a matter that had begun to weigh on many a football player most heavily, as he saw men left jobless and without income when a serious injury took them out of the lineup.

Probably no one, until Paul Brown arrived on the scene, scouted the small or the faraway schools as systematically as Curly Lambeau did. He was so thoroughly devoted to building a championship club at Green Bay that until the club finally began to show a steady profit, he gave his mind to nothing else. (Eventually he did move out to California to keep his aging carcass warm in the off-season.) His early recruits came not just off the All-America and All-Conference lists but off the squads of colleges that sounded as if somebody had made them up. In the twenties there were men from St. John and St. Thomas, from Beloit, and from Carroll. There were several local boys who had never been to college at all, and a large contingent from Marquette. Ripon, Carleton, Milwaukee Teachers, Northern Michigan, and St. Ambrose also contributed heroes to the Green Bay roster.

One of the brightest names, a man who remained a hero in Green Bay, even to the police who occasionally had to guide him home, was that noted itinerant athlete already mentioned—John "Blood" McNally—who often treated the Green Bay fans to wild improvisations on the field. But they saw Johnny Blood under several different flags both before and after he put on a Green Bay uniform for keeps. Johnny played for the Chippewa Falls Marines, for the "Old Style Lagers" of La Crosse, and for the Kenosha Cardinals. After starring for Green Bay for one season (after a long lapse) Johnny switched next season to Kenosha and helped them beat the Packers. He had come to Green Bay first from the Pottsville Maroons after playing (during the same seasons) for both the Milwaukee Badgers and the Duluth Eskimos. Curly Lambeau talked Johnny into returning to Wisconsin (Curly, when he joined the league, had insisted on receiving the Milwaukee territory) by offering him $100 a week, then making it $110 if Johnny would promise to stop drinking on the Tuesday before the game. "I could never do that," said Johnny. "Make it Wednesday." Wednesday it was, and Johnny moved to Green Bay to help adorn the legend there.

The Packers Remain the Green Bay Packers

It was Curly's aim that the Green Bay club should represent the whole state of Wisconsin, which was one reason why he insisted on the territorial rights within seventy-five miles of Milwaukee. Some sourpusses predicted that once he had developed a winner, he would take the whole gang to Milwaukee, but Curly, a loyal home town lad, never had any such plan. Before the club had grown all its feathers, it did have to play some of its games in Milwaukee to gather money enough to get by on. But it remained the Green Bay Packers through good times and bad.

Bad times came, as they must to all men, to the Green Bay Packers soon after they joined the league. But a man named Andy Turnbull, general manager of the local newspaper (and George Calhoun's boss) came to their rescue just as

a spell of wet weather was about to sink them. He recruited three more local enthusiasts who, with himself and Lambeau, became known as The Hungry Five. It was their job first of all to get up the $2500 needed to move the creditors off the playing field. Then they were all to scrounge about the Fox River valley to find what nickels and dimes were needed to *keep* them off.

In the course of their scrounging, the plan developed that turned the Packers into the only community-owned football club in the league. They sold shares at five dollars each to every fan who would agree to let himself be taxed up to $100 to meet the needs of the club. These shares were sold with the understanding that they would never pay dividends or provide any cash return whatever. Nor could any one corporation hold more than a limited number. As a result the Packer franchise is locked tight into Green Bay (where the big industry now packs toilet paper rather than canned meats) for as long as the world (or at least the National Football League) shall stand. It cannot be sold or transferred except by vote of two-thirds of the stockholders and they are as likely to vote for that as they are for moving the city fifty miles inland.

The Packers soon rewarded their backers by coming up with several imaginary league championships. They were imaginary because they were won on a percentage basis and sometimes the Packers did not even play against the runners-up. In 1931, for instance, the Packers finished some percentage points ahead of the Portsmouth Spartans. But they clung to the title only because they refused to play the final game of the season (already agreed to)

Don Hutson, the Alabama Antelope, wide open for a pass, turns to gather the ball into his tremendous hands, as an anguished defender comes up too late. In eight seasons out of ten, Don led the league in pass receiving.

with the Spartans. Crafty Curly Lambeau, after dropping a game to the Chicago Bears (whom they had beaten previously), saw that a defeat by the Spartans would leave the Packers in a tie for the championship and so he backed out of the game. "Green Bay Pikers!" the Spartans howled.

Sometimes Curly's own players called him such names, for he was a tight-fisted man when arguing salaries—even though he did for a long time offer the best deal (year-round employment) of any club in the league. Curly also was given to trying to enforce discipline by fat fines. He cut some sizable chunks out of Johnny Blood's income when Johnny overshot the Wednesday drinking deadline. But Curly at the same time was an inspirational leader. He dearly wanted to win and he would throw himself into the contest with all his heart, even long after he had quit active play. Spectators at the Green Bay games in Curly's day can remember him well—dressed in his go-to-meeting best, with a brilliant necktie floating under his chin, storming up and down the sidelines, exhorting his boys, screaming invective at the officials, giving defensive signals with both arms, and pounding himself on the head when some pet piece of strategy fizzled.

The Packers' original and seemingly natural rival had been the city down the lake, Milwaukee, and fans had taken special delight in watching the home town boys demolish the sorry aggregations that came up from the big city. But after the Packers (for a while, after the packing company stopped buying the jerseys, the club tried calling itself the Behemoths, but nobody could say it twice the same way) had joined the league, representing Milwaukee as well as Green Bay, the favorite enemy became the Chicago Bears. When the Bears came to town, blood was sure to flow. And when the Packers went to Chicago, the Lumberjack Band pranced all through the Loop and in and out of hotel lobbies, scaring kids in carriages and defiantly playing their battle songs.

The Packers also in time built up a nice hatred for New York, exacerbated by the patronizing manner in which their "little" team was welcomed by the New York press and radio. One announcer, noting that Eddie Kotal, the Green Bay ball-carrier, appeared without a helmet, spoke disparagingly of the "underequipped" club from that little town far off, not realizing that Eddie went without a helmet, not because there were not clothes enough to go around, but because he thought he could run better without one.

"How Sweet It Is"—The Packers Beat New York

The victory the Packers scored over New York on a chill, wet, and dreary afternoon in November, 1929, was therefore one of the sweetest the town had ever known. The game was played in New York's Polo Grounds on a thoroughly slimy surface that should have made it impossible for anyone to move the ball more than a few yards up and down the middle of the field. But the Green Bay gang took to the slippery going like big-horn sheep and pounded the Giants into the mud, 20 to 6. Curly Lambeau, who had broken a rib in an earlier game, had permanently retired from play by the time the Packers met the Giants. But he was as active as any halfback as he stamped and leaped along the sidelines.

The quarterback who ran the club that day was Johnny Blood, the man who could do everything, who might pass, or run, or kick, or all three on the same play if his demon moved him. But the real hero was Cal Hubbard, that big barn-door of a man who would eventually become one of the greatest of major league umpires. Cal had been cut loose by the Giants as being past his prime and he took a fervent and loud delight in dumping Benny Friedman's handymen into the mud that afternoon. Lambeau, determined to keep Benny Friedman's passing attack from gathering steam, tried what was for that era a daring maneuver. He pulled big Cal out of the line and let him roam around behind it, along with the fullback and the roving center, to spot and bump any receivers coming through and to plug up whatever holes might open. Cal gloried in the linebacker job and he played it like a man in a frenzy. When a crowd of blockers came roaring around end, as they often did in those power days, Cal would dump the whole herd of them into the lap of the ball carrier. Or he might single out the lonely ball carrier, collar him with one sweep of his paw, then splash him on the sod. Cal did not fail to call the attention of his ex-employers, Tim Mara and Steve Owen, owner and coach of the Giants, to what he was doing to their loved ones.

Cal's activities as one-man defensive line allowed the rest of the Green Bay huskies to charge in upon Benny Friedman as if the whole purpose of the game was to lay hold of the quarterback. Benny was so overwhelmed by this sudden influx of unfriendly bodies that he swallowed the football an uncounted number of times and spent much of the afternoon on his pants in the mud.

The details of this game were reported back to Green Bay, where half the town had crowded into one smoke-filled room to watch, on a big green board called a Grid-Graph, a sort of reconstruction of the action on the field as it was given to the operator. There being few outdoor loudspeakers in that day, this was the only way a large crowd could be given the news. And when word came finally that the Packers had put the Giants down, the crowded room exploded with a roar that must have set men wondering a mile away. But not even this delirium could have matched the glory the players themselves took in the game, as they yelled in triumph or wept in frustration if some play went wrong. They played the whole game as one devoted and angry family, with no substitution until the right guard, Jim Bowdoin, obviously groggy, had to be removed. Then the whole club yelled in dismay. They had wanted to finish the game as a unit.

This victory did not in itself bring the championship, for there were more games to play. But it practically settled matters for that season, as the Giants were the only strong rival the Packers had. The Green Bay club finished the season without a loss and when the heroes came home the whole town turned out in the freezing cold to greet them. Crushed together in the downtown area, the frantic fans filled each street from wall to wall. And the bellowing they set up on that drear December night would have outdone a herd of triumphant bulls.

That was the beginning of a string of championships for Green Bay that provided the investors with all the dividend they had ever hoped for. Their team, now the darling of the whole state, grew

Still playing in their familiar pre-war jerseys, the Green Bay Packers take on the Washington Redskins in a pre-season game in 1945. Ted Fritsch is returning the kick-off. That's Wilbur Moore, of the Redskins, who is leaping clear over defensive back Larry Craig to get at Fritsch.

in fame, both individually and collectively. And of course it became easier to recruit ballplayers, with championships and yards of newspaper space awaiting those who joined the flock and made good.

Don Hutson Leads the Packers in Their Days of Glory

Among their most famous recruits of the pre-war era was a long-legged young man known in the newspaper columns as the Alabama Antelope but properly named Don Hutson. Don was a slippery ball carrier and an expert place-kicker. But he did best what ends at Green Bay were supposed to do—catch forward passes. Teamed first with Arnie Herber, an expert at the jump-pass made popular by Bronko Nagurski, Don caught flying footballs with either hand or with both, at all distances in every sort of impossible circumstance. It seemed to his fans for a long time that all a passer had to do was to get the ball within two yards of Hutson and he would clutch and hold it.

Arnie Herber, who was recruited from a college named Regis, was succeeded by another great thrower of the football—Cecil Isbell of Purdue. For a number of seasons they were both throwing the ball to Don Hutson, and with Hutson's help each one in turn became the leading forward passer in pro football. Both were cool and accurate. But whether they would have shone so brightly without the impeccable Antelope to make so many of their passes good is a question. For Don caught passes that lesser men would have merely waved at. He caught them over his head, at his knees, just off the grass, at the absolute end of his straining fingers. In one game, Hutson, closely

covered at the goal line, sped straight at the goal posts, grabbed one post as he was going by, swung around in a vicious pivot that left the defensive man running top speed away from him, and then reached back with his free hand to snake a pass out of the air for a touchdown.

But Hutson did not become the Antelope just because he could make next to-impossible catches. Once he had the ball in his hands he was swift as a horned animal, with the elusiveness of a waterspider. Although he weighed 195 pounds he could run the 100-yard dash in 9.8 and there were few men who could overtake him once he had gained a stride. Hutson as a defensive end was mediocre indeed, despite his fighting qualities. His weight was spread over too lank a frame to permit him to apply it with proper ferocity against a heavy lineman. But once his coach had learned to move Don to defensive halfback (he would be a safety man in today's game), he proved wary as a wolf and just as hard to duck away from. With the same swiftness he used to snare thrown footballs, he could reach out and capture a dodging runner, yanking him up short and downing him.

Hutson was not, of course, the only great man on the Packers in their first days of glory. Also among those early champions were Buckets Goldenberg, the guard who was built like a buffalo, Clark Hinkle, the driving fullback who many said was the equal of Bronko Nagurski, and Mike Michalske, another guard who was about as easy to budge as a freight car. Still, the men who drew the cheers and set the spectators to throwing away their hats were Arnie Herber, who loved to pass the football twice as far as anyone had ever seen it travel, and long Don Hutson, who was sure to be near the ball when it came down. Hutson, for a time, owned almost every pass-receiving record the Al Munro Elias bureau could devise. He is still named, by men who saw them all, the greatest receiver who ever played on the shores of Lake Michigan.

With men like these to further its fortunes, the Green Bay club put hard times far behind it, and its non-profit stockholders gave it a security no other team in the league owned. So as many another small city hastened to sell its franchise, or just let it go back to the soil from which it sprang, the Packers remained as the only undersized city in the league, and remained too for many years as a strong contender. Its leadership, however, finally began to falter. Curly Lambeau, always a fierce advo-

cate of his own cause, and the unifying spirit of the team, was eventually left without a contract. He had got in the habit of spending the non-football months in California and the executive board could not forgive this lack of patriotism. He had fallen out with George Calhoun, and Cal, ailing now so he was less and less able to get about, no longer served as publicity man and comptroller. Yet even when Lambeau had gone to Chicago to ally himself with George Halas, a kindred spirit despite their ancient rivalry, he still remained a Packer at heart and still gave out his annual predictions of triumph.

As for the team itself, it found new heroes to replace old. Long before the call went out for Vince Lombardi to come make it into a champion again, it had begun to flourish like a Green Bay tree.

Vince Lombardi and his soon-to-be successor, assistant coach Phil Bengston, during the second Super Bowl, in which Green Bay defeated Oakland. Substitute quarterback Don Horn looks unnecessarily worried.

The Cowboy and the Redskins

NO matter what Curly Lambeau may have thought or said about his own part in the task, the man who really taught the pros how to use the forward pass was Sammy Baugh, who joined the Washington Redskins in 1937. Sammy was a Texas cowboy who never saw a cow except across a fence until after football had provided him with enough money to buy a ranch of his own. He was also a baseball player who came to the pros with what was thought to be a minimum of skills. (He was a punter and passer.) Actually, at Texas Christian, he had been more of a baseball player than a football star—good enough to have had an offer to play for the St. Louis Cardinals. His strong arm seemed at its best in gunning long throws across from third base to first.

When he did come to Washington, attired in ten-gallon hat and cowboy boots ("They hurt mah feet!" he complained), he at first just seemed a walking publicity stunt invented by that notorious old showman George Preston Marshall. Marshall, whose Redskins had worn out their welcome in Boston after George had betrayed his loyal and patient followers there by jacking up the admission price as soon as the Redskins won a championship, insisted on the

163

George Musso, veteran guard of the Chicago Bears, vainly tries to point out to a skeptical official the error of his ways. Chicago vs. Washington, 1942.

cowboy get-up at least until the first pictures were taken. And Coach Ray Flaherty of the Redskins, who had been a receiver for Benny Friedman in New York for seven seasons, warned Sammy that he could never get by in pro football on passing alone—not even on passing and kicking. "You'll have to learn to run," Ray told him.

Sammy did learn to run but as it turned out, he *could* have stayed in the league on his passing, for there had never been anyone in all the game's history who could throw the way Sammy did, or had the guts to do it as often. Even his first college coach, Dutch Meyer, urged him to practice punting so he could really be of some use to a football team. But when Sammy and Dutch moved from the freshman team up to the varsity (Dutch was promoted the same year Sammy became a sophomore), the two of them startled and enlightened the Southwest Conference by the brand of football Sammy manufactured. Sammy, brown, leather-skinned, and cool-handed, just had the flesh spread too thinly on his frame to offer much of a threat as a power runner. But the world had never before seen such fast-moving aerial-type football as he demonstrated. With forward or lateral passes or quick kicks on almost any down and from anywhere on the field, the TCU eleven turned Texas football into the greatest show on earth. George Preston Marshall, always concerned with spectaculars, had heard about Sammy Baugh long before his name came up in the draft. George had second choice that year and when the man with first choice passed Sammy over, George could hardly believe his own good luck. He grabbed Sammy at once

and began to envision his arrival in Washington all booted and spurred and twirling his lariat. He had to skip the spurs and the lariat but he insisted Sammy become a cowboy.

Sammy Baugh Wins Games on Passing Alone

Sammy's skills at passing had not come by accident. As Ted Williams practiced hitting in every spare minute, Sammy practiced throwing the football. He dangled an old spare tire on the end of a rope in his backyard and set it swinging, then gave himself the job of firing the football through the hole from varying distance and every angle.

Working from the tailback position in the single-wing formation Sammy continued to throw the football from every conceivable angle and for long, short, and medium gains. It was he rather than Friedman or Lambeau who really convinced the pro football world that games could sometimes be won on passing alone. The pro rules by this time of course permitted passing from anywhere behind the scrimmage line, and Sammy took full advantage of the rule. He would sometimes let a forward pass go while he was running full tilt toward the sidelines, apparently intent on sweeping the end. He could release the ball faster than any man before him. He threw baseball style (in this era, there were many sidearm passers who balanced the ball on their hands and slung it with a sweeping motion of the arm), with bent elbow and cocked wrist, so that the ball was impelled with the full strength of his arm, and as accurately as if he had fired it from a gun. Sammy was not a man to come up with a pass when running became sticky. He would throw three, four, five, even six passes in a row—with the defense assuring itself that *this* time he would surely hand the ball off or run with it.

The forward pass not only brought victories to the Redskins, it brought them sudden increases in gate receipts and it was this that aroused all of pro football to the true possibilities of the air attack. So it was Sammy who started the trend away from the triple-threat star toward the day of the specialist. For when Sammy Baugh played, the air was full of footballs. And many of the great powerhouses of the league, who could send small herds of beef through and around the massed opposition, found themselves outscored and utterly confounded by this lean, long-armed young man who apparently had never learned that there was a time when passes should *not* be thrown. To Sammy, who helped make winning clubs out of mediocre ones, it was always a good time to throw the ball. Yet he would sometimes utterly befuddle the enemy by drifting back with his arm cocked and suddenly booting the ball over the heads of the bright-eyed defenders who were poised ready to pick off his pass.

Sammy had learned the job of kicking very well indeed. The quick kick became one of his favorite weapons and helped make him the leading punter in the league for four seasons. The single-wing formation, being just a variation of the short punt formation, lent itself most readily to this maneuver, and Sammy used it often with startling results. In the 1942 championship game against the Chicago Bears, the Bears had kicked off to the Redskins and then smothered the Washington ball carrier on his own twelve-yard line. It would have been typical of Sammy to heave a long pass to get his club into the ball game and the Bears were ready for him, alert and eager to grab a thrown football and run it in for six points. Sammy took a direct pass from center and dropped back, the fat football held loosely in his two hands, his eyes apparently in search of an open receiver. Then, with hardly a half-moment to get set, he just laid his foot into the ball and booted it far far downfield, out of reach of even the deepest defender. It struck the ground at about the fifty-yard line and bounded

Sammy Baugh, whom George Preston Marshall made into a cowboy, turns George into an Indian for some forgotten publicity stunt.

A Sammy Baugh pass to Redskin halfback Wilbur Moore prompts this bit of ballet as Roy Zimmerman of the Eagles vainly stretches to intercept.

"He was over!" Sammy Baugh declares, as Washington halfback Jim Castiglia is pushed back from the Chicago goal line. Slightly bored spectators are George McAfee, Chicago halfback (5); Clyde Ehrhardt, Washington center (31); Ed Sprinkle, Chicago end (7); and H. Allen Smith, Chicago end (30), no kin to the humorist.

Wilbur Moore of the Redskins is pulled up short by his jersey on a kickoff return, 1941.

Someone in the Polo Grounds in New York tries to pull down Sammy Baugh by *his* jersey. Sammy has no intention of going. (1942.)

After grabbing the ball from the quarterback on an old-fashioned statue-of-liberty play, Wilbur Moore of the Washington Redskins is off to a touchdown. End Pete Marcus leads the way. Defense has been successfully outflanked, with most of them well out of the play. (1944.)

away, away, away toward the Chicago goal. When a Chicago man reached it at last, he had half a dozen Redskins for company and all he could do was down the ball. It was on the Chicago five-yard line and the game situation was turned right around.

In that same game, with the Bears telling each other at every down *"Now the s.o.b. will throw it!"* Sammy sent twelve plays right into the center of the line, where the Bears were playing "soft," to keep him from hitting on one of his sudden passes over the middle. On the twelfth plunge Andy Farkas carried the ball across the Chicago goal line.

These triumphs however were the prized exceptions that proved the value of Sammy Baugh's rule. Had he not already shown he would pass whenever the mood was on him, the enemy would not have been so vulnerable.

Baugh Was the First
Modern Passer

Sammy of course is no longer in the books as the greatest passer in the game. Other players and other formations have helped wipe out Sammy's records. Yet Sammy was the first of his kind and deserves the title of the best. He had to play both ways and was as agile and swift on the defense as he was while running the attack. (He once set a mark for pass interceptions.) And it was Sammy who taught all future quarterbacks they *never* needed to run except to get on and off the field when the ball changed hands. Also he helped break the ancient thralldom that had made the game, especially when it was played on a wet field, a grunt-groan affair that was hardly more exciting to watch than an honest wrestling match.

In the pre-Baugh era, there had been many a slogging scoreless game played on a muddy field, on which the two clubs slithered about in an aimless and fruitless struggle, with only an occasional juicy (and wobbly) punt to illustrate to the spectators that the men had been playing with a football. But neither mud nor snow nor glare ice could make Sammy cuddle the ball to his breast. In Sammy's first year with the Redskins he led them to a championship in a game played in the snow at Wrigley Field, Chicago. It was not a feathery snow but a frozen one that could cut a man's fingers or even break them. The players all wore rubber-soled shoes, because cleats would not bite into the stuff. Sammy had never tried to play football in the snow before. Just getting used to it took him most of the game. But in the last quarter, with the Redskins trailing 21 to 14, Sammy let fly a pass to Wayne Millner that scored a touchdown from seventy-eight yards away. The next time Sammy got the ball he threw a thirty-five-yard pass to Choo-Choo Justice and won the game with it.

Sammy lasted a long time in football. He was never overweight and never out of condition. He quit playing baseball when, after a tryout with the Cardinals and with two minor league clubs in the Cardinal system, he found he just could not straighten out those curve balls. But he stayed active in the off-season just the same. The salary that George Preston Marshall paid Sammy was modest by today's standards, but Sammy had no expensive habits and was given to spreading his dollars over a wider area than most people could manage. Before long he was able to buy himself a small ranch where he could really play at being a cowboy, doing tricks with the lariat and raising a few cattle. He kept his muscles tough by roping calves in rodeos and even milking wild cows.

There was probably never a better regulated athlete than Sammy Baugh. He had no taste for drinking or for late hours. He divided his day and evening up into definite sections for play, practice, and diversion. His one vice was playing pinball machines for money, and this was hardly calculated to put him in hock to the Mafia, or even keep him up much past his regular bedtime. It was even whispered (and even said out loud on occasion) that Sammy had been known to lay a fat bet on his own club in a football game, sharpening his own incentive just as professional baseball players had been known to do in the pre-Landis days.

Sammy Baugh continued to play for the Redskins until he was almost forty, sticking with them through good times and bad and remaining their bread-and-butter man despite shifts in coaches, in style of play, and reckless interference by the owner. Coach Ray Flaherty was fired by George Preston Marshall, who had decided that his genius extended into game strategy and the hiring of players—a point on which Ray Flaherty and some subsequent coaches disagreed. Marshall not only allowed himself to order shifts in game strategy and to scold ballplayers he felt were not giving out enough effort; he even supplied himself with a walkie-talkie radio so he could dictate the calling of plays in a ballgame from his private box. When coaches rebelled at such interference, George never hesitated to scold them

like an angry parent. He even broke a long-time friendship with Curly Lambeau (whom he had hired as coach) when he engaged in a childish fistfight with Curly (in which no blows were struck) in a hotel lobby, after Curly had refused to fire two players who had smuggled beer into their rooms.

The damage that this sort of upstairs bickering did to the morale of the team was obvious in the dismal record the Redskins began to post. But Sammy stayed with them, and succeeded often in turning defeat into victory, or at least in providing the home town fans something to marvel at. When the new "T" formation came in and it seemed certain that all the old single-wing heroes would be ticketed to the dump, Sammy became a T-formation quarterback, and learned to fade back, to stay in the pocket, to fake, roll out, and bootleg like the best of them. And of course he continued to fire spectacular passes at almost any point in the game.

In 1952, Sammy, nearing forty, entered his final season. Aching in a dozen places and wearing half a hundred dormant charlie horses from years of constant walloping—and wearing too the same ancient dinky little shoulder pads he had bought from Ernie Pinckert in 1937—Sammy was still capable of hitting the height of his skills when the pressure demanded it. Sammy had spent a relatively poor season in 1951, with only 67 passes completed out of 154 attempts and with a higher percentage of interceptions than had ever fallen to his lot before. But he still closed out his passing career, against the Chicago Cardinals, in a manner befitting the greatest of them all. In training that year he had broken his hand and he was re-

Scarred and muddy champions rejoice for the camera after Redskins beat the Chicago Bears in 1942 playoff, 14 to 6. Sammy Baugh (33) sticks out his chest. Wee Willie Wilkin wriggles his bare toes. Choo-choo Ed Justice (13) looks thoughtful.

ported to have lost his touch completely. The Cardinal defensive unit, scenting Sammy's blood, set out to divide his poor carcass into individual helpings and ship it back to Texas in a box. The big Chicago tackle, Don Joyce, made a special project of beating Sammy into the ground, even though Sammy might long before have unleashed the ball. On play after play, big Don would come roaring in and hurl his full weight into lean old Sammy Baugh. But Sammy never complained and never flinched. Nor did he stop calling pass plays, one after another. And he completed them all. On the eleventh pass play, Joyce, like a tree trunk propelled by a Mack truck, slammed into Sammy again and bang went Sammy into the ground. But this time Sammy rose up and celebrated the closing of his career by deliberately pasting the merry monster from Tulane right on the chin, shivering the big man right to his heels. Sammy was promptly thrown out of the game, and Joyce with him.

In his middle years (he was nearing forty-five) Sammy came back to professional football as coach of the New York Titans, owned by Harry Wismer, a former associate of George Preston Marshall and a certified eccentric (some might have said "weirdo") in his own right. But Sammy found it impossible to coach when both Harry and his wife insisted on sharing the burden of deciding which players to put in the line-up and what plays to call. So after struggling in vain to turn his discontented, demoralized and sometimes unpaid charges into a football team, Sammy, still lean and tough as a trail-worn steer, packed his duffel and hied him home to Texas once again.

171

Football Full Time

IN one year the Chicago Bears had three quarterbacks whose names began with "L". One had been there for nine years and the others were just beginning. They were all T-formation quarterbacks and so could not all play at the same time. They were named Luckman, Lujack, and Layne—and the greatest of these was Luckman.

Sid Luckman indeed was perhaps the greatest T-formation quarterback ever, for he had been sought out, traded for, and hand-raised by George Halas of the Chicago Bears, the man who, while he did not actually invent the modern T-formation, at least had a strong hand in perfecting it. And George was credited too with inventing the man in motion that enabled the new formation to turn all football upside down in the 1940's.

The man-in-motion T, as developed in the post-war years by the pros, had almost nothing in common with the early T-formation, which had been used from the 1890s on. In this new T-formation the center had merely to thrust the ball into the quarterback's hands without looking, for the quarterback kept his hands in contact with the center's pants. The center therefore was able to look straight into the enemy's eyes

173

Grown older, but not gray, Sid Luckman shares his gathered wisdom with Bill Wade, Chicago Bears quarterback.

and became more useful in the front line on that account. A rule change eventually enabled the center to hold the new skinnier football in one hand, if he wanted to, with just the front end of it in contact with the ground, so he had a forearm free to block with.

As the new T-formation was used, every play was a potential touchdown run. Linemen did not surge forward to shove head and shoulder into the defensive man and half lift, half shove him backward as far as they could. They just rose up swiftly to "brush" the man back with forearm and chest, so the blocker and runner could slip quickly through the sudden opening and the blocker could give his attention to the men downfield.

In this style of play the quarterback was not counted on as a runner. But his ability to handle the ball, to pivot deftly to one side or another, to hand the ball off cleanly, to fake, and to keep the ball concealed, were more important than ever. The ball, being easier to hold in one hand than the old fat balloon, could be kept out of sight a great deal more easily and coaches came up with plays of all sorts in which the ball was hidden behind the quarterback's leg or body while his free hand went through the motions of giving it to a runner. (Sid Gilman, the Cincinnati University coach who would eventually become coach of the Los Angeles Rams and then the San Diego Chargers, is supposed to have invented a maneuver to which the T-formation was well adapted—the "ride" method of pretending to give the ball off without really letting it go. (The quarterback in this play would hold the football momentarily against the charging runner's belly and actually let it go along a step or two with the man before pulling it back and giving it to someone else.) The T-formation quarterback, playing close up against the scrimmage line, had to keep his head and keep his feet beneath him. The ball had to be handed off in such a way that it did not hit the runner in the neck or in the knees, but nestled comfortably into his abdomen where his hands could fold over it. The quarterback also had to be able to fade back swiftly with the ball out of sight, to stay calm and cool as the prospective "pocket" formed about him, and to step *forward* into the pocket as his protective blockers rode the enemy pass-rush right on around him. He also had to own the skill to roll out with the ball "bootlegged" behind his thigh, ready either to pass the ball over a charging defensive man's head, or to keep right on going toward the goal if the defense failed to move up on him. Above all, of course, he had to be able to deliver the ball through the air to moving receivers. And he needed to be cool-headed enough to know when he should tuck the ball safely into his gut and accept the loss.

Developing the skill to handle the ball deftly and turn this way and that without stumbling over one's own feet was a task of rather large dimension. Backs who could take a ball and run, or even pass it when need be, sometimes found the foot-and-hand work of a T quarterback far beyond them. It was necessary on every squad therefore to have at least one experienced quarterback in reserve. The new T without a sure-handed quarterback was a total disaster in the making, for hand-offs would pop into the air or roll on the ground, or backs would go sprawling or come suddenly chest-to-chest with a man on their own side.

The man in motion that added so much flexibility to the new formation was, according to legend, invented or rather discovered in the heat of play by George Halas himself. When one Chicago backfield man, in accordance with the prescribed pattern, but prematurely, took off for the sideline before the ball was snapped, Halas was bemused at the sudden consternation in the defense as they set out to adjust to keep the man covered. Spreading the defense in some manner had long been an aim of the architects of the game. This maneuver seemed to open the game up wide, and George decided promptly to keep this bit of business in the act. And for a long time defensive coaches were asking themselves if it was better to move an end out to play head-and-head on this man, to send a halfback out to "cover" him, or just to let him run.

The single-wing formation had unsettled the defense with its unbalanced line that enabled the linemen to two-team the opposite tackle when the play came his way. But this man-in-motion bit for a time opened up the defense as nothing had before. It occasionally left the man in motion wide open to receive a toss, or it took a backfield man far out to the sideline and left a wide open space where a pass receiver could roam. Eventually the defense learned to deal with this maneuver and with the other new deceptions the T-formation could practice, by using a five-man line with an extra line-backer to help outnumber the attackers at the point of attack. But

This innocent-faced collegian, posing with Columbia's lion, owned as much fame as a Broadway star when he led Columbia to victory over Stanford in the Rose Bowl in 1934. But Cliff Montgomery played only one unhappy season in pro football, with the Brooklyn Dodgers.

in the beginning, the offense earned a sudden edge.

Sid Luckman Becomes the Perfect T Quarterback

Sid Luckman was probably the man who learned best how to exploit this edge. But when he reached the Bears he was no quarterback at all. He was, as a matter of fact, a reluctant lion indeed and had to be coaxed to take money for playing. Luckman had been a triple-threat star at Erasmus Hall

High School in Brooklyn and at Columbia and it was said that George Halas, through his elaborate system of volunteer scouts (made up of "graduates" of the Bears) had known about Sid since the boy was in high school and George had started then scheming out ways of landing Luckman. When, in 1938, Sid became eligible for the draft, the Bears did not have first choice and so Halas had to make an undercover agreement with his friend Art Rooney of Pittsburgh to draft the big handsome boy, then trade him promptly to Chicago. In this way, George snatched him out of the eager hands of the New York clubs, either one of which would have traded its hope for salvation to have Sid running, passing, and kicking for their side. Dan Topping of the football Yankees said he would have swapped his whole team and started from scratch with just Luckman.

But when Halas set out to sign Sid to a contract, Sid said no. He had been beaten pretty severely about the thighs and shoulders in his years of trying to drag a mediocre Columbia eleven across the goal line often enough to win. Now he had put football behind him and was impatient to make his start in the trucking business with his brothers. He had been "advised against pro football." He did not sign with the Bears until seven months after he had received his first letter from Halas. In those seven months there were, you may be sure, gallons of honeyed words expended by the sweet-tongued seducer from the Staley Starch Company. And George never had occasion to regret a single phrase, even though Luckman at the start looked like one of the worst performers ever to wear a Chicago jersey.

Turning himself from a left halfback into a T-formation quarterback seemed like more than poor Sid could manage. He had never even seen the T-formation in action anywhere before he came to Chicago. When it was explained to him that halfbacks in this new system went unattended through the line, he could not believe it. By Sid's light that was certain suicide.

When Luckman began handling the ball in T-formation, he seemed to have lost all knack for the game. When he pivoted to hand off the ball, he invariably got his feet twisted and sometimes he tripped himself up. He handed the ball off so clumsily that it continually popped free. After about three weeks of this, Halas gave up. If he could not fit Luckman into this new formation he would have to fit the club to Luckman. So he instituted the formation Sid was familiar with—the Notre Dame box. Sid returned to his usual post—left halfback —and called the signals from there, with everyone else having to learn new blocking assignments and new plays.

The Bears actually managed to win a game with Sid in this spot. But the confusion that seized the whole squad as they tried to learn a new brand of football while the enemy was right upon them decided George Halas he must go back to the T, no matter what the move did to Sid Luckman's psyche. So from that time on Sid had to practice quarterback moves in all his waking hours, not merely on the practice field, but in the locker room, in his hotel room, on the train, in his room at home. Hour after hour, he took the ball from center, turned right, turned left, handed off, faded back, pitched out, and made as if to pass the ball downfield. The job he was learning is one that ordinary players are supposed to take several seasons to master. But Sid Luckman mastered it before his first season was done. By the time the final game came around, Sid knew the entire playbook, and was familiar with every move by every man on the team. He also knew a great deal about the enemy defenses, so he could pick out their weak spots almost by instinct.

Sid not only learned the plays they gave him but was able to cook up plays of his own, to the loud dismay of the men who were trying to run the club from the sidelines. But his ability to anticipate enemy moves was so uncanny, and his eye for weaknesses in the enemy defense so sharp that his inspirations on the field of play often brought even more dismay to the opponents.

Sid studied the game of football as some men study the physical sciences. He never begrudged an extra few weeks at the start of the season to sit with his coaches and plan or re-think strategy. And when he ran into a new situation on the field of battle, he often had a devastating answer to it. When he first came back to New York as a professional he offered Giant coach Steve Owen a sample of Luckman improvisation that almost did Stout Steve in. The Giants, under Steve, always made use of a defensive huddle, so alignments could be called in secret, with assurance that every Giant would know where and how he was to play. Sid, having made note of this, decided to take advantage immediately of the fact that the Giants were not immediately ready for battle. The Bears took the kickoff and lined up immediately without a huddle. Sid had called the next two plays before the opening whistle. While the Giants stood in the defensive huddle Sid took

the pass from center and ran thirty-five yards before they caught him. The Giants huddled again but the Bears did not, and Sid this time ran thirty yards. Then Steve Owen gave up on the defensive huddle.

The Bears Humiliate the Redskins 73-0

But Sid's greatest day as field-boss of the Bears came without doubt when the Bears met the Redskins in a return game in Washington in 1940, and humiliated them by a score that still lives in the memories of fans who were not even alive at the time: 73 to 0. (The Redskins had beaten the Bears earlier that season by a score of 7 to 3, and the manner in which the numbers 7 and 3 "jumped out" again must have sent a thrill down the greedy spine of many a numbers player.)

The preparation for this game, at least on the part of the Bears, was far more intense than for any previous game all season. The Bears had dedicated themselves to evening matters with the Washington club. After the first Redskin victory, George Preston Marshall had given out the word that the Bears were a "first-half club" who could be counted on to fold in a game where the opposition refused to give up. In the lexicon of the Redskins, the Bears were already "the crybabies" because George Halas was so given to pulling out the rule book to read lessons to the officials when a tight decision went against the Bears. Now the Bears were determined to shove all these taunts down George Marshall's throat. As the game approached, they steadily "psyched" themselves with reminders of what Marshall had said. And they grew red-eyed from studying the motion pictures of the previous loss to the

Redskins. So often and so devotedly did the Chicago squad study each step, stumble, fake, or maneuver by the Redskin defense that it might have been possible to call any member of the Bear squad out of bed at two in the morning, ask him how the Redskins would react to this or that play and get an accurate and detailed answer.

Of course there was no assurance that the Redskins would be using the same defenses they had used in the previous game. But it seemed most likely that they would not be dwelling on Redskin mistakes quite so assiduously as the Bears were studying their own. Luckman therefore set out immediately to test the Redskin defense, to see if it would react as it had before to one of his favorite maneuvers. He sent Ken Kavanaugh, the Chicago left end, out wide, leaving a gap of over fifteen yards. The opposing halfback, exactly as he had done in the movies, drifted out to cover Kavanaugh. Then, as the play started, Sid sent Ray Nolting, the Chicago left halfback, in motion to the right. The Redskin halfback moved out to cover *him*. The play, a drive through tackle, gained eight yards. But Sid Luckman was far more interested in how the secondary had reacted to the spread. On the next play, Kavanaugh again split wide, and again the halfback moved out, leaving an open alley. This time it was McAfee, the right half, who went in motion the opposite way, to his own left. And Luckman, after faking the ball to Nolting, reversed and gave it off to Bill Osmanski, who was traveling under a full head of steam as he came up to the ball. Osmanski streaked right out to the spread side and headed down the open alley. Bill was supposed

to go inside the enemy end, but the tackle had not been completely blocked and was still in the play, so Osmanski, after a brief fake toward the off-tackle hole, rounded the end and sprinted into the open spaces. Two Redskins—Choo-Choo Justice and Jimmy Johnston—converged on him, trapping him along the sideline. But right end George Wilson of Chicago, running at furious speed, was closing on *them*, and they never saw him. They felt him, however, for George threw one of the most fearful blocks ever seen in any football game. Coming in on Justice's blind side, big George took Ed right off his feet with so much force that Justice flew into the air as if an auto had run into him. In flight, he slammed right into his teammate, Jimmy Johnston, taking him too unawares and sending him into a spin that saw his heels flying over his head. That double block was all Osmanski needed to spring him and he went all the way—sixty-eight yards—to a touchdown. Jack Manders kicked the extra point.

This touchdown, although it may have shaken the Redskins a little, did not intimidate them by any means. They clung to their conviction, imbued by boss George Preston Marshall, that the Bears were given to folding up as soon as a good club got ahead of them. And, with invincible Sammy Baugh running their ship, they expected to haul even immediately and then steam ahead. They very nearly did even the game up on the very next play, for Max Krause, the former New York Giant, took the kick-off and sped away just as if he did not intend to stop at all. He carried the ball sixty-two yards before the Bears caught up with him. The next play should have led to an immediate tie ball game, for it was perfectly executed, except in one small detail, by the Washington club. Sammy Baugh took a direct pass from center and dropped back, gentling the ball in his two hands, getting it adjusted to his grip as he looked downfield for receivers. Everyone in the park spotted the logical receiver almost at once, for there stood Washington right end Charlie Malone on the Chicago two-yard line, alone and apparently (until now) unnoticed. The fans screamed in delight as Baugh spun the ball directly to Charlie's arms. It hit the target too. But—that miserable detail—Charlie dropped it. The low-hanging autumn sun shone directly in Charlie's eyes and he never caught sight of the ball until it hit him. There was a groan of utter dismay from the crowded stands. And, while it cannot be said that the fight went out of the Redskins then, there must have been a sneaking wonder if perhaps this was not going to be their day.

The Redskins could gain no more and Masterson missed a field goal. Thereupon Luckman drove his club from their own twenty down to the one-foot line of the Redskins in sixteen plays. He did not throw a single pass along the way. With the ball just a foot from the goal line Luckman called a play he almost never used—his own signal—and he "sneaked" the ball over for the second touchdown.

After that the Bears could do no wrong. The new "touchdown-every-time" system that the T had instituted seemed finally to be operating just as the theorists had planned. And in addition the manic Bears became true monsters on defense. Luckman said afterward that he had never known such a build-up of fierce determination as he had seen before that game. There was no goofing off or horseplay, just a sort of hushed anticipation as each man concentrated on psyching himself for this golden moment.

At half-time the score was Chicago 28, Washington 0. And George Preston Marshall, who counted over every dollar he was paying these men to perform, sought to inspire them with the reminder that the first half was over and the time had come for the Bears to quit. But George Halas needed only the quote from Marshall to work his own boys up to the point of violence. The Redskins did come out for the second half full of fight and determination, ready to dismember any outfit that tried to restrain them. But the Bears were doubly inspired. Not only did they smell fresh blood, as they noted the scoreboard, but they were still afire with rage against the man who had suggested they were lacking in manhood. So they pounded out on the field for the second half just as if they had at last cornered the street mob that had yelled dirty words at their baby sister. They were so hungry to score and score again that they seemed about to tear the football away from the Redskins. The Redskins took the kick-off and Sammy Baugh tried a short forward pass on the second play from somewhere near his own twenty. It proved short indeed, for Hampton Pool, the Chicago right end, smelled the play out immediately and sped in to intercept. He had carried it across the goal line before some of the Bears even realized the play had busted. If anything could have finished the Redskins that was it—to have Sammy Baugh himself throw an enemy touchdown. The Skins never for a moment surrendered or even relented. Their big barelegged tackle, Wee Willie Wilkin, had to be led off the field by his teammates, weeping with rage and frustration. But no matter how fiercely they tried or how many stratagems the Redskins resorted to, the Bears, so far ahead that they could play like wild men, outplayed and outwitted them.

In the third period the Bears scored four touchdowns, one on an interception by McAfee, who carried the ball thirty-four yards to score, and another on an interception by Bulldog Turner, the indestructible center, who could outrun many a backfield star. Turner reached up and stole the ball on the Redskin twenty-one-yard line and after Hampton Pool had flattened Leroy Zimmerman, who had thrown the ball, Turner carried it over the goal line. About the only real trouble the Chicago Bears ran into was trying to find a man who could miss the extra point. They used four different men on conversions and made them all until Dick Plasman missed in the third quarter. The scene ultimately developed a nightmare quality for the Washington fans, who had come to the park ready to celebrate a championship. About every time a fan looked up from covering his eyes in anguish he would see another Chicago man galloping free and headed, more than likely, for another score. There was a forty-four-yard run by Harry Clark that brought six points when Harry just ran right over safety man Frank Filchock. There was a bad pass from center that Turner covered on the two-yard line, which resulted in a

score on the next play. There was an interception by Maniaci that led, after a few plays, to still another score.

Something of the madhouse tone that the game acquired may be deduced from the fact that before the game was over the teams were down to their last football and the officials had to ask the Bears not to kick any more points after touchdown. The kicks had been sailing into the stands and the fans were keeping the balls for souvenirs. The Redskins had supplied six new footballs—more than enough to furnish a full game. But soon they had to put their practice balls into play and eventually the last scuffed and discolored ball was brought out. After that the Bears tried passing for the extra point, and missed both times. But in every other way they kept insisting on more and more points. As substitutes would leave the game they would exhort their replacements: "Pour it on! Pour it on!" And even the enemy fans took to encouraging them and deriding the futile efforts of their own heroes.

After the game, George Preston Marshall, in a typically sportsmanlike gesture, berated his club, called his own lads quitters and accused them of being too busy counting the house to bother coping with the Bears. George Halas contented himself with announcing that he thought his club "deserved to win." And the Bears hugged each other in rapture. They had done exactly what they had hoped to do. They had not just beaten the Redskins. They had routed, ruined, disgraced, demoralized them. The mighty Redskins had gained a total of three yards by rushing and had had eight passes intercepted.

This game would live on in most

minds as Sid Luckman's greatest. But Sid himself, who most relished a victory over New York, must have known another day that was equally joyous to him. That was when New York fans, many of whom had followed Sid from the days when he first ran the football for Erasmus Hall, staged a "Sid Luckman Day." This was one of those stale rituals that athletic brass seem devoted to—a "day" in which an athlete is loaded down with gifts from admirers (and from those who hope to shine somehow in his reflected glory) and at which he is expected to deliver over a badly adjusted microphone to a crowd that is probably not listening a modest little speech of acceptance and gratitude. Almost invariably the speeches are stumbling, vacuous, and full of "I certainly want to thank" phrases aimed at almost everyone. It is traditional that the "honored" athlete then goes out on the field and turns in the worst performance of his career.

Sid Luckman however wandered far from the script. He spoke modestly enough, but lucidly and succinctly. And he went out on the field and put on a performance that has never been outdone. A few moments after the kick-off Sid threw a touchdown pass to Jim Benton, the left end. And before the second quarter ended, Sid threw a pass for a second touchdown to Cornelius Berry, a substitute end. Sid's third touchdown came on a pass to Hampton Pool. The fourth Chicago touchdown came on the ground but Sid threw a pass for the fifth, thirty-three yards to Harry Clark. Now the professional observers in the press box began to ask each other if Sid could possibly, in the time left, throw two more touchdown passes and thus tie Sammy Baugh's record of six in the same game. Sid quickly completed a pass to Jim Benton for his fifth score. Was there time for another? There was indeed. A short pass over the middle to George Wilson made it six for Sid and seven altogether for Chicago.

Now what set the writers and commentators to staring at each other in wild amaze was the possibility that big Sid might throw still another and celebrate his day by setting a new record. By this time most of the fans knew what was afoot and they began to yell for Sid to complete his seventh. In the very final seconds of the game Sid connected—a long pass to Hampton Pool that the boy from Stanford just managed to snag in his fingernails and cling to long enough to count the score. Thus Sid provided himself with at least one scoring record he did not have to split up with Sammy Baugh.

But Sid was far more than a completer of passes. His years of losing football at Columbia had provided him with a skill not many T-formation quarterbacks had developed. Because Sid almost always found his club overmatched in college (and in spite of this it scored some famous victories) he had grown used to getting his passes off with a horde of unfriendly linemen storming about him and straining to lay their hands on his frame. Sid had learned to duck and dodge them almost subconsciously, while he concentrated on picking up the distant receiver. No college passer had had to scramble any more than Sid had, just to provide himself with the free time needed to get a pass away. He had developed great peripheral vision, so he could discern the foes on both sides of him without ever once taking his eyes off his target.

Sid did of course often fail to find a target and he went down under a storm of bodies times without number. He once got up with a broken nose, in that day before the face mask had been introduced—and when nose guards had long been outré. But these seasons of throwing under direct fire provided Sid with unusual agility at staying out of danger and escaping the hungry hands of the pass rush.

Sid, having begun his pro career in complete ignorance of the T, was perhaps the man who convinced all of pro football that it was turn to the T or perish. Before Sid was through demonstrating what wonders could be worked with this formation, coaches had begun to modify the T— to recover a little of the momentum of the wing-back formations and to open up the defense to give the backs and receivers running room. But from that time forth every pro club sought a quarterback built in Sid Luckman's image, who could keep his feet when all around him were losing theirs and trying to cut his out from under him too, and who could hand off to a running back without telegraphing his every move to the opposing linemen: The Bears, when Sid grew too old to suit up any more, found good use for their new L's—Layne and Lujack, who each had days when he looked like Luckman all over again. But actually Sid was never replaced—because he did not have to be. When the war (which took Sid into the Merchant Marine) brought free substitution, there was no more need for a fellow who could not only call the plays but could run, block, kick goals, throw forward passes, inter-

cept enemy throws and cut down runners in the open field.

While a few men still insisted on playing both ways, a quarterback who was also a kicker and runner soon became an anachronism. And one who played safety on defense would have been deemed a mad extravagance. A T-formation quarterback has trouble enough, what with four or five men on every play roaring in to belt him down, to climb upon him, to ram their knees into his gut, even to scratch his face. Asking him also to carry the ball downfield on every third or fourth play, courting torn ligaments and concussions, would be like asking a twenty-five-game winner in a baseball game to try to set a base-stealing record.

Actually, Sid himself did not often carry the ball, and when he did, George Halas practically stopped breathing until he saw Sid safely up on his feet again after being tackled. (One time, when Sid was a little slow in getting up, Halas, in defiance of the rules, raced right out in the field to make sure his prize pass-thrower was still breathing.) Sid did take special satisfaction in one run he made, however, a run that scored the winning touchdown in the championship playoff against the Giants in 1945, when Sid was supposed to be finished as a football player. (Actually he had four more seasons to go.) The Bears had been practicing, for use in an emergency, a bootleg reverse in which Sid would carry the ball. But Halas had been reluctant to permit its use, especially with Luckman having arrived at an age when he was about due for some crippling injury. But the score was 14 to 14, there was little time left in the game, and the championship was

k and handsome as a movie star, Bill Dudley posed for this picture when, as a ball-carrier for
oit Lions, he was the highest paid football player in the league.

in reach. The Bears had the ball on the New York 19. Sid called time and walked to the sideline to speak to Halas. He did not really have to ask the question that was in his mind and Halas answered it without its being put into words. Sid turned and trotted back to the huddle.

"Ninety-seven bingo, keep it!" he announced to his teammates. Keep it he did, hiding the ball behind his leg while McAfee started around the left end with a phalanx of blockers. Sid trotted off in the other direction and had got clear of the scrimmage line before the Giants realized he had the ball. By that time the Chicago blockers had moved in ahead of Sid to sweep out the secondary. Straining every muscle in his frame, Sid sprinted for the goal, while Giant after Giant was felled around him. When he scored at last he ran back to be overwhelmed by his own blockers who all tried to pound his back at once.

This was an era when pro football was just beginning to grow up. While a few clubs were filling their parks many times a season, there were still a number that played to half-empty seats except when a particularly devoted rival was due. It was still possible then for a coach or a general manager to pick a fine football player right off the street, or to pass one up without ever realizing what he had missed. (In 1948, Emlen Tunnell, destined to be one of the mightiest defensive backs who ever played pro football, walked into the Giants' office and asked for a job. It was two weeks before the Giants decided to hire him. And it was eleven years before they got the uniform off him. Em played in 126 consecutive games, and intercepted 74 passes.)

There were other full-time footballers besides Luckman back from the wars. And ready to be recruited, out of the millions of veterans with their termination pay in their pockets, was a whole new generation of fans who would learn to rate professional football six or seven notches above the college game, which so many of them never had a chance to enjoy anyway.

Bill Dudley, the Last of the Great Two-Way Men

One of the greatest of full-time footballers, and one of the last to hang up his going-both-ways cleats, was a three-quarter-sized fellow with a slightly flattened nose who had been bred in the Virginia hills. This was Bill Dudley, sometimes called Bullet Bill although he never frightened anyone with his speed. There were many players who could catch up with Bill on the field, even when Bill got a head start, but there were few indeed who could lay their hands on him when he was trying to elude them and fewer still who could put him down without a company of two or three mates to help them. Bill was the only football player ever voted "Most Valuable" in three different areas: College, Armed Services, and Pro.

Some who watched Bill when he first came to the University of Virginia— where he was recruited as a kicker— insisted that he had learned to do everything wrong and so could never make good with the pros. He passed sidearm, in the pre-World War One manner. He ran, said some critics, "as if he was staggering." And he kicked placements without stepping into the ball: he just swung his leg like a pendulum. He was also, admittedly, too small to be much use on anything but a high school gridiron. But using his own private style for everything, and adding his fierce desire and his squint-eyed determination, Bill led the pack at one time or another in almost everything.

In high school, Bill had never missed an extra point. It was this skill that won him an athletic scholarship at the University of Virginia, after the coach at Virginia Polytechnic had turned Bill down. Even in Graham High School at Bluefield, Virginia, Bill had at first been refused a chance to play. He weighed only 136 when he tried out and the coach would not give him a uniform. Two years later Bill had gained six pounds and the coach relented. Bill promptly became the star left halfback and took over all the kicking. By the time he was ready for college, Bill had attained his full height of five foot nine and his top weight of 152 pounds.

The University paid Bill five hundred dollars a year for playing football, and out of this he was to buy his books and pay his board and room. In return he played football with every ounce of his strength and with a grim determination that amounted to a frenzy. He *never* let up and he would never allow a teammate to let up either. He seemed charged with an urge to win every contest he ever entered. Yet he was unfailingly courteous, actually gentle off the field, and was not a man to vaunt himself even mildly. The only way you could be sure Bill Dudley was around was to observe the explosive manner in which he got off the mark and the indomitable way he banged, shoved, dodged, twisted, squirmed, spun, and clawed his way through the opposition.

Despite the predictions of the experts,

Bill was an instant success in professional ball. He joined the Pittsburgh Steelers in 1942 and led the league in yards gained on the ground. But after returning from the service in 1945, Bill locked horns with Dr. Jock Sutherland, the dour and dedicated Scot who had built invincible football machines at the University of Pittsburgh and had then resigned in protest when some fanatics seemed bent on turning the school back to the pursuit of knowledge. When Bill had first reported to the Steelers in 1942, he carried an injury he had earned at the university, a bad ankle that still pained him intermittently. Despite this, Bill, in the very first game against the Philadelphia Eagles, broke loose and carried the ball fifty-five yards for a touchdown. The following Sunday, in a game against the Redskins, Bill Dudley's ankle gave way and he had to be carried from the field. But he insisted on going back into the game for the second half, with his ankle taped up tight. He took the kick-off that opened that half and ran all the way to the other goal line with it.

Activities of this sort, one might surmise, would give a man a certain standing with his club, even after a span of years. But Jock Sutherland was the old type of "disciplinarian" who apparently concealed a good deal of private venom behind his stern facade. He had taken a dislike to Bill and seemed to be looking for ways to vent it. Perhaps what irritated him most about Bill was the young man's impatience with any form of foot-dragging on the field, either during a game or in practice. Bill, who believed as devoutly in football as some men do in General Motors, had no patience at all with any man who would hinder him,

Below: The Pittsburgh Steelers lost this game to Chicago 28 to 7. But Bill Dudley of Pittsburgh, two weeks out of the Army Air Corps, carried a load of enemy players across the goal line to make the Pittsburgh touchdown. Bill, head up and face partially obscured by an enemy foot, is at the bottom of the heap in the center of the picture. *Right:* Tom Fears of the Los Angeles Rams seems to be coaxing the football in as he strives to outrun Bill Dudley, then of the Redskins. Tom led the league in catching passes three years in a row. *Above:* Bill Dudley, playing with the Redskins at the end of his career, was still a hard man to corner. Here he carries the ball against the Green Bay Packers in 1951.

be he ally or enemy. When Bill found one of his teammates dogging it a little he undertook to give the man a few sharp reminders. For this habit, Bill was dubbed "Beefy" by his mates, who would sometimes call him "coach" to suggest that he was trying to take charge. But Bill owned the admiration of all the men he played with just the same. No football player could resent a man who was so obviously ready to spill his guts on the ground to bring the club in first. Often Bill, in a game, would lift the whole team out of itself by the strength of his own spirit.

But Jock Sutherland was no man to allow a mere ball player (and far from the best paid one) to encroach on his own prerogatives. He gave out word that Bill was "hard to handle," although in all Bill Dudley's career there had never been any coach, other than Sutherland, who found Bill less than a joy to have on the squad. Bill never complained, never sulked, never disregarded advice. He did, however, speak his mind whenever he thought it needful. And that was a bad habit to fall into in Jock Sutherland's presence.

Jock first grew irritated at Bill when Bill showed up at noon for practice instead of at nine o'clock in the morning. Bill had been honestly mistaken. He had forgotten that wartime football, short of money and short of organization, held only brief morning practices and one or two "team meetings" each week. Bill thought the pro football day ran, as it had before the war, from lunch time until it grew dark. But Jock pretended to look on this as evidence that Bill's election as Most Valuable Player in the service had turned him into a prima donna. His first opportunity to snarl at Bill came in a practice session when Bill missed his receiver on several passes. Bill showed no anger at Sutherland's sarcasm. He merely observed, in his mild Virginia manner, that it "would be a damn sight easier to find those receivers if you let them wear different-colored jerseys."

"Answering back" in this manner was behavior the good Doctor would not tolerate. The veteran players, knowing Bill had committed a great naughtiness, stood wide-eyed, awaiting the lightning to strike—as children in a more innocent age used to draw in their breaths if a classmate dared talk back to teacher. Jock Sutherland's face took fire but when he spoke his tone was fiercely controlled.

"Are *you* coaching this team?" he demanded.

Bill was no more perturbed than if he was facing a determined tackler.

"No sir," he said, in his ordinary voice, "I am not."

The coach, who must have stood near the end of the line when they gave out the gift of tongues, tried to wither Bill with the sharpness of his command: "Then you take orders like anyone else." Bill nodded, unabashed, and after the practice session he sought Jock out and apologized for whatever he might have done to injure the Doctor's feelings. Of course Bill had known right along that Jock's view of Bill Dudley was more than a little jaundiced and he suggested now that perhaps, if Jock was so thoroughly dissatisfied, it might be the time to contemplate a trade.

Ah, no, said the Doctor triumphantly. It is the other players who are dissatisfied. But Bill knew better than that. The only men on the club who ever resented

Bill were the few who had assumed that pro football was a sort of racket where you went through the motions and made sure you did not get hurt. Bill had simply been raised in a different school, where even the hired hand tried to give full value for his dollar, and where it was deemed a sin to let a teammate down.

Dispite Bill's apologies, the grim Scotsman continued to study ways to sear Bill's hide in practice. Mere performance on the gridiron was obviously no way to the Doctor's heart. But Bill was damned if he'd seek out any other. He accepted Sutherland's sarcasm in polite silence until his contract expired—two years after he had returned from the service. Then, despite his having been named Most Valuable Player in the league, Bill declared he was through with pro football, and he refused to bellyache about the treatment he had received. "I'm too small for this game," was all the reason he would give. Not a word about the number of times Jock Sutherland, apparently to punish Bill for his lack of humility, shoved him in the line-up in spite of injury.

Bill took a job then coaching at the University of Virginia. But the Detroit Lions could not accept the fact that a man who led the league in yards gained on the ground in his first year as a pro could be "too small" for further effort. They received permission from the Steelers to negotiate with Bill and their emissaries trailed him out to the Pacific coast, where Bill was honeymooning. Bill would not say yes or no. He agreed to come back and talk about a new contract. When he came to Detroit Bill was offered, and accepted, the highest salary ever paid, to that date, to a professional football player: $20,000 a year.

Bill's teammates at Detroit were uneasy at first, for his reputation as the man who had tried to take Jock Sutherland's job away had preceded him. But Bill went to work as if he was going to have to struggle to make the club. He spoke little, listened to every word the coaches offered and oozed several pints of sweat every day. By the time the season opened (in Forbes Field, Pittsburgh, of all places) the Detroit players had, in secret ballot, named Bill Dudley captain of the club. He received every vote except his own.

Bill's willingness to mortify his flesh and squeeze the last gasp of breath out of his lungs to serve the cause of victory had made his teammates marvel. This guy, they decided, was *really* the most valuable player.

Bill was of course playing on defense too, like everyone else—the wartime unlimited substitution rule not yet having been made part of the pro game's commandments. And on defense he was just as determined to keep the ball moving toward the other guy's goal line as he was on offense. It was one of Bill's basic tenets, when he played safety man, that every punt should be returned if there was as much as a foot to be gained by trying. If a kicked ball seemed to be sailing out of bounds, Bill begrudged its loss and would strain his neck to catch it before it escaped. This determination led to what was probably Bill's greatest run, and the one that remained longest on the record books.

This came in 1950, when Bill was playing for the Washington Redskins, against the Pittsburgh Steelers. The day was cold, the field was wet, and the footing was uncertain. It was a great day for fair catches, or for letting kicks bounce over the sidelines. Joe Geri had kicked a mighty punt some sixty yards, at an angle sufficient to carry it right over the sideline on the fly, or bounce it over the goal line. Everyone on the field—except Bill Dudley—having acknowledged these possibilities, seemed immobilized. Bill, however, sensing the chance that he might be able to lay hold of the ball before it hit the ground, was on his way at the top of his speed toward the sideline. If the ball did go out, it was going out on the five-yard line or thereabouts, and would leave Bill's team jammed against its own goal line. So Bill felt he had to catch it, though he courted a double hernia in trying. He halted his flight with his toes nearly on the sideline, and reached out to clutch the ball. He took hold of it, pulled it to his chest, then turned to look at the nearest official. The official answered Bill's silent question with a nod, meaning "Yes, it was inbounds." Bill took off for the other goal line.

The whole Pittsburgh team was scattered about between Bill and the distant goal and once his mad purpose was clear they began to converge on him. The nearest potential tackler stood just ten yards away. Bill faked a turn in across the field. The man moved to intercept him, and Bill was back on the sideline, speeding away, with the man unable to recover soon enough to catch him. By this time Bill's teammates were busy knocking people down to make Bill's path more pleasant. By the time all the Steelers had awakened to what Bill was trying to do, there was a solid rank of blockers to lead Bill downfield unharmed. Bill went the whole way without feeling the touch of an enemy. He had run ninety-six yards for a touchdown. Years later Bill was to look back on that run with wonder.

"I still don't understand it," he said.

But everyone else understood that this was the manner in which Bill always played football. There was no such thing with Bill as getting "up" for some games and not for others. He was always "up," no matter who the opponent, what the weather, or how great the prize. There was some motivation built deep inside him that made it impossible for him to quit trying. Once Bill actually took his place in the huddle when he was completely unconscious. The team moved to line up and Bill's muscles simply would not respond. Bill had, a few plays earlier, completed running a punt back for a touchdown. The Lions, for whom Bill was playing then (1947), were leading the Chicago Bears 14 to 0 and now they had the ball again. Bill was handed the ball and started around left end. Tackle Fred Davis, from whom Bill had slipped away, swung his heavily taped forearm and just caught Bill on the temple. Down went Bill. But when the ball had been placed he got up again, made his way into the huddle, and then, as his teammates moved into postion, just stood there, swaying like a bush in the wind. His mates called time and led Bill to the sidelines where it was some minutes before he could even understand what was said to him.

Finally Bill began to come around under the devoted attention of the team doctor.

"Where am I?" he whispered.

"Chicago."

"What's the score?"

"We're ahead 14 to 0."

Bill chewed on these facts for another moment or two, then shook his head as

Steve Van Buren, Philadelphia's nearly unstoppable ball-carrier, is off on a seventy-one-yard run to a touchdown against the Brooklyn Tigers in 1944.

if to awaken his drowsy memory.

"Am I married?" he whispered.

He was. That summer, before he signed with Detroit, he had been married to the sweetheart of his schooldays.

Bill once made a longer run for a touchdown but he did it in a post-season game, between the champion Redskins and the pro All-Stars, in 1942, just before he entered the Army Air Corps. The All-Stars that year were almost all members of the Chicago Bears, who had lost out to the Redskins in the play-off. This being a benefit game, with no effect at all on league standings, there was no real motivation other than a natural urge on the part of the Chicago men to square matters with the Red-skins. And even that urge was mitigated somewhat by the fact that Sammy Baugh, the chief architect of the Bears' defeat, had already taken off for home.

As for Bill, he had less motivation than anyone for he was still with the Steelers and had not even got close to the play-off.

The game was played in Philadelphia. If there were more dismal scenes where young men might celebrate the closing of the football season—and perhaps even the closing of a football career—it might be difficult to discover one that would outdo Philadelphia in wartime. But pro football players even in that distant day were resourceful young men and they managed to delve deep enough into the surrounding backwaters to fish up a few opportunities for dalliance, drink, and other fleshly indulgences. As a result, when the two teams met, the fine fierce flame of competition was barely aflicker. Just the same Bill Dudley was there to play ball and within moments he had infected all his teammates with this urge. It was impossible for prideful men to share the field with a man as ready as Bill was to burst his own veins for the sake of victory and not share some of his desire.

The All-Stars beat the Redskins 17 to 14, with Bill scoring six of the All-Stars' points after a pass interception on his own two-yard line and a ninety-eight yard run to the Washington goal. On his way to the score he had the superhuman assistance of George Wilson, the very man who had started off the 73 to 0 defeat of the Redskins two years earlier by demolishing two tacklers with one block. He wiped out two tacklers on Bill's run too, but he did it one at a time. First he rubbed out the very first man who made a grab for Bill. Then he rose up, chased downfield after Bill, caught up with him at midfield and promptly destroyed the one defender who still had a chance to bring Bill down. It was really the least you could do for a team-mate who would put out the way Bill always did.

Steve Van Buren, the Modern Era's First Great Runner

Bill was, of course, at that time not yet earning his top salary. Nor had football wages anywhere even begun to approach the heights to which competition would eventually send them. But there were still men who were willing to pour out blood and sweat as if they had sworn an oath of fealty to the club owner. One of these was Steve Van Buren, a curly-headed and determined young man from Louisiana who joined the Philadelphia Eagles just before the war ended. Steve, like many other great athletes, operated with a physical handicap. But hardly anyone ever noticed it. In fact, Steve's handicap forced him to develop a skill that helped make him impossible to stop. His shoulder had been so badly lamed that he was not only unable to throw forward passes (and so could never be a triple threat) but he had to carry the ball always in his right arm and could not use his other arm to fend off the opposition. Instead, if he could not dodge a man, he just ran over him, in the Bronko Nagurski style. And Steve ran with such terrorizing power, with choppy, fierce strides, that there were few men who could hold their feet alone against his drive.

Steve did not run into men when he could elude them, however, and he was best at skittering about in an open field after slipping through the line on one of coach Greasy Neale's quick-opening plays. (Greasy had dumped the single-wing formation as soon as the Philadelphia club became unmerged with Pittsburgh in 1944 and had installed George Halas' T-formation.) Steve led the league in ball-carrying for four seasons but he was at his best at the tail end of his career. In 1948, when the championship play-off was staged in a blizzard that half the time hid the action from the spectators and sent lightfooted halfbacks sliding on their chins, Steve made the only score that defeated the Chicago Cardinals 7 to 0. The Cardinals that year sported their "dream backfield," made up of Charles Trippi of Georgia, Elmer Angsman of Notre Dame (each of whom had made two spectacular long touchdown runs to take the championship from the Eagles the previous year), plus field-goal kicker Marlin Harder of Wisconsin, and Marshall Goldberg of Pittsburgh. But Steve Van Buren was the man who made dreams come true that year, and the next year as well. In fact, the next year was Steve's finest. He ran through every club on the schedule, banged inside for short yardage, sprinted outside for long yardage, caught passes, and piled up touchdowns.

Steve had made his very longest runs in 1945—a ninety-eight-yard kick-off return for a touchdown against the Giants and a sixty-nine-yard touchdown run from scrimmage against Detroit—but in 1948 his gains added up to about 600 yards short of a mile (specifically, 1146 yards) and established a record that stood until Jimmy Brown broke it. And when the championship game (against the Los Angeles Rams) was played in sloshing rain, Steve once again proved a master in slippery going. Spattering pints of mud at every step, Steve gained a total of 196 yards.

Tommy Thomson, the One-Eyed Quarterback

Teamed with Steve in his best years and helping to make him great was a sharp-eyed quarterback who never wore shoulder pads. (He thought he had the easiest job in football, sometimes spoke of taking a rocking chair out on the field with him, and saw no reason why he should not last for twenty years. He lasted nine.) This was Tommy Thompson of Tulsa, who could see clearly out of only one eye, but saw clearly enough out of that to lay forward passes on Steve Van Buren's fingertips when Steve was forty yards away and gaining. While Sammy Baugh was a better all-around passer than Tommy Thompson, no one ever excelled Tommy in throwing those long, long bombs for touchdowns. Greasy Neale had taught his linemen to provide tight protection for Tommy, so he seemed to have half the afternoon to wait for Van Buren or some other receiver to gain a step on the defense.

In 1946, in a game against the Washington Redskins, the Eagles were behind by twenty-four points when the second half began. Tommy Thompson, in the third quarter, finally managed to rally his troops. He quickly threw two long touchdown passes, while Steve Van Buren (whom Greasy Neale rated the equal of Jim Thorpe in carrying the ball) broke through the Washington defense practically on his own to make a third. With a minute and a half to play, the Eagles were still three points behind and they had the ball deep in Philadelphia territory, with a long uphill drag to the other goal line. Tommy reasoned that the job had to be done at once or not at all. He had an enormous, hard-to-knock-

Bobby Layne when he wa leading—or driving—the De troit Lions and making rec ords for running, passing an scoring.

down lad named Jack Ferrante playing end that day, and playing both ways. Jack had never attended college but he could run like a starving hound and he would storm through the stadium wall to catch a pass. Tommy called what would be known in today's jargon as an "up" pattern, featuring big Jack, and when Jack broke free, far down the field, Tommy, from his imaginary rocking chair, floated him a lovely pass that reached him just as he was going by. Jack never had to slow half a step and continued on until the ball was worth six points.

Tommy's accuracy made men gasp for several more seasons. He had grown strong in school from hurling javelin and discus, and putting the shot. It is not likely that there was a man in the pro game who could fling a football any farther than Tommy Thompson could. Despite his near-blindness in one eye he seemed able to spin footballs through spaces so small the leather would scrape on all sides. He simply despised being intercepted—as a good fast ball pitcher resents having home runs hit off his delivery—so he worked overtime to make sure his throws were always on target. But Tommy, despite his own prediction, did not last until the era when passing became almost the only job a pro quarterback needed to know; the records he set were soon extinguished. Men came along then who passed four times to Tommy's one and who worked with receiver-specialists who never had any need to weary their winged feet by playing on defense. Still, no one ever turned up a forward passer who could fire bull's-eyes from as far away as Tommy Thompson could, or lay them into a receiver's hands any more gently.

Bobby Layne, Who Could Beat You Many Ways

There was one sassy young fellow who lasted all through the both-way era and on into the days of unlimited substitution and two platoons, without ever suffering any dampening of the fires that seemed to burn eternally within him. That was tough Bobby Layne, understudy to Sid Luckman in Chicago and fighting leader in a number of lost causes in several difficult cities. Bobby, who lived to be the only player on the field who would not wear a face-mask, was never an easy man to deal with. He hated to lose and yet often found himself trying to goad a gang of losers on to victory. He would remove the hides of his teammates with the rough side of his tongue and hand a little of it to his bosses too if he felt they were doing him wrong.

Bobby was a back who could do everything. He carried the ball himself without a qualm, or he passed when he thought he could complete the pass. He also kicked field goals and extra points. And he relished bodily contact. His favorite play was the option, which left him with the choice of flinging the ball over the heads of incoming defenders, or carrying it downfield himself among clutching arms and banging shoulders. He was indeed a man who, as the stale phrase has it, "could beat you many different ways," for Bobby might pass for a touchdown, kick the ball over the crossbar, or tote the ball right over the goal line in his own hands.

Bobby did best when he was at Detroit, in the "modern" era, when running backs no longer had to play sixty minutes in a game, nor make tackles in the open field. Bobby earned himself the quarterback job at Detroit by sheer anger and obstinacy—and startling skill. The Lions had just been humiliated by the San Francisco 49ers (in 1952), after they had won all their exhibition games and seemed headed for a championship. Coach Ace Parker and the whole Detroit squad were in a dismal mood when young Bobby announced that the quarterback job was going to be his no matter if he blew a gasket in his upper abdomen from trying.

He took over the job grimly and even arrogantly, refusing to accept any suggestions from the sidelines and barking his signals in the huddle without hesitation or discussion. The players who did not hustle to position and perform their jobs with sufficient violence had their ears scorched to their skull by Bobby's invective.

The club, largely veterans who still looked on Bobby as an upstart, did not immediately respond to the lash of Bobby's tongue. And they were up against a belligerent group of young men from Los Angeles. At the half the Los Angeles Rams were leading 13 to 7. Bobby left the field with emotional smoke coming out of his ears and used the intermission to build a throbbing head of steam. When he led his gang back on the field the Rams could not restrain them. Bobby scolded, threatened, exhorted, passed, ran, and dodged about the backfield. At the final gun, the score was Detroit 24, Los Angeles 16.

From that moment on, Bobby was boss of the Detroit Lions. He had the assistance of course of some musclar and talented men before and behind him, men like Marlin (Pat) Harder, the field goal kicker, Cloyce Box, the thundering end, and Bob Hoernschmeyer, who was given to running all the way home when he got the ball. But they all responded to the fire that burned in Bobby and played with a ferocity that matched Bobby's own. They scored some overwhelming victories over clubs that had seemed their equals—52 to 17 over Green Bay and 43 to 13 over Dallas. They were finally downed by the Bears but Bobby never forgave that defeat. And when he took his bunch to Chicago to get even, the Lions took the game by 45 to 21. (The Bears had won the first game 24 to 23.) The Lions won the championship that year and Bobby carried the ball himself ninety-four times, for a total of 411 yards.

Bobby's career, which lasted fifteen years, was interrupted now and then by serious injury. But troubles that had dimmed or even ended the careers of other passers and runners just seemed to inspire Bobby to wilder efforts. After he had been out of the game for almost the entire season in 1955 with a banged-up shoulder and the club had lost six games in a row, Bobby came back in 1956 and reversed the record: He won the first six games and barely missed leading them to the championship. Bobby led the league in scoring that year, with 99 points, including five touchdowns. Then in 1957 Bobby was badly injured again and Tobin Rote won his job away by helping Detroit to a championship. In 1958 Bobby could have split the job with Rote, but he would not accept second chair no matter who was ahead of him. Coach Buddy Parker had gone to Pittsburgh and Bobby insisted he be sent there too. In Pittsburgh Bobby ended his career, but not until he had posted one more sensational year, with twenty touchdown passes, two touchdowns on his own, and eleven field goals. But Bobby could not yank the patched-up Steelers much over the .500

mark and before long the Pittsburgh fans made Bobby their least-loved athlete—booing him consistently whenever anything went wrong and loudly calling for his replacement. Bobby eventually left the field for good, but not meekly and not in despair. He left snapping, snarling, cursing, ready to fight any man or group of men who would belittle him to his face.

Bob Waterfield, the Come-from-Behind Quarterback

In Los Angeles, in Bobby Layne's day, there was another great quarterback named Bob Waterfield, who could also do all the things with a football that a man needed to do to earn points with it. There were plenty of men in the league who could punt or pass better, run faster, and even kick field goals from farther away than Bob could. But there was no one man, in the 1940's, who could do *all* these things as well as Waterfield. Bob was like Bobby Layne too in his ability to set a team on fire, to drive them to outdo themselves in a ballgame and then spark them up to do it all over again the following Sunday. He seemed to specialize in re-igniting the flame in a half-beaten team so that the Rams, with Waterfield, began to make a specialty of winning football games in the final seconds after coming from far behind.

For one thing, Bob Waterfield loved, as Tommy Thompson did, to throw the football for impossible distances to land in the outstretched fingers of a man who was running at the very top of his speed. Bob Waterfield was like Bobby Layne in that he did not often make league records in any particular department on his own account (he led the league only twice, in average pass yardage) but still managed for a number of seasons to

win the most ball games for his team. When the Rams won their first league championship in 1949, after many misses, it was Waterfield who led them there. And Bob Waterfield, in his eight active seasons with the Rams, scored more points than any other player who ever wore the Los Angeles uniform. He also kicked the most field goals and booted the longest punt. And in 1945 he was the first player ever to be voted "most valuable" without dissent.

There Was No Defense for Frankie Albert

No red-blooded resident of San Francisco, however, would have agreed that Bob Waterfield could even stand comparison with their own hero, star of the All-America Conference club, little left-handed Frankie Albert. For Frankie could pass, run, kick, and invent new plays in the heat of the struggle. As he told the first college coach who tried to discourage him because of his small stature: "I'm strong as a bull and six times as smart."

One time, in a game against the New York Yankees, on fourth down, Frankie illustrated his mental and physical agility by recovering a bad pass from center, starting on a dead run to the left with a half-dozen opponents slavering after him, and booting the football sixty-four yards downfield, where it went out of bounds on the New York twelve-yard line.

Frankie shared Bobby Layne's love of rolling out with the ball in his hand. In fact it was often said of Frankie that he practically invented the bootleg play, in which the quarterback holds the ball (it was nice and skinny in the 1940s and anyone could hold it easily in one hand) behind his hip as he trots away in the opposite direction from the movement of the rest of the backfield. There was never anyone more skilled at faking than Frankie was and when he first began to use the bootleg it was almost a certain scoring play, from anywhere inside the ten-yard line. The opponents just never were able to follow the ball as Frankie pretended to hand it here and there before taking off with it himself. All Frankie had to do when he wanted a touchdown from ten yards out, his coaches insisted, was call an end run by the halfback and then hold onto the ball. Sometimes as he idled along with the trophy hidden back of his own thigh, enemy linemen would go charging right by him in pursuit of the halfback, with never an extra glance at Frankie.

But Frankie also had exteme confidence in his ability to complete a pass. It was not unusual for him to call the exact same pass play three times in a row until he made it work. But the 49ers under Frankie were not originally a pass-crazy club, as some said the Redskins were under Sammy Baugh. In a game against the Los Angeles Dons in 1948, Frankie attempted only twelve passes all day and that season his backs averaged six yards a carry (but Frankie *did* throw twenty-nine touchdown passes in 1948).

Frankie was not really small compared to the average human but compared to the general run of professional football player, even in his day, he was of less then moderate size. He stood five feet ten and weighed 170 pounds, bigger than Bill Dudley and a great deal smaller than Bob Waterfield. He had been an All-America choice in college and even starred in a movie ("The Spirit of Stanford") before he became a pro football player. He joined the Navy during the war and when he refused to play football for the training station team he was shipped to the South Pacific. But Frankie came back alive and full of confidence. After starting off as a single-wing operative in college, and hardly ever winning a game, Frankie learned the T-formation moves under Clark Shaughnessy and became one of the best. His faking and improvising were so spectacular when he finally became a pro that he grew to be the despair of the television crews, who were just beginning, in Frankie's day, to learn how to keep the camera's eye on the ball. But when Frankie's own teammates sometimes did not know if he had kept the ball or handed it off, how could the poor cameraman decide? An enemy coach once said of Frankie, after Frankie had demolished the coach's defenses: "There is *no* defense for Frankie Albert."

Mr. Brown's Messengers

EVEN after the coming of peace had turned loose a swarm of football fans with money in their pockets—thanks to the 52–20 bonus (twenty dollars a week for fifty-two weeks) that Roosevelt had wrung out of Congress—professional football knew more hard times. A few of the clubs had begun to organize more tightly or at least to present a sharper appearance, thanks largely to the influence of Dick Richards of Detroit, who not only added class and uniformity to the appearance of the club but even hired the director of the Wayne University band to help keep the customers from growing too restive between the halves.

There were still franchises in the league, however, that no amount of sweet music would revive. Before football could ever settle down into a modicum of stability there were more fortunes to be lost, more clubs to be shifted about, and more players and fans to be orphaned by the collapse of a club they had pledged their ticket money or their tender hides to. Chicago still had too many football clubs and so did Boston, which had only one. New York, which might have supported two, for a time had three and sometimes four.

All signs indicated, however, that somebody was going to get rich at this business. The championship game of

Paul Brown (in hat) keeps a close eye on his latest charges, the Cincinnati Bengals.

1946, played in New York between the Giants and the Chicago Bears, drew the biggest football gate of all time, with the exception of the 70,000 who had come to see Red Grange some twenty years before. There were over 58,000 people at the 1946 game and the players, divided the fattest pot pro football had ever offered, with each member of the winning club taking home almost $2000 extra.

Television had just begun to creep into the football parks and Commissioner Bert Bell had been farsighted enough to rule that local areas should be blacked out of broadcasts, so that fans from the normal spectator-shed would have to go to the park to see the game. There was disaster ahead for

many promoters still, as struggles began to wrest football franchises away from their long-time owners or to win fans to follow the clubs belonging to a brand new league.

Many players back from the war found themselves wooed by emissaries of both football leagues—the National Football League and the All-America Football Conference. The conference had lived on paper through the last of the war years, after several men had agreed to field teams and pay for franchises as soon as the coming of peace made such moves practicable.

The first effect of the coming of the new league was a sudden upward surge in football salaries that made it twice as hard to finance a ballclub. Major

Touchdown amid general rejoicing. Willie Gallimore of the Chicago Bears crosses the goal line as teammates applaud, spectators scream, statistician looks for penalty flag, policeman offers embrace, and crippled man seems about to abandon his crutches.

colleges, especially on the Pacific Coast, had always offered handsome stipends and bonuses to football stars, prompting many of them to expect the same sort of wooing from the professional clubs.

But until the new league came along, a pro football prospect, having been "drafted" by agreement by only one club, had to accept what he was offered or go find some other way to earn his keep—unless by chance he chose to live in Canada. The All-America Conference however paid no mind to the draft agreement of the other league. They not only bid against the National League for college stars, they even set out to lure established players to jump the fence and earn higher salaries.

Eventually, as in all such situations, peace was arrived at and the AAC was "absorbed" by the National League. But there were many who insisted that the AAC, despite the fact that many of its franchises evaporated in the merger, really absorbed the older league. For the men largely responsible for the success of the AAC became major figures in the "old" league. And the one man who had injected into the AAC the brilliance of planning, play, and organization that insured its existence, also wrought major changes in the structure and style of play of the older league.

It was Paul Brown who brought to professional football the discipline, the tightly organized teamplay, and the intricate forward pass patterns that turned it into the finest public spectacle a man could find. Paul also helped demolish, by simply ignoring it, one of the "rules" the original organizers of the conference had adopted—the "lily-white" rule, the one that had long disgraced professional baseball. Paul, like Tony Morabito of the San Francisco club, just went ahead and hired black players anyway and the bigots were reduced to private exhortations about "making it tough on the guys who didn't hire them." Black players, the men in Buffalo and Chicago whispered, were troublemakers and their league was going to prosper from being free of them. But Paul Brown had coached football at every level, from the time he decided he did not want to be a lawyer, and he had observed that his black stars usually made trouble only for their opponents in a football game.

Paul Brown first won fame in the very seedbed of professional football—Massillon, Ohio—at a high school where, it was whispered, there was as much athletic recruiting as there was at Ohio State University, where Paul also served a successful term. Brown coached as well at Severn Academy and at Great Lakes Naval Training Station, where he saw in action for the first time a few of the players he decided to sign for his Cleveland club when the new league should start.

A slender, balding, diffident and cultured man who looked less like an athlete than any other coach in the business, Paul Brown owned the shrewdest and most active brain that had ever been bent upon the simple game of football. He gave almost all his waking hours to devising stratagems for advancing the ball by ground or air against opposition of every sort—and, perforce, invented along the way numberless devices for preventing the opposition from moving the ball the *other* way.

Nearly every professional football coach can be said to love the game, else he would not likely have given himself to it in those days when demands on time and nervous energy were high and returns were low indeed. But there has probably never been a man who really derived from football as much soul-deep satisfaction as Paul Brown did. Others have thrilled at victories, have savored the petty power the job offered, have relished the outdoor experience, the happy intimacies with their own kind, and the seemingly limitless extension of their youth. But Paul Brown, essentially a cerebral type, made the game

of football into an academic discipline and discovered in it satisfactions for the brain, the imagination, the ego, and the psyche. He very early in the game discovered that, riding the surfboard of the future as he was, he did not need to concern himself with his cash return at all. He just kept on creating teams that could win football games and there were men forever eager to thrust money upon him.

Paul Brown changed almost every aspect of the game—the recruiting, the training, the equipping, the planning, and the performance. And before long every coach in the business was imitating his methods down to the tiniest detail. First of all, he systematized the recruitment of football players. Other coaches had recruiters as ubiquitous as his own and for a long time now professional coaches had been seeking football players far outside the "All-America" lists, in the small universities and the "phys ed" colleges. And George Halas of the Bears had long had his "alumni" to spot prospects for him and steer them to Chicago. But Paul Brown developed a scouting staff as tireless and as professional as that of any major league baseball club and he sent them far into the fresh-water reaches of the nation to size up players hardly anyone else had heard about.

The Pros Discover *Esprit de Corps*

There had long been one feature of the college game that the pros had only periodically been able to reproduce—that was the fierce *esprit de corps* that provided cohesiveness and inspiration to the squad so that petty personal ambitions were submerged in the unified desire to down the common enemy. Professional football players scorned dis-

No Paul Brown needed here. Rookie quarterback Virgil Carter of the Bears prepare for a game by writing plays on his pants.

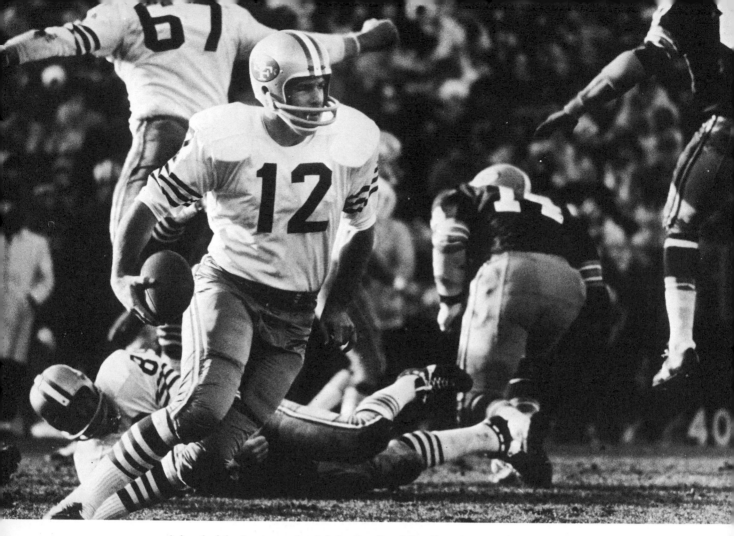

A lovely fake by quarterback John Brodie of San Francisco sends the entire enemy force off in the wrong direction, while John heads for the outside on a keeper play.

plays of emotion in the locker room and too often the stars of the club just walked through the motions in practice and came to life only when the opening whistle blew. Not under Paul Brown, however. His charges studied their tasks like schoolboys and practiced the same move over and over and over.

In school and college there was always wide variation in talent, with continual failures and memory lapses that led to broken plays and improvisations. But every member of a pro team not only knew his own job but could recognize quickly how well the man opposite was going to do his. And with Paul Brown every member of the squad knew not only his own move on every play but the move of every other man on the team. The ball-carrier knew precisely what sort of blocks would be provided—whether a tackle would be blocked out or in and who would work on the linebacker. The blockers, at the same time, knew just where the runner was going, which way he was going to fake, and what exact path he meant to follow. There was no such thing under Paul Brown as sudden improvisations by the quarterback or surprise dips and dodges and twists by the pass receivers. On a pass play, every potential receiver had a precise pattern to conform to. He was going to proceed downfield at a given angle, and turn out (or in) at a certain spot, while other receivers ran patterns designed to draw coverage away from him or outnumber the defenders in a certain zone.

This sort of blueprinting had never been done before. Other coaches had provided patterns but none had ever insisted on such absolute and minute cooperation. Paul Brown, unlike any of his rivals, conducted schoolroom classes in football, with regular written examinations to discover if every man knew *all* the moves of every player on every play. These examinations—based on lectures, blackboard diagrams, and voluminous note-taking, were not a joke, and were not optional, no matter how great a man's reputation.

Some petted athletes from the big colleges were appalled at what life was like among the Cleveland Browns. The team, in the training season and while traveling, lived together, ate together, and dressed alike, obeyed a curfew, shunned both drink and dalliance, and carried notebook and pencil to class, where Paul Brown or his assistants lectured on the intricacies of offense and defense. If they came late to class or practice, there was a fine to pay. If they needed time off, for an aching tooth, an ailing aunt, or a drunken uncle, they had to seek permission to absent themselves. Of course mild regimentation of this sort had long been the lot of many people who worked for small wages, so the ordinary man or woman was not likely to have his hair raised on hearing about it. But a few well-publicized players who joined the Browns in the early days treated this schoolboy stuff with open scorn.

Actually the classroom lectures were only a minor aspect of the Paul Brown system. The player-scholars under his care learned the game as some men learn science. They not only heard each move explained and saw it diagrammed. They wrote it down, committed it to memory and then went out and rehearsed it on the field—and rehearsed it and rehearsed it, until it became almost as automatic as buttoning a shirt. And they learned to perform the move on signal and in unison, with as much precision as a ballet group.

No matter how long a man had been with the club or how many times he had performed his moves, or how often he had set them on paper before, he still had to write them all over again each season on a fresh page in his notebook. And he had to practice them with his mates until the moves all meshed together like the gears of a machine.

A member of the Cleveland Browns was a Cleveland Brown all year long, no matter that he sought some minor means of staving off the butcher and baker in the off-season. He reported to the training camp at Hiram, Ohio, in midsummer and lived like a member of some armed forces special mission, hardening his muscles and sharpening his reflexes and learning the moves he was to make. Naturally enough at these midsummer sessions, where beer was scarce and girls even more seldom, and where sweat and blood were spent in greater quantity than most men like to spend them, there would develop, especially among the old-timers, a grim resentment. This, however, was really just a symptom of the development of that sought-after *esprit de corps*. This sharing of hardships and pooling of gripes brought about a sense of unity

Completed pass, the main objective of the modern T. Detroit's Pat Studtsill grimaces with effort as he jumps high to take a pass in front of a defender.

that would serve the club well on the field of battle.

Brown also bolstered the organization in other ways. The front office was no longer a haven for hobbyists who sought to "stay close to the game" or a hole into which idle rich men might drop a few dollars that otherwise might have gone to the Internal Revenue man. The men and women who worked for the Cleveland Browns office worked the year around, as Paul Brown did himself. For the season itself now lasted from midsummer until after Christmas and the off-season was given to seeking and signing recruits.

Paul Brown himself had a sharp eye for football talent and often developed it where other coaches hardly noticed its existence. Marion Motley, the first in a series of piston-legged black ball-carriers that were to make Cleveland a power in pro football, was first observed by Paul Brown as a schoolboy star at McKinley High in Canton, Ohio. Motley attended the University of Nevada and played at Great Lakes Naval Station, something of a forgotten man, not usually taken along when the team played out of town. But Paul helped turn Motley into one of the greatest pass blockers in the business and a running threat so potent that no enemy ever dared unload his full strength on the quarterback, lest Motley have the ball and explode into the open with it.

Paul Brown had no compunction about passing up highly touted ballplayers whom other coaches might have spent half their careers catering to. A few years after Marion Motley was recruited by the Browns the University of Nevada spawned a passer and runner named Stan Heath, who became the leading ground gainer in the nation, first choice of nearly every pro coach in either league. Heath accepted the Browns' offer but immediately let it be known, when he came to camp, that carrying notebook and pencil to any sort of "class" was not for him. He already knew the fundamentals and all he wanted to do was play. Paul Brown immediately cut him loose to go play for somebody else. He was obviously not going to adjust to Paul Brown's ways and Paul wanted him to have a chance to sign elsewhere. (He joined the Green Bay Packers and lasted one season.)

Brown, besides immediately repudiating the "lily-white" rule of the new conference, refused to countenance any agreement either to avoid raiding the rosters of the National League or to leave college players alone until they had finished college. Some of the college stars Paul coveted had returned from long hitches in the service and did not have many good football seasons left, so Paul wanted them playing for him now. From Ohio State Paul hired tackle Bill Willis, end Dante Lavelli, and halfback Eugene Fekete. He did not, as some thought he might, try to steal any ballplayers from the Cleveland Rams. But when the Rams, dismayed by the success of the Browns, ducked out to Los Angeles, then Paul persuaded some of their players to stay in Cleveland with him.

Paul Brown Required a Different Breed of Player

The Paul Brown brand of football owed nothing to Pop Warner. It was T-formation football, with quick openers, traps and passes replacing the spinners, power plays, and reverses. And to operate this attack, Paul needed a strong-armed and accurate quarterback to go with the fast and powerful fullback. And

he needed ends and halfbacks who could get out into the open to take passes in full stride, or to fake their way into position to catch a spot pass in the clear.

Despite its dependence on the forward pass, the Paul Brown method did not, as some seemed to think when he started, ignore the ground game, altogether. It is true that Paul Brown teams would resort to the pass under circumstances that would give other coaches a rash of goosepimples. But he always maintained a proper balance between the passing game and the ground game, for he realized that without a serious threat to gain on the ground the passing game could be stifled. And so he often managed to catch the opposition off guard with a forward pass when everyone in the stadium, except Paul and the other Browns, was looking for a run. Once when Cleveland was two touchdowns ahead, with the ball on their one-yard line, Paul had his quarterback, Otto Graham, fade into his own end zone and throw a short swift pass to Mac Speedie on the line of scrimmage. Speedie, who was paced to fit his name, then scurried all the rest of the way—ninety-nine yards—to make a touchdown. In 1948, a move like this was deemed practically immoral. To put the ball in the air from your own end zone, with a fourteen-point lead. That was the act of a nut.

But if Paul Brown was a nut he soon had infected the whole football world with his insanity, so that for a while the reckless manner in which other coaches tried to imitate Paul Brown's wide-open game began indeed to make pro football look like basketball, just as a number of aging sportswriters had been saying for years. Sometimes in that day a spectator might sit through most of a quarter and not see anything but forward passes. And coaches who a few years earlier were warning their backs that they could not get by in pro football on passing alone were now teaching that "passing is 75 percent of the game." But Paul Brown never taught that. Indeed his greatest passer, Otto Graham, was also one of his most successful gainers along the ground and his threat to take off upfield with the ball under his arm made his passing far more effective. As a passer, Graham had no peer.

Otto Graham, a "Paul Brown" Quarterback

Paul Brown first saw Otto when the rangy young man was playing tailback for Northwestern against Brown's Ohio State club. Working from the single-wing, Otto ran with the ball, blocked for other runners, passed, sometimes called signals, and did much of the open-field tackling on defense. What impressed Brown most was a single pass that Otto threw in that game. Running to his left, while his receiver moved across the field in the opposite direction at a dead run, Otto turned and dropped a pass right in the other fellow's hands without even causing the receiver to break stride. In something less than two seconds Otto had timed the receiver's speed and his own speed and had fired the ball in the perfect trajectory to land it right where it was supposed to go.

Brown remembered that pass long after he had forgotten most of the other details of the game and the memory moved him, when he and Otto both found themselves in the service, to sign Otto to a professional contract with a team that did not yet exist. (Paul had already signed his own contract, for

$20,000 a year, to run the new club that Mickey McBride of Cleveland was financing to start operations after the war.) After Otto's first playing season had started, Paul tore up the contract and wrote his new quarterback a better one.

When the All-America Conference opened for business in 1946, the game was still handicapped by the rule that permitted only three substitutions in any one series of downs—just enough to allow the coach to rescue his kicker or some other specialist from the vicissitudes of defensive play—so Otto Graham, being the strongest defensive man on the club, played both ways. The unusually wide peripheral vision that enabled Otto to keep the movements of three or four receivers in his range all at the same time served him well on interceptions too. There were few enemy receivers who could outrun him and fewer still who could break Otto's tackle, if Graham could attack him from a proper angle.

But it was Otto's passing that earned him his fame and his nickname of Automatic Otto, awarded him because of the frightening precision with which he reached his targets. Targets, in the Paul Brown pass patterns, were of all types, for Brown's fertile invention had turned the spectacle of football into something inexpressibly thrilling. First an end would "flare" out, then a back might appear suddenly, running a parallel course, with a third back cutting diagonally across to the other side of the field, and another end moving across just beyond the line of scrimmage. Or one end might suddenly sprint far down in what became known as the "fly" pattern, while another receiver cut diagonally across in the middle distance.

Some spectators gasp, some yell, some watch unmoved as Detroit's tight end Jim Gibbons snares a pass just as Rich Petitbon of Chicago slices him down.

Other coaches had had several potential receivers downfield and had worked out plays that set decoys to dodging and faking about to lure the defenders away from the prime receiver. But in Paul Brown's patterns, every eligible man had a specific job to do, a course to run that was blueprinted for him before he started. The aim of all the moves was to open up the area where the number one receiver would appear. If one receiver were to cut inside a defending halfback (they were not yet named strong safety and free safety) then another man might be sent deeper, to draw that defender with him and there would be another with the job of luring the safety man away from the selected target area.

Inasmuch as Otto knew in just what order these potential receivers were to "come out" and exactly where they would be on the field, as well as which direction they would turn in, he could shift quickly to receiver number two or number three if the first choice were too closely covered. Paul Brown found no fault if the prime receiver could not be reached. He would rejoice to see the pass completed to any of them (although he did not favor too frequent passing off to the safety valve back who remained behind the line of scrimmage).

The Free-Substitution Rule Returns for Good

In 1950, the permanent return of the free-substitution rule made a quarterback's life easier, for he no longer had to

stay in the game and administer blows to the opposition with body and shoulder to keep men from crossing the goal line, nor was he any longer required to catch punts on the fly and try to carry them back through a sudden convocation of tacklers. The quarterback in the up-to-date game had become as priceless as a pitcher was in baseball, whose well-being was never laid on the line merely in order to gain an extra base. For the quarterback not only passed the ball once or twice, and even three times in every series of downs, but directed the attack, appraised the defenses, charged up his teammates, digested the intelligence they brought back to him from the skirmishes, and usually selected the plays. So when the offense was stopped short and had to take to punting the ball, the quarterback would be recalled to the sidelines, deposited on the bench, wrapped in wool and tenderly ministered to until his club had the ball in its hands again.

But Otto Graham, big as a fullback, fast as an end, light-footed as a tennis player, often played defense even after the rules permitted him to seek immediate sanctuary in the bench before the ball carriers started coming his way. There was no better safetyman on the squad than Otto, for he was quick to size up a play, agile enough to anticipate and adjust to an approaching runner's fakes, and a sure-shot tackler who could down a runner with force enough to make him wish he had gone the other way.

A feature of Otto Graham's play—and a stratagem he never resorted to except when Paul Brown required it—was the quarterback draw, one of the most devastating plays in the game when it works. In this maneuver, the quarterback retreats in the same manner as if he were falling back to pass, then reverses himself suddenly and charges straight down the middle, which is often left open when the other side is certain a pass is coming. This play, with which Otto accomplished many long gains, often looks like a sudden improvisation by a quarterback who has found all his receivers covered. But it was one of Paul Brown's standards and he sent it in for Otto to use most often when the opposition were least prepared for it. And no quarterback ever worked it better than Otto could.

Paul Brown Calls the Plays

Paul Brown was not able to send in plays as often as he liked until the coming of the free substitution rule. Then he adopted the system that became his trademark—and eventually, in the eyes of his critics, his besetting fault. Every time the ball was whistled dead with Cleveland on the offense, Brown would send a guard panting in with the next play. (Once for a joke a Cleveland quarterback told the messenger guard: "That play is lousy. Tell Brown I want another one." And the guard, used to following directions, turned and had already started back, before the raucous laughter behind him wakened him to reality.)

Originally, Paul had allowed Graham to call many of the plays, for he had great respect for Otto's ability as a strategist. But finally even Graham had to stand in the half-formed huddle and wait with the rest of them until the Word came in from the sidelines. And Paul continued to call the plays (not *all* the plays, he would insist, for he permitted occasional "check-offs" or

Getting rid of the football (1). Green Bay's Willie Davis slips his hand inside arm of Tom Matte of Baltimore and knocks ball loose.

changes at the line, provided passes were not substituted for runs and vice versa) despite muttered gripes in the clubhouse, complaints from the stands, and sarcastic comments by sportswriters who accused him of taking the game away from "the boys."

Professional football players however were no longer boys and the duty of the coach was simply to win football games, not to build character or instill a sense of responsibility. Paul always felt that, with the aid of observers in the stand (who needed to know what play was coming in order to check on the carrying out of assignments) he was in a better position to call the play than the quarterback. He also owned a conviction that he knew more football than any man who worked for him—a conviction based on a long series of successes. Paul had started planning how to win ballgames when he was a 152-pound quarterback at Miami of Ohio. His ability to win them as a coach was, one might think, sufficiently demonstrated by his taking top prize in the All-America Conference in every one of the four years of its existence.

But commentators and coaches continued to find fault with his "tyrannical" system of taking all the strategy on his own shoulders. In response, Paul did not hesitate to suggest that some coaches found it a lot more convenient to have it appear that major decisions had been made by the quarterback, it being so much more comfortable to lay the blame for busted strategy on a dumb quarterback than to turn one's own tender hide to the heat. Paul Brown made no secret of his responsibility for making major decisions and he willingly accepted the criticism and the howls of derision on the few occasions when a play-choice blew up in his face.

Paul Brown Takes His Methods to the NFL

When Paul Brown brought his Browns into the National League he of course took his methods along, and the National League coaches set out earnestly to rearrange his gears for him. They feverishly sent pictures, diagrams and scouting reports on to Greasy Neale, who, as coach of the Philadelphia Eagles, was to be the first to face this eccentric outsider in a league game. Neale at this time was particularly proud of having spiked the guns of the T-formation with his five-man line in which the ends withdrew a few strides and played head-and-head on the offensive ends, the normal pass receivers. The five linemen then were all guards and tackles, charged with jamming the enemy's play in the backfield, with no need to step inside and wait to prevent a runner from getting loose around one end.

But Paul Brown had done some preliminary observing and plotting of his own and he came to the meeting with a very simple scheme for opening wide holes in that five-man line. Each time his warriors, on offense, came out of the huddle the linemen took their regular positions, then sidestepped about a foot away from each other. The opposing five-man line, coached to play head and head with the offense, moved likewise. Before many plays had been run there were gaps in the line through which the backs could waltz two abreast. And the Browns thereupon made hash of Greasy Neale's defense.

It was a pleasant Saturday night in mid-September and there were 71,000 people gathered at Cleveland's Municipal Stadium to watch their heroes break into the National League. The Browns had been drawing big crowds at home (and on the Pacific Coast) since the very beginning, when 60,000 Clevelanders came to watch them open the 1946 season against Miami. But never had the fans known rarer delight than this—to watch their darlings destroy the pride of the haughty National League, who had rated the Browns as just a cut above a mediocre college club. Paul Brown, as a matter of fact, still relishes that game as his dearest victory, even after twenty years and eleven championships. The final score was 35 to 10, in favor of Cleveland. Greasy Neale's geniuses had hardly been able to make a scratch on the scoreboard.

Whether Paul Brown's methods were "taking the game away from the boys" or not, they were certainly not taking it away from the fans. The Browns never knew a lean season after that. In their first six years in the National League they won the conference championship every year. And three times in that period they won the championship of the league.

The championship game in 1955 was Otto Graham's last appearance as a player. He won the game 38 to 14, by scoring two touchdowns himself and passing to Ray Renfro and Dante Lavelli for two more. His victims were the Los Angeles Rams, who had fled Cleveland almost ten years before, unable to live on what was left for them at the gate. The gate for this game, played in Los Angeles, was the largest ever known to that time—85,000 spectators plus TV providing a total of over half a million dollars. Each player on the winning team took home the biggest check ever awarded (until then) to a player in a pro football championship game—$3500. Five years earlier the Browns had beaten the same team for the championship and had earned thereby only $1100 apiece. Ten years *later* a winner's share of $3500 would have looked skimpy indeed. But in 1955 it was for some players close to a season's wages.

Otto Graham and his boss had had differences while they worked together, of the sort any athlete has with a boss who exercises tight control. (Some of John McGraw's charges used to go home and dream fondly of beating Little Napoleon over the head with a bat.) But there never had been any feud, or any bitterness. And while Otto may have said more than once or twice that he thought a quarterback should call his own plays, when it came his turn to coach the All-Stars in their annual game against the pros, behold, Otto sent every play in from the sideline. Coaching at the Coast Guard Academy, where he spent a number of happy seasons before being lured back against his better judgment to coach the Washington Redskins, Otto agreed that the game looked very different from the coach's point of view, and his respect for his old coach grew deeper still.

Paul Brown eventually became sensitive to the constant criticism of his messenger system and took pains to remind inquisitive folk that he *did* allow his quarterbacks to check off at the line. And sometimes the message that the messenger brought in, Brown confessed, was simply "Surprise me!" (It would not do, he felt, to give up the psychological advantage of persuading the opposition that the messenger was bring-

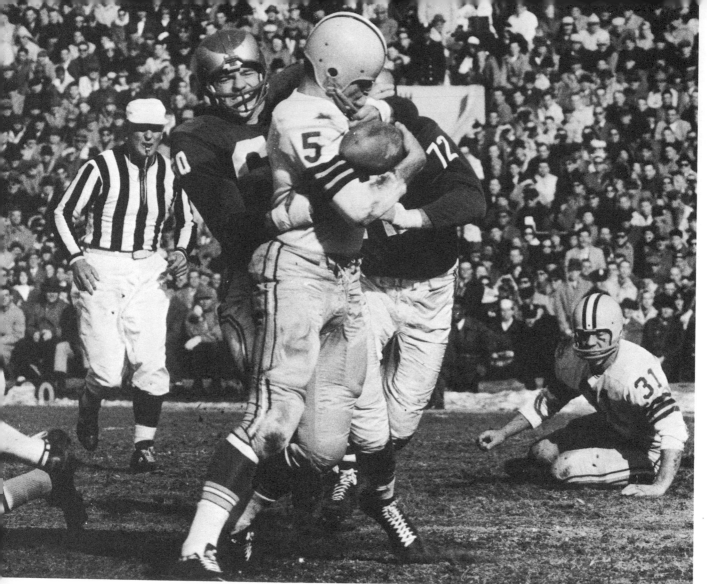

Getting rid of the football (2). Ball slips away from Paul Hornung of Green Bay as Philadelphia's Chuck Bednarik puts squeeze on ribs and face mask.

Getting rid of the football (3). Terry Barr of Detroit is amazed at the way the ball keeps going when he is pulled up short.

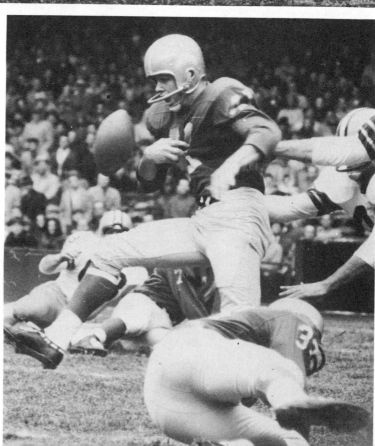

ing some word from on high.) When, in 1962, Brown began to allow his new quarterback, Jim Ninowski, to call the plays without benefit of messengers, there were those who said out loud that finally the old guy had yielded to pressure and was beginning to phase out his system of sideline control. But Brown firmly denied this. All it was, he insisted, was an effort to help Ninowski establish his leadership over the club. And he always started sending his messengers in regularly before the game was half over.

Brown of course was not the only coach who sent in plays from the sideline. Before the unlimited substitution rule permitted the use of messengers Greasy Neale employed baseball type signals—hands on shirt, hand on cap, hand on hand, hand on knee—to get advice to his quarterback. And Curly Lambeau of the Redskins, who was not confident enough of his grasp of the T-formation to give signs to his quarterback, still used to range up and down the sidelines using gestures and postures and wild waves of the arms to indicate to his team what sort of defense they should set up. And when Tom Landry, coach of the Dallas Cowboys, had two quarterbacks of equal skills for a season, he would alternate them from play to play, sending each man in all primed with wisdom called down from the observers in the press box high upstairs.

One of the chief values of calling each play from the sidelines, Paul Brown would explain, was the opportunity it provided an observer to learn just why this play or that play would not work. Only when the watchers on high knew what to look for could they make such decisions. And sometimes when a play did not work, there would be some easily remediable error in performance which did not at all affect the value of the play. Other times, failure would indicate that the play should be promptly discarded from the "game plan." (Brown usually started each game with a list of plays in his hand, and would try one after the other to test their effectiveness.)

Ultimately, what with the narrow loss of a championship or two, an accretion of sharp criticism from the press, and a sort of concentration of gripes that broke out finally into rebellion, the new owner of the Cleveland Browns, Arthur Modell, was persuaded that the club needed a new coach. Brown, said a clique of rebels led by star Jim Brown, was "robbing the players of dignity" by running their lives and their play so closely. This, apparently, rather than the factionalism Jim Brown himself had helped engender, was the cause of Cleveland's fall from power. So Paul was deposed, but not until his lawyers had worked out a handsome settlement that would have made Paul Brown the highest paid amateur golfer in the continent had he chosen to spend his remaining years in that pursuit.

Just what dignity his players lost when Paul Brown was leading them to the top of the mountain season after season would be hard to descry. It is true that he demanded of his charges perfect execution of the maneuvers he tried to teach. He did not find fault with men for lack of talent—only for failure to perform up to their abilities. He did, it is true, ask Jim Brown to carry the ball again and again and again. But he was paying Brown enough to insure that player took home a reward equal to his effort. And, as Paul Brown said, if you have a big gun, you have to shoot it.

As a matter of fact, the whole world of professional football would have had

Otto Graham, the perennial winner as a Cleveland quarterback, became a loser when he took over as coach of the Washington Redskins in 1965. He gave up in 1968.

difficulty totting up its debt to Paul Brown, for he influenced it in so many ways that some of them have been forgotten. He preserved the profiles for instance of one or two budding male movie stars by outfitting all his men with a special face mask that eventually became *de rigueur* throughout the game. He introduced the notion of pencil-and-notebook studies that systematized the game so that its intricacies no

Getting rid of the football (4). Jim Taylor of Green Bay loses the ball when a fierce Chicago Bear hits him with a flying tackle.

longer lay within the grasp of the semi-alcoholic vagabonds who once peopled almost every roster. He helped squelch forever the indecent "whites only" rule that would have shunted the league into a backwater. He set the example of recruiting football talent assiduously in whatever distant garden patch it might grow. He demonstrated the value of year-round organization in creating not only a more smoothly functioning staff but in helping instill that sense of family unity and brotherly devotion that prompts football players to outdo themselves on the field of battle. And these were just a few of the "messages" that Paul Brown imparted to his colleagues and that they chose to take to heart.

In Black and White

EXCEPT for the grubby attempt on the part of the organizers of the All-America Conference to bar black ballplayers, professional football never extensively degraded itself by trying to establish the "color line" that used to shame baseball. There were clubs of course that tried to honor the traditions of the slave-holding south by studiously overlooking black football players who sought jobs. But right from the beginning, almost, there were black football players on the rosters of National League clubs. Fritz Pollard, the All-America from Brown University, played the game for money with Akron, Hammond, and Providence. In Hammond, Fritz had a black teammate who had also played at Brown—Jay Mayo (Inky) Williams, a mighty end.

Before these men had joined the pros, however, there was one of even riper vintage, a black ball carrier named Henry McDonald, who had played football at Canandaigua Academy before joining the Rochester Jeffersons in 1912. McDonald, a handsome, long-legged man, who was an accomplished boxer, traveled to Canton, Ohio, with the Jeffersons to play against Jim Thorpe's Bulldogs—in those days when the merry followers of the Bulldogs usually carried

219

Joe (the Jet) Perry, his toe grabbed by a hungry hand, jets forward for a healthy gain.

a coffin on to the field to indicate to the visiting team what might await them. Early in the fray McDonald carried the ball and was met on the open field by a quarrelsome character from West Virginia, who later became a National League coach. The confederate delegate, instead of tackling McDonald, or trying to, laid hold of him and pulled back his fist. "Where Ah come from," he declared, in the gallant manner usually affected by Southern sportsmen, "black is black and white is white. And they nevah mix!" McDonald looked the white man coolly in the eye, for he had not much doubt of who might come in first if that raised fist were ever delivered. But Jim Thorpe, who, being part Irishman and part Sac and Fox Indian, might have been said to be racially

neutral, promptly laid hold of the glaring Southerner and pulled him away.

"We're here to play football," he growled. "So let's play football!"

What the consequences might have been had that punch ever been thrown no one will ever know. Certainly the Dixieland type would have carried home a mouse under one eye, or a newly fattened lip, or both, if not some more permanent scar. And the rancor of the encounter might have lasted into the league. As it was, other black men besides Henry McDonald were threatened, roughed up, or hazed in various indelicate ways when they tried to make a living at football. But, inasmuch as the big northern colleges often had black men on their rosters, some of them were continually turning up in the

National Football League. Duke Slater, the swift-footed and strong-armed tackle from Iowa, who could outpace many a halfback, put in ten seasons with National League clubs. Paul Robeson played end for Akron and Milwaukee before taking to the concert stage.

But professional football was never as green a pasture for the black player as for the white man of equal or lesser skills. When there were two leagues big enough to bid against each other, a black star, particularly if he were a ball carrier, might command a comfortable salary. But the run of the mill stalwart— the blocker, the lineman, the substitute ball-carrier—would, if he were black, be almost certain to take home a slimmer pay envelope than the white man at the next locker. A black man after all had no "business opportunities" to turn his head from athletics and no professional career, ordinarily, upon which he could embark when he was ready. Whatever he was tendered for offering his hide to the bangs and bruises of the professional game was bound to exceed the menial wage that was pretty nearly all he could look for elsewhere.

And young black men who had led, by some happy accident, lives somewhat sheltered from the spurns and daily humiliations that would befall every black citizen in the Southland, were sometimes cruelly jolted to discover the extremes of spite, vilification, and naked cruelty that awaited them, not only on the football field but even in their own locker rooms.

Black men who played in the early years on clubs that were nearly all white were expected to accept as well meant, or at least as their just due, names like "jig," "dinge," and "burr-head." (In the late nineteenth century a black ball-player on a small-town Pennsylvania semi-pro baseball team was known to fans and teammates alike as "Nigger" Johnson.) They were also expected to "know their places" to the extent of giving a white mate all the best of it in choice of locker, place on the bench, turn at the water bucket (a number of white men refused to follow "a nigger" in drinking out of the common dipper) or use of any of the facilities. And if they traveled it was taken for granted that the black player would go find accommodations for himself in some "colored" lodgings.

Joe Perry Meets Violent Opposition

Even after the war, when the country had started to grow up sufficiently to observe without wincing white men and black men sitting at the dinner table, the black football player often ran up against practices that he might have imagined had been buried with Theodore Bilbo. Joe (the Jet) Perry, who still holds records for yards gained on the ground, joined the San Francisco club in the All-America Football Conference in 1948, hired by Tony Morabito in the face of earnest requests and dire warnings from some of his fellow club-owners, who averred that he was just buying trouble for himself and all the other clubs. (A few years earlier Branch Rickey had been presented with an "eyes only" resolution adopted by his fifteen fellow major league baseball magnates that it would not be in the best interests of baseball to take Jackie Robinson into the league. The copies of the resolution were then gathered up and destroyed. Branch Rickey and Commissioner Happy Chandler did even better than that. They ignored it.)

On the field Joe Perry met even more virulent opposition. He had never in his life before (and he had played football at Compton Junior College and in the Navy) heard such volleys of what on TV and in the public prints can only be described as "racial epithets" from opponents and occasionally from a spectator. "Monkey" and "nigger" would have sounded like pet names alongside some of the choicest of what Joe had flung at him. Joe, being, like so many blacks, adjusted to a certain amount of ignorant behavior from whites, was still not the sort of man to accept such treatment in silence and he more than once undertook to stop up the stream at its source.

When the 49ers joined the National League in 1950, they had their first chance to meet the Bears, renowned as the roughest and toughest club in the game. In one play Joe's job was to perform a false run around end while the play went in the opposite direction. Joe did his decoy job, the whistle blew, and Joe turned back toward where the ball had been downed. As he stood there, relaxed and unwary, the Chicago defensive tackle, George Connor from Notre Dame, smashed into him full force from Joe's blind side. He flattened Joe and left him with two broken ribs and a burning determination to even the score.

From that time forth Connor and Joe Perry became bitter enemies and whenever the opportunity offered and the most trifling excuse could be found, they would take to trading punches to head and body. But it was two more seasons before Joe found the perfect opportunity to repay George Connor

in full measure. In the game with the Bears when Joe was carrying the ball, he found only George Connor between him and a certain touchdown. The normal move—and one that would have produced a score—would have been for Joe to fake George out of position and dodge away from him. But Joe had waited too long for this very moment. Putting on all his speed (he had been clocked at 9.7 in the hundred-yard dash) Joe headed straight at George Connor. Joe and George were nearly equal in weight—both over 200 pounds—but Joe was flying and George was standing still. They collided with the sound of a leather trunk falling five stories to the sidewalk. George went flat on his back and Joe staggered another six yards before losing his balance. It cost Joe the touchdown, but it rang George Connor's bell and turned off his lights for several moments. The strangest result of this encounter, and one from which wiser men than I might draw a lesson on human behavior, was that the next time they met Joe and George discovered they were good friends and they remained that way throughout the rest of their careers.

Joe took part in another row a few years earlier that probably still ranks as the greatest fight in pro football, engaging as it did all the members of two squads as well as the marching band, and involving much racial bitterness. It began when Joe Perry undertook to help a black teammate respond in kind to some of the illegal roughing up and name-calling he had been accepting from the Philadelphia Eagles. When Joe turned the argument into a fist fight, the entire Eagle bench erupted upon the field. And the 49er bench

Dick Bass of the Rams, given to running right over tacklers, was known as the human manhole cover. Here Charlie Cowan leads the way.

thereupon came roaring out to meet them. So many individual fights broke out then, and so fiercely did the players have at each other, that it seemed the day would end with players still wildly belaboring one another in every sector of the field. But it subsided, as all such ructions do, and the men went back to playing football. Bert Bell named the affair "a disgrace." The paying customers thought it a delight. And it may have been the first time that white football players had ever joined in to avenge the dirty names and dirty deeds awarded a teammate just for being black.

Joe Perry, of course, was one of the best men who ever carried a football, of whatever skin hue. He opened his career with a blaze—breaking loose against Buffalo for fifty-eight yards and a touchdown—and he kept the fire burning bright for thirteen seasons. When he first took his job with the 49ers, he had received lush offers from a number of colleges, some of them offering more than his 49er contract mentioned. But Joe was looking for a steady job. In a game against Green Bay in 1957, Joe carried the ball twenty-seven times. In his thirteen seasons with San Francisco he averaged just over five yards a carry.

Joe was not a man to slow his pace because of bruises and abrasions. Playing against the Los Angeles Rams, one day, Joe had seven teeth knocked adrift by enemy elbows, forearms, and knees, and he scored three times without his teeth. (But in a later game against the Rams, Joe, playing for Baltimore at the end of his career, broke loose for a touchdown and then fell in a dead faint in the end zone. Joe, the doctor said, had torn a leg muscle by the ferocity of his effort.)

Most coaches, athletes, and club owners—at least those whose bigotry was no more than the congenital type so many of the country's whites have been infected with—found it relatively easy to accept black men as ball-carriers. It was, after all, a black man's part, in the cultural legendry, to run extremely fast, to dodge nimbly, to squirm readily out of trouble. Thus a fellow like Buddy Young of the New York Yankees, who could scurry about like a spider as men tried to capture him, awakened no special animus for his speed. But Buddy was not afraid of contact, despite the fact that he was of a size that would have looked more at home on a race horse. And there were a number of men of Confederate persuasion among his opponents who made the mistake of thinking Buddy could be scared into immobility by a few fierce tackles.

Black Linemen Begin to Appear

Soon after the leagues had merged, and the unlimited substitution rule permitted coaches to develop big powerful men into defensive specialists, black linemen began to appear by the dozen, many of them men whose ancestors had grown iron-muscled through unremitting toil and who had themselves grown tall and wide, responding like most of the nation's males to more advanced methods of nutrition and more con-genial environment. These were all well motivated men, barred by their blackness from envisioning a flowered future in the corporate pastureland, where physical bigness was often more sought after than intellect as a means of impressing potential customers with the firm's importance. Most black men knew that they would have to seek their fortunes in athletics and that when their careers were done their future lay in some civil service type job at starvation salary. So they could be counted on to give their whole hearts to football and to yield easily to the persuasion that they must visit the utmost violence on those who would try to take their jobs away. Before the Second World War, it would have been possible to list on a very tiny piece of paper the number of black linemen—except for ends—in football. Outside of the all-black colleges, black football players had found their best opportunities carrying the ball, where they would not be guilty of committing what might look like an unprovoked assault upon an opponent. After 1950, white quarterbacks had to adjust themselves to having black monsters as well as white descend upon them with intent to commit violence.

It took football a long, long time however to dare to start drafting and training black quarterbacks. The club owners still whispered to themselves that it would not *do* to impose black leadership upon white men who might nurture in their hearts the ideals of the slave states. But long before organized baseball had sufficiently matured to talk out loud about some day hiring a black manager, football clubs in both leagues were offering opportunities to black men to call the signals and take charge

of the attack. It seemed even distantly possible that there might be a professional football club in our lifetime that would sweat and strain and pour out its blood at the behest of a coach whose skin was the same color as that of the man who created the Republic of Haiti. But it seemed certain that the ballplayers would be ready for it long before the club owners were.

Among the football players—in such quarters where white players might find themselves momentarily segregated—it was still possible to hear, from Confederate lips, muttered comments on "niggahs" and even "darky jokes" of the sort that most sane people find particularly offensive. But the behavior of these subdued bigots when in company of black teammates offered hope that they had been just acting out without any special zest the part long assigned to them in the sidewalk culture of our land.

On major league *baseball* teams the appearance of a black recruit always meant some scurrying about by the club's road secretary as he sought to

match the new man up with a roommate of the same color, lest the club be put to the expense of giving him quarters by himself. In this matter too professional football showed itself far more adult than the National Game. Football roommates on the road were often of both shades, with never a hard word, a dangerous "incident," or so much as a single rock torn loose from the foundation of the republic. When football players staged parties during the season, as they usually did some six or seven times each week, there would always be black players and white players in attendance, with girls to match, and again there was hardly the least talk of lynching.

In the training camp dining rooms it was noticeable that black players tended to segregate themselves, although there would always be at least one table where skin color had been forgotten. Undoubtedly among the black professional football players there was a sprinkling of those who believed in separatism as a political goal, as there must have been a number of whites who nursed some

Running back Mike Garrett of Kansas City shares his joy with teammates Otis Taylor (right) and Gloster Richardson, after making a touchdown against the Vikings in the 1970 Super Bowl.

Ray Nitschke of Green Bay, one of the toughest defensive men in the game, seems to challenge Redskin Charley Taylor to get up and try it again. Taylor doesn't seem at all interested.

far-out theories of their own. But generally the segregation seemed quite accidental, of the sort that would prompt boys from the same town to associate when they found themselves among strangers.

In the world outside the stadium or the training camp, however, bigotry was often in full flower. In the Southern cities, among the older citizenry and those who had not learned to dress their prejudices up in sheep's clothing, there was sometimes a special impulse to put down a black athlete, particularly if he were a man of some reputation. Finding a place to live without daily embarrassment, to eat without having to ignore studied insult, or to get a haircut without an appeal to a Federal Court was, in such areas, almost a full-time task for a black man. The fact that he was accepted as equal among his mates, even deified by fans of every shade, and allowed his dignity in most other areas, still was not enough to reconcile a black man to indecencies of this sort. Indeed his irritation may actually have been increased by the knowledge that there was a world where such nonsense need not be tolerated. And talk about the "great progress your race has made" would be designed to drive a man under those circumstances to say some extremely bad words out loud if not to committing some act of violence, it being so obviously the white race that needed to make progress in that area.

Realistically, however, it had to be agreed that professional football offered to a black man one of his best chances of escaping not merely the ghetto, but the whole vicious pattern of exploitation and segregation. The race, in pro football, was clearly to the swift, and the battle to the strong. And while a black athlete was not likely to discover Wall Street personnel men crouched shivering on his doorstep on cold mornings, come to beseech him to lend his face and personality to the peddling of shares of stock under some famed aegis, he might still find outside sources by the score for swelling his daily supply of bread.

Also it is worth remarking that the wholesale entrance of black athletes into professional sports has enriched, or at least enlivened, the jargon, if not actually the language, of sports, and even added variety to its gestures. Locker room profanity, to the utter distress of management, is now replete with all the hair-raising and ingenious epithets of the ghetto, echoing the bitter cynicism of the dispossessed and their lack of regard for some of the straight world's most sacred symbols. Both black and white performers learned to exchange congratulations with the joyous whacking of one man's hand upon another's outstretched fingers or palm—a gesture that once belonged to the black man alone.

White athletes in general had remained thoroughly square, most of them being products of football factories where boys were brought up to believe that any questioning of the verities that grandfather had been required to subscribe to was a form of far-outism that was akin to perversion. It was the black athlete, with his inbred impulse to set the world right, who taught the white athlete to expand (if not actually to blow) his mind and to make welcome at least one or two ideas that might have scared poor grandpa skinny.

Passers and Runners

NO one could ever have called Hugh McElhenny a triple threat. He did not punt or kick field goals or throw bull's eye passes. All he did was *run*. But this single threat was all he needed to become in his time the acknowledged King of pro football.

Like so many famed athletes before or since, Hugh developed his greatest skills in spite of a severe handicap. There had been many others who had done much the same—boys who had suffered severe leg damage and had become champion milers; lads doomed to a short and sickly life who had turned themselves into big league baseball players; "ninety-pound weaklings" who had grown up to terrorize the prize ring. But it is doubtful if any of them ever had more physical woe to cope with than did Hugh McElhenny from the time he was not quite in his teens.

When Hugh was eleven years old, a rambunctious youngster in Los Angles, he stepped on a broken milk bottle and cut all the tendons in his right foot. He spent five months in bed after that and for seven months he got around on crutches. Doctors had hopes that he might eventually graduate to a cane but they told his parents that little Hugh would never walk normally again. Hugh,

229

Sonny Jurgensen, streamlined and charged up, yells his signals in the face of the enemy. Center is Lenn Hauss. Washington, 1969.

however, was possessed of a fierce desire to play football, even at that age, and he started at once on a series of special exercises designed to return strength to his mangled foot. He succeeded too, and by the time he was in his second year in high school Hugh was playing halfback on his football team. But he required a steel plate in the sole of his right shoe to make it possible for him to run and he required hypodermic shots before every game for the next several years to deaden the pain.

Hugh's high school fame as a ball carrier extended so far that Frankie Albert of the San Francisco 49ers wanted to sign Hugh as soon as he had graduated. But Hugh, with his eye already on the top dollar, decided there were better opportunities in college. He attended Compton Junior College, where athletics was almost everybody's major, and where Joe the Jet Perry had also matriculated. At Compton, Hugh not only ran off with a great many footballs, he also took to running the high hurdles and set records there. It was not long before he had cash offers to the number of more than half a hundred to transfer to a larger university almost anywhere. He decided on the University of Washington, because they offered not only a fat wad of cash but a job for his new wife as well. At Washington, Hugh earned himself a reputation of being hard to deal with, as well as being the best ball-carrier most men of that time had ever seen. Hugh was so often late for practice that his coach stopped speaking to him and urged all his teammates to ignore him too. So Hugh simply did all his warming up by himself in a far corner of the field and then came by on Saturday to win the ball game.

For one reason or another, either because of his sudden affluence or his emotional conflicts, Hugh took to drinking steadily in the off-season. His wife, who resembled Hugh in having a mind of her own, gave up trying to keep him straight and left him. So Hugh quit college and devoted himself to making up with his wife.

Hugh (the King) McElhenny Takes a Pay Cut

His very signing with Washington had caused a scandal that wound up with the fining of the university by the Pacific Coast Conference. Apparently the $20,000 price the university was reputed to have offered Hugh was a violation of the salary ceiling. At any rate, when Hugh finally did yield to the blandishment of the 49ers, he was, said Frankie Albert, the only man Frankie ever knew who actually took a pay cut to come play for the pros. The 49ers had not been over-eager to draft Hugh, nor were there many other clubs who wanted him. His "temperament" was in some doubt. He was a man, it was reported, of violent temper (he once knocked a motorcycle cop clean over his motorcycle with a blow to the head), owned a fat collection of speeding tickets, and had earned almost as much renown in neighborhood taverns as he had on the football field.

But Hugh turned out to be a thoroughly devout and disciplined performer, willing to carry the ball in any sort of going and always keyed up to go all the way. He was, said observers, a far greater runner than Red Grange had been, for he was faster, heavier, and could change his speed more quickly. Like Grange, he used to set the spectators to gasping and yelling by his unearthly skill at avoiding tackles. Time after time, men who seemed to have a clear shot at

Hugh would be left flat on the turf behind him, or would just seem to bounce off his sturdy thighs. Part of Hugh's ability to elude the men who would cut him down could be ascribed to his unusually wide peripheral vision. Without taking his eyes off the man dead ahead, he could still pick up in the corners of his eyes the men who might be closing in from either side and would dodge and shift and turn in time to slip away from them.

All Hugh's peculiar skills were beautifully exemplified in a run he made against the Chicago Bears in 1952. Standing on his own six-yard line, Hugh caught a punt as two Chicago defenders bore down on him. Hugh stood on his toes for several seconds, seeming to shift his weight from one foot to the other as he surveyed the field ahead—a typical move of his before turning on his top speed. Just as the two tacklers drove in upon him, Hugh seemed to rocket forward, and the two men, finding only atmosphere between them, collided and fell to the ground. As Hugh sped toward midfield, one tackler approached from the right. Hugh promptly slowed down to a "controlled pace" and watched the man warily. Then, just as the man committed himself to the tackle, Hugh, turning slightly to the left, jabbed hard with one foot and accelerated to top speed again, leaving that tackler too with two arms full of Chicago air. By this time the rest of the Chicago club had zeroed in on Hugh and tackle Bob Toneff ran just ahead to blast a way for him. Hugh dodged, faked, twisted and sprinted away and never stopped until he had crossed the goal line. George Halas, who had been performing gymnastics on the sideline as he sought to hurl fresh bodies in Hugh's

way by sheer mental power, let out a hoarse yell of grudging approval "That," he roared, "is the God-damnedest run I ever saw in football!" And George, remember, had been right on hand when Red Grange was at his best.

As for Hugh, he ran a little semicircle in the end zone, then kneeled to look back up field, to see if any fouls had been called. Hugh's critics called this habit of his "show-boating" but he merely shook this complaint off. He *never* counted a score, he said, until he found out if there had been a penalty in the play. As for this punt return against the Bears, Hugh's mouth fell open in dismay when they told him how far he had run.

"Six-yard line!" he exclaimed. "My God! I thought it was the *twenty*-six! If I'd known it was the six, I'd have let the damn ball roll for a touchback!" It is not recorded whether his coach believed him.

The very first run Hugh McElhenny made in pro football was in an exhibition game against the Chicago Cardinals in 1952. Determined to put a stop forever to the undercurrent of talk about his "temperament" and general unfitness for serious effort, Hugh broke loose from scrimmage and ran sixty yards for a touchdown. The play had been an improvisation by quarterback Frank Albert, who had first urged his boss to draft Hugh and was also determined to show that the big lad was an honest-to-God ball-carrier. He sent Hugh wide, pitched the ball out to him, and let him fly practically unattended downfield. Hugh was across the line of scrimmage almost before the defense could read his number. Later in his first season, Hugh ran eighty-nine yards from scrimmage for a touchdown against Dallas. He com-

1. Frank Gifford of the New York Giants loses his grip on the ball as he carries it across the goal in a game against Washington in New York in 1956. But he had already put the ball over the line and he fell on top of it.

2. Gifford loses the ball at the goal line again. This was in the East vs. West game in 1957. Teammate Kyle Rote fell on the ball for the score.

3. All-time champion Jimmy Brown cuts downfield behind tackle Monte Clark. Jimmy's left forearm was a mighty defensive weapon.

4. Hugh (the King) McElhenny of San Francisco scoring a touchdown in typical style—with frustrated tacklers strung out behind him on the turf.

5. McElhenny, with the Minnesota Vikings, was no longer King, but he still performed with his old ferocity.

6. One more touchdown by Paul Hornung. Referee lifts hand to signal a score as Jim Taylor trots along in the rear.

7. Cleveland's great offense before the 1965 championship playoff at Green Bay: Jimmy Brown, in the rear, Lenny Green (48), and quarterback Ryan (13). Coach Blanton Collier, at right, shivers in the chill. Brown did not score once, as Green Bay won 23 to 12.

8. The last game. Paul Hornung, who suited up but did not play in the first Super Bowl, sits disconsolate and forgotten. Number 60 is linebacker Lee Roy Caffey.

pleted that year with an average gain of seven yards per carry.

Hugh was on hand to lend his fierce "temperament" to that greatest fight ever staged on a football field, the one that Joe Perry had helped turn into a free-for-all. Hugh, using his plastic helmet as a sort of mace, managed to discourage a number of foes and he was even suspected of having called in the 49er band to club the enemy with their clarinets.

But the fire that burned so fiercely in Hugh's soul availed him nothing in 1955 when his bad foot betrayed him. In the exhibition season he seemed merely to have bruised his foot badly but when the injury did not heal, the club sent him to specialists who could do no more than report that his boyhood injury had been aggravated. With a hideously sore foot to slow him down, Hugh played out the season but his speed and elusiveness seemed to have disappeared. Hugh had overcome this very ailment once, however, and he grimly undertook to beat it again. When he returned to the battles in 1956, he ran as fiercely and as swiftly as ever. Against Green Bay, he took the ball eighty-six yards from scrimmage for the score that spelled victory. Teamed with Joe Perry in his best years, Hugh McElhenny helped bring his club within a finger's breadth of a championship. He made his best effort with a seventy-one-yard run from scrimmage against Detroit in a game in which the 49ers lost the divisional championship. If Hugh had made it all the way, his club would have won it. But a collection of Detroit players, all clinging to some piece of him, managed to drag Hugh out of bounds on the nine-yard line.

Like all speedsters, Hugh McElhenny eventually found that he had begun to lose a half-step or more. But his remarkable wide-angle vision, which some men called his sixth sense, kept him out of the arms of tacklers often enough to get him where he was headed. He also retained one of his finest weapons—an old-fashioned straight-arm such as had not been seen in football since the days of the Canton Bulldogs. With it Big Hugh turned many a prospective tackler into a casualty. He had learned that trick in high school, Hugh said.

Hugh closed out his career with the New York Giants—no longer the King, for, after thirteen seasons, there were many pretenders who had succeeded him. But for brief moments his wiliness, his remarkable ability to elude a pair of clutching arms, and his unique skill at changing direction in full flight gave the New York fans a final glimpse of the man who had once been best of them all.

Frank Gifford Becomes a Sixty-Minute Man

New York by this time had seen some of its own great heroes earn fame and start to fade, for by this time Frank Gifford had completed ten seasons of football—with one year out to recuperate from the mightiest blind-side tackle ever wreaked upon any man.

Gifford, in college, was a triple-threat man, a sort of throwback to the days when such creatures were common. He played tail-back in the single-wing formation at the University of Southern California and played quarterback in the T-formation. He carried the ball, passed it, punted it, kicked field goals and made extra points. He also looked and lived like the incarnation of Frank Merriwell. Had he been born thirty years earlier he would have been described as an Arrow-collar type, for he

wore the impossibly neat and regular
features of the man in the advertise-
ment. He lived a regular, if not completely abstemious, life. He was modest,
soft-spoken, inherently courteous. And
he married the girl who was chosen
campus queen at the college.

But when Frank began to play professional football, he felt the heart go
out of him. He put in a number of frus-
trating and bruising sessions of practice,
in which he discovered that professional
football defensive players *invariably* hit
ball carriers with all the force they could
summon. He felt ignored by the coach,
disliked by the veterans, and forgotten
by the homefolks. One day he packed
his bag and started home and if assistant coach Allie Sherman had not
stopped him and persuaded him the
coaches had faith in him, Frank might
have wound up acting in the movies.
(He had been a Hollywood bit player
while in school.)

The Giants made triple-threat Frank
into a sixty-second man—using him, as
only a few were still employed, both as a
ball carrier and a defensive back. This
was during the days when the $21,000
salary paid to Y. A. Tittle of the 49ers
was a matter to write newspaper stories
about. Rookie backs, even All-America
backs such as Gifford was, did not bank
six-figure bonuses or spend evenings
sorting out business offers. (Frank actually did turn down an "enormous"
bonus—$6,000—offered by a Canadian
football promoter and accepted a modest tender—$3,000—from New York,
because, he said, he felt he belonged in
"American" football.) Football players
who played for money in that day had
their worn football shoes tapped by the
neighborhood cobbler, ate the blue-
plate special in the nearby restaurant

Iron Man and Golden Boy. Coach Vince Lombardi, chest out, takes the sun with his (at that
time) favorite football player in Green Bay, Paul
Hornung.

and checked over their thinning wallets every other day. Frank's wife was expecting a baby and while they were by no means broke, the Gifford's were not living entirely on sidemeat. And Frank, working earnestly to hang on to his job with the Giants, stripped twenty pounds off his frame in a single season.

A decision by Vince Lombardi, New York offensive coach, to keep Frank on the offense saved Frank from withering completely away—and helped save the Giants too from stumbling on into futility. For Gifford soon began to match men like McElhenny and Ollie Matson and Doak Walker in yards gained. Having been a single-wing tailback, Gifford took easily to Vince Lombardi's new offense that returned to football some of the thundering power of the single-wing end sweep. Carrying the ball for the Giants in this new-old play, Frank began to look once more like the unstoppable back he had been in college. To run this play it took, besides speed and deeply instilled instinct, a quick mind to decide in a flicker exactly when to make the quick cut upfield that would leave the outside defenders flat-footed and blocked out. This is where Frank excelled, for he was a thinking football player and he played with intense concentration. Charging upfield, Frank carried his head high, as if he were sighting over the enemy tacklers' heads to spot some far-distant goal, even beyond the end zone. He was not a McElhenny type speedster and could probably have been beaten in a long race even by some linemen. But Frank was exceedingly quick off the mark and full of that almost ecstatic desire to attain the impossible goal. This made him harder for defensive men to stay up with when he took off

and harder to stop when he was under full steam. Gifford was a steady rather than a spectacular player and it is ironical that of his few spectacular plays the one that seems most likely to live in horrid memory is the fearful blindside blasting he took from two-fisted Chuck Bednarik, fearsome both-ways linebacker of the Philadelphia Eagles.

Right out in front of 60,000 devoted New York fans Chuck caught Frank looking the other way, after he had snuggled a pass in his arms, and hit him so hard he nearly rattled the perfect white teeth out of Frank's handsome head. Down went Frank, so limp and obviously senseless that more than one faint heart thought him dead. The ball rolled free, a Philadelphia man pounced upon it, and Chuck Bednarik did a little war dance of triumph, punching his fist upward into the air.

The fans took this as a vulgar rejoicing over Gifford's having been knocked loose from his senses. Frank lay exactly where Chuck had deposited him, flatter upon the sod than a conscious man would ever lie, and he stirred not a finger, even after men rushed out with restorative medications. Bednarik did not really know that Gifford had been hurt. He was rejoicing in the fact that his side had the ball, with only two minutes to play, and now victory was practically certain. But Gifford did not get up and he had to be carried, still unknowing, on a stretcher and taken by ambulance to the hospital, not merely out of the game, but out of football for a year, afraid, as well he might be, that he might now incur some permanent injury to his central nervous system.

The New York fans, devoted to their handsome hero, would not forgive Bednarik. A few of Gifford's teammates called Chuck a cheap-shot artist. But a cheap-shot is a fierce blindside block thrown against a man obviously out of the play. Who was to say just how hard and from what direction a player should hit the ball-carrier? Frank, gracious as always, held no grudge against Bednarik (although there was some talk in New York of "getting even" when the Giants played in Philadelphia). Chuck sent his good wishes to the hospital where Gifford lay, and followed up with flowers. Gifford did not acknowledge them. The Eagles were to meet the Giants again the very next week and Gifford decided Bednarik might be psyched into pulling his punches a bit if he was left wondering about whether a grudge was smoldering. (Almost a half century before, George Stallings of the Boston National League baseball club, meeting Connie Mack's Athletics in the World Series, added some white hairs to Connie's thinning thatch by pretending to harbor some deep resentment against the gentle old man.)

Gifford's recovery was quick and complete. The predicted feud never did eventuate. The Eagles beat the Giants again but with no bloodshed. All the same, Gifford, who was now thirty years old, decided he had played enough football. His investments in California promised him a good income, he had a steady broadcasting job in New York, and he did not feel he required more concussions to remind him he was no longer a boy. He had never taken home a particularly munificent salary from playing football and even though this particular injury was of no lasting consequence, he felt that, after missing the remainder of the season, he had come to the logical point at which to bow out.

But one season on the sidelines, watching the excitement without really savoring it, was all Frank could take. He came back to play again in 1962, had to learn a new job—flankerback—and after dropping more passes than he felt he should, began to shine again. He caught thirty-nine passes and made seven touchdowns. He ran with the ball only twice but made an eighteen-yard gain on one carry. In 1963, however, Gifford found himself standing too often on the sideline while some of the flock of new receivers caught the passes. This jolt to his pride did more to Frank than the concussion did, and he finally did retire from the game.

Gifford's greatest play was always said to be an impossible catch he made of a pass from Y. A. Tittle, in a game against Pittsburgh—a catch that the Pittsburgh coach said really cost Pittsburgh any chance of victory. But Frank took no special credit for it. He never expected to catch the ball that way he said, just tried to knock it into the air and hope to grab it as it fell. But he got his fingertips on it and the ball, as some such balls occasionally do, just stuck there long enough for Gifford to pull it in. The fans screamed in half-disbelieving joy and the Pittsburgh defenders, who had been congratulating themselves at having forced old Y. A. into overthrowing the ball, wondered what the hell you had to *do* to beat this crowd.

The play that some fans like to remember, because there was something so typically Giffordish about it—alert, unselfish, and effective—was the improvised lateral Frank threw in a playoff game against the Cleveland Browns. He had wound up with the ball on a double reverse in which quarterback

Baldest man in the game. Y. A. Tittle, veteran of many seasons in Baltimore and San Francisco, waits on the sideline preparatory to leading the New York Giants in an exhibition game at Green Bay.

The sort of protection that makes a quarterback a star. Johnny Unitas, safe inside the (momentarily) impregnable pocket, chooses a target. Alex Karras of Detroit is held out long enough to permit Unitas to get his pass away.

Green Bay's Jim Taylor, about to hit the ground. And the ground, in this 1962 playoff game at Yankee Stadium, New York, was like the floor of a garage. The cold was bitter, wind blew hats and overcoats and frozen dust across the field, and ball-carriers wore rubber-soled shoes.

Veteran field goal kicker Don Chandler of Green Bay scored 11 of the 23 points Green Bay made to win the 1965 title. Bart Starr is holding as Jerry Kramer strolls by.

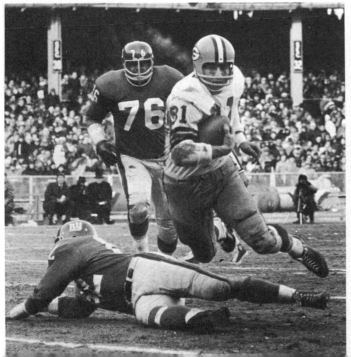

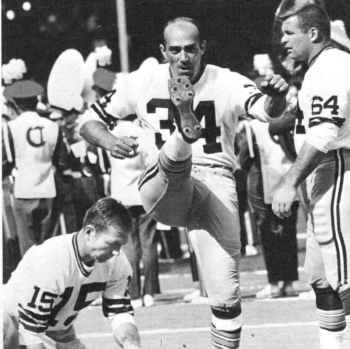

Charley Conerly handed off to fullback Alex Webster, who then slipped it to Frank, who was coming against the grain of the play. The play worked with almost perfect precision and Gifford was off to the goal line with six points in view. Somewhere behind him tottered ancient Charley Conerly, thirty-five years old and growing older step by step. Charley, who always ran rather like a pregnant woodchuck, had not scored a point since some day that the oldest fan had forgotten. But Gifford, who was Charley's closest friend on the club, saw Charley running free and suddenly pitched the ball out to him. It was perhaps a foolish move, for the slowest man on the Cleveland club could probably have given Charley a five-yard start and caught him. But it took the Clevelanders so utterly by surprise it was several seconds before they believed that Conerly really had the ball. Those seconds were all Conerly needed to pant his way into the end zone and become a hero.

Jimmy Brown, Symbol of the New Pro Game

On the same field that very day—and brought almost to a full stop by the aroused New York club—was the greatest ball carrier the game, up to that day, had ever developed. He was Jimmy Brown of Cleveland, symbol of the new pro game, in which great size and strength was added to great speed and desire to produce a contest that looked and sounded like college football multiplied by ten. Jimmy Brown had played football in college—or at least in a football plant where a fellow could attend four years without any real danger of his learning English grammar. Not that Jimmy showed any deficiencies in grammar. He had had a fairly strict upbring-

ing and had attended a good high school, in Manhasset, Long Island, New York, where he spent almost all his spare time conditioning his growing body to run, run and run. For Jimmy was a trackman in high school as well as a baseball and basketball player. He needed no pep talks or sententious lectures to keep him in school or keep him trying. Living in a high-income neighborhood where his mother worked as a domestic, Jimmy's pride demanded that he earn respect through athletics.

Jimmy grew into a very large man—six feet two inches tall, weighing 230 pounds, with shoulders wide as a windshield, a size eighteen neck and a thirty-two inch waist. Jimmy was lured to Syracuse University, where he became the greatest athlete ever to graduate from that athletic manufactory. There were many who insisted Jimmy might well have become a heavyweight boxer, for he had dazzling reflexes, fast hands, and a great ability to absorb punishment. Jimmy, however, wanted to play football. He was a halfback at Syracuse but when he came to Cleveland Paul Brown made him into a fullback, perhaps seeing in Jimmy the reincarnation of Marion Motley, who had helped make Otto Graham invincible at quarterback. Jimmy however was never the blocker that Motley was. He preferred to run and at running there was none better. Jimmy had a teammate named Bobby Mitchell who had come very close to matching the record in the 100-yard dash. But many who saw Jimmy and Bobby run together would vow that Jimmy would be leading for the first fifty yards.

This ability to get an explosive start had much to do with Jimmy's success. Pro football defenses are not to be toyed with, for the charging linemen come ravening in upon the runner as soon as the ball is snapped. In college ball a man could often jitter about a little behind the scrimmage line in order to "pick a hole." But the man who tried that in pro football most often found himself being pried up off the sod right about where he started.

Jimmy, however, not only took off at top speed from a standing start but kept on going no matter how many defenders laid hold of him. Jimmy was agile and shifty. Undoubtedly he shared McElhenny's ability to hold the entire field in his range of vision and to adjust quickly to slip a tackle. But he could also blast through on the inside, bowling over the men who had failed to get a clean angle on him, tearing through arm tackles as if they had been cotton string, and twisting out of the grip of even the most powerful defenders. Time and again, fans seeing him submerged in a clot of tacklers would count him stopped, only to see him burst free like a bull through a broken fence to charge another twenty or thirty yards.

If Jimmy failed to provide all the blocking other fullbacks had given at least he made up for it in ball-carrying. Paul Brown saw to that, for he called on Jimmy to tote the ball two, three, four, five times in a row, inside, outside, and at the end of short passes. There was talk that Jimmy resented his being "overworked" this way. (Other ball carriers had been known to complain that they did not get to carry the ball often enough.) But if he was being overworked he was certainly not being underpaid. It had always been Paul Brown's theory that the laborer, even if he labored in the heady vineyards of sport, was still worthy of his hire. In his

day, Jimmy was probably the highest paid performer on the gridiron.

The lack of a sharpshooting passer at his side made Jimmy's way often difficult, for when the defense was not too overawed by the quarterback's arm, they could afford to key on Jimmy steadily, so that two or three big men could set upon him almost before he could get a sure grip on the ball. Yet Jimmy plugged along in all sorts of going, averaging over five yards a carry in season after season. In the first five years as a pro, Jimmy led the league in total yardage gained—the only man ever to have done so.

Lacking a spectacular quarterback, the Browns might still have gone to a championship with Jimmy Brown if they had owned a halfback who could carry the ball on the inside track. But they had instead fleet Bobby Mitchell, a man who could generally break away only when he could be shaken loose on the flank or just outside the tackle. The only "inside" threat was Jimmy himself, who was the man they counted on when short yardage was needed, either on third down or when the ball lay near the goal. But Jimmy was also the man the opposition counted on to get the ball on such situations. Consequently the defense could key on him with complete confidence. Jimmy did not therefore get loose as often as he might have. And the Browns did not finish in the money even when it seemed certain they would.

Still Jimmy made a habit of gaining 1000 yards or more every season, to lead all the rest. In 1962, however, the year when it seemed the Browns had finally packed in the horsepower they needed, Jimmy ran into disaster, and so did the Browns. The Browns had drafted, to play at Jimmy's side, the only ball carrier who had ever matched Jimmy Brown's mark at Syracuse—big, strong and fleet-footed Ernie Davis. Bobby Mitchell had been traded off for the right to draft Davis and Ernie seemed like the inside threat necessary to give Jimmy more running room. Jimmy, however, badly sprained his left wrist and thus rendered his ball-carrying arm useless. Forced to tuck the ball into his right arm, Jimmy could no longer let fly with his mighty right forearm—a weapon more potent even than Hugh McElhenny's straight-arm and one that had forced a pathway for him through many a pack of hungry tacklers.

Total disaster fell when it was learned that Ernie Davis was dying of leukemia. So Jimmy Brown, bad wrist and all, became even more the solitary threat. He did not flinch either but smashed right ahead with the football in his right arm and his left arm practically immobile. For a wonder, he actually did gain 1000 yards that season, only to be thrown for two losses in the final game that reduced his total yardage to 996.

This year, 1962, being Jimmy's worst and the worst the Browns had known since Jimmy joined them, it was predictable that Jimmy should start to gripe. Paul Brown, he muttered (within the hearing of the writers) was using him too often, was not giving consideration to the special skills of certain players (Jimmy Brown for instance) and was in general too strict, too set in his ways, too overbearing, too lacking in sympathy. The real beef of course was that the club was not winning, for when a club is winning the coach, whatever may be his character, his habits, or his style of speech, becomes the darling of the players and fans alike.

But the rebellion Jimmy led having split the team into factions, the management was moved to relieve Paul Brown of his coaching duties and let him go play golf. Under the new coach, Blanton Collier, Jimmy came to life again. For one thing his arm had healed. For another, the Browns had a new quarterback named Frank Ryan who was a constant threat to hang on to the ball and run with it. This loosened up the defenses somewhat and made the attack more flexible. For a third thing, there was a new halfback, Lenny Green, who could also take the ball on the inside path and allowed Jimmy to go wide more often.

Jimmy went wide most often on the flare pass that Coach Blanton Collier added to the repertoire. This got Jimmy out beyond the end and on his way with the ball in his arms before the monsters could move in on him. With their big gun in working order once more, the Browns won six games in a row and Jimmy became again the top ball carrier in the game. In the opening game with the Redskins, Jimmy scored on one pass play that covered eighty yards. After the first six victories Jimmy was averaging seven yards a carry and rival coaches were silently praying that he might soon suffer some convenient accident. Even the New York Giants, who had bottled Jimmy up so effectively in seasons past, could not contain the new Jimmy Brown. In the game that year in the Yankee Stadium Jimmy gave one of his finest exhibitions, delighting even the enemy fans who had so long cheered his frustrations.

At the start of the game, Sam Huff and the other cannibals of the New York defense were stifling Jimmy in the same old way—breaking past his

Mel Triplett of the New York Giants looks as if nothing will stop him as he roars toward the goal line in a game against the Cleveland Browns. But Cleveland guard Chuck Noll, shown bracing himself for the impact, stopped Mel just shy of the line. Ken Konz (22) gave Noll a hand. New York got the score a few seconds later and won the game.

Crippled quarterback Johnny Unitas glumly watches the 1965 playoff game, in which he should have been the field general.

Jurgensen, back in top form now that victory is in the air again, gets a kind word from an admirer, coach Vince Lombardi. Washington, 1969.

blockers to spill him at the corners, smashing in through the middle to down him before he could take a forward step. But in the second half, coach Collier loaded up his big gun and let fire. With the ball on the Cleveland twenty-eight-yard line, Ryan called the flare pass to Jimmy. Both tight and split ends, along with the flanker, raced downfield and to the right. Jimmy flared out to the other flank, while the left side of the line, along with the center, slid over to provide blocking. Then quarterback Ryan flipped the ball to Jimmy Brown. Center and tackle held the linebacker out and Jimmy just trolleyed down the sideline the whole seventy-two yards to the New York goal line without even an angry finger to try to stay him.

But the most spectacular deed Jimmy performed that day was a later run that did not evolve out of a pass and that covered a shorter distance. But it was managed by shrewd use of his blockers, a lightning reversal of his field, and his usual rocket speed. Jimmy, with the ball in his arm, started out to his left. Two good blocks got him through the line and he poised on his toes for the smallest sliver of a second to size up the gathering opposition. Then, with a shift of gears so sudden that it took the enemy entirely uprepared, Jimmy sped laterally across the field to his right. One defensive man got a good shot at him along the way but Jimmy, sighting his approach, stopped short. The man got only half a hold on Jimmy and Jimmy twisted free and kept going. As he reached the open spaces on the right, Gary Collins, the tall end from the University of Maryland, wiped out at one slice two Giants who had been taken unawares by Jimmy's sudden reversal

and were trying to recover themselves and pursue him. There was no one else near him and Jimmy just opened a wider and wider gap on his pursuers until he was able to coast the last ten yards, grinning happily. He had faked the entire Giant defensive team out of position in one lightning-fast change of direction. New York fans stood up to cheer the effort.

In Jimmy's next triumph, against the Philadelphia Eagles, he piled up yards enough to take the total-yardage record away from Joe the Jet Perry. Big Joe had set *his* record in 13½ seasons. Jimmy beat it in 6½. Later in the season, against the Cardinals, Jimmy carried the ball twenty-nine times for 179 yards. There was one sixty-one-yard run for a touchdown. That was enough to set a one-season record of 1,677 yards. (The old record had been owned by Jimmy too.)

Jimmy never did become a heavyweight boxer, although there was a good deal of "confidential" information afloat to the effect that this could be his next move. He was so fearsomely muscled (many people, seeing the muscles that bulged on his thighs, thought he was wearing pads there) that it is not certain many men would have been persuaded to enter the ring with him. What Jimmy did become was a movie actor and a surprisingly good one. (Frank Gifford, who seemed to have been fashioned by fate into the ideal movie actor, was a surprisingly unsuccessful one, although a polished TV commentator.)

Jimmy also earned himself many columns of unpleasant publicity, invariably in connection with some alleged moral transgression, but none of the charges ever stuck long enough to injure him. And the fans who watched him break loose with a football and make his way to the goal line while splattering foemen right and left remained without any deep concern over how Jimmy spent his off-gridiron hours.

Paul Hornung—Sex and the Single Football Player

A contemporary of Jimmy's, and one who also sometimes had his name in the papers in connection with the company he kept while not playing football, was Green Bay's Golden Boy, Paul Hornung. Paul, an All-America from Notre Dame, whom Vince Lombardi changed from a frustrated quarterback to a dazzling halfback, also seemed endowed with movie star features and physique. He was something of a triple-threat type, like Gifford. But unlike Gifford he was given to uninhibited rejoicing in his youth, in his bubbling appetites and in his attraction for the opposite sex. He played football with the ferocity that Vince Lombardi required of all his charges. But he played young man about town with nearly as much devotion, never cringing at having his picture taken in a low-slung sports car laden with young ladies.

Hornung's career had been headed for a rather dismal end when Lombardi arrived to build a new attack around him. Running then in the Lombardi-type offense, which Vince had first introduced while coaching the offensive team for the Giants, Hornung became another McElhenny. Lombardi football used the T-formation still but instead of relying on quick "brush" blocks to spring a runner loose, it went back to two-man blocking at the point of attack, to gain three, four, five yards at a time. It also brought back the pulling guards who would lead the halfback on power

sweeps around the end, exactly as Lombardi had used Gifford in New York.

Paul Hornung was big enough (six feet two and 215 pounds) to carry the ball right into the beef of the line. He was also swift enough to outrun the defenders on end sweeps. His ability to pass the ball made him every bit as effective as Gifford had been on the "option" play— in which the halfback throws the ball if the linebackers move in on him. Paul could also kick field goals and if they asked him to he could get off a respectable punt. Sometimes he would score all, or almost all, the points in a game. Against Baltimore one day he scored thirty-three points, with four touchdowns, six extra points, and a field goal. Paul was also a seasoned and aggressive blocker, who was not at all hesitant about hurling his body at a linebacker to make a clear path for his fullback, Jim Taylor. And Taylor's presence in the backfield, where he was a constant threat to break right through center for a dozen yards made Hornung's football life easier too, by keeping the defenses looser and preventing them from keying on the Golden Boy. (Hornung's gleaming blond locks had begun to grow thin at the edges before he was finished running up and downfield with a football in his arms.)

Made into a national hero by Lombardi's success in leading the Packers to the championship. Hornung was one of the first of pro football heroes to be recognizable wherever he showed himself. In the 1950's, although there were many, like quarterbacks Norm Van Brocklin, John Unitas, and Bobby Layne, whose names were known from coast to coast, and others, like Gifford and Jim Brown, whose great good looks might be expected to draw a crowd, it was still possible for most of these men to walk into a busy restaurant and pass along a street in a strange town and not be called by name. Hornung was known nearly everywhere. Most pictures and TV shots revealed the pro football heroes only with their enormous plastic helmets and face masks in place. But fans were used to seeing Paul Hornung with his golden hair agleam, so that when he appeared among a mob of strangers at the Kentucky Derby for instance, he would find several hundred at his heels, hoping for his signature on a piece of paper or just a close look.

It may have been this adulation that helped persuade Paul he was not to be subject to the same rules that guided lesser men. He was one of the few ballplayers who did not slavishly obey the strict regulations that Lombardi laid down. And Vince Lombardi was wise enough to know just how tight he could draw the rein on his triple-threat mustang. When Hornung stayed up late or engaged rather openly in mildly riotous living, Lombardi managed to keep his head turned away. But eventually there was some part of Paul's off-gridiron behavior that could not be ignored.

Professional, and even college athletes, grow used to being courted by hearty men with big bankrolls, who acquire, or think they acquire, some added stature among their kind through talking on intimate terms with any of today's heroes. But often among those who hasten to pick up the bar tabs, arrange introductions to lissome ladies, or stage merry celebrations, are divers sharp-eyed types who are in the business of gathering useful information from working athletes to acquire an edge in picking winners. Paul Hornung, and other

athletes, found themselves associating with some such men and saw no harm in it. Paul even got into the habit of betting on his own club through some of these leisure-time acquaintances—just as professional baseball players, boxers, and horsemen had been doing since the sports began.

When Paul was caught at this, and freely confessed his fault, he was rusticated for a full season. But this was in 1963, after a year that saw Paul often sitting on the sidelines nursing a painful neck. (Although the Packers won all but one of their games that year, Hornung carried the ball but fifty-seven times and averaged 3.8 per carry, well below his usual figure.) When Hornung returned to the Packers in 1964, he teamed with Taylor and Tom Moore, a man who could outrun both of them, to become part of a backfield that should have been invincible. Jim Taylor gained more yards and scored more touchdowns than Paul himself. Tom Moore, replacing Paul for a season, had not prompted a single fan to wish aloud for Paul's return. Without Hornung, they had lost only two games. *With* Hornung, why should they lose any? The trouble was that Hornung, strong as he was and eager to play, had lost the fine edge of some of his skills, chiefly his ability to kick the ball between the goal posts. He missed in two contests conversion points that would have tied or won the ball games. In a game that Baltimore won by a three-point margin, Hornung missed four field goals. Out of thirty-eight attempts that season he made good on only twelve field goals. (In his last good year, 1961, he put fifteen out of twenty-two across the bar and between the uprights.)

Yet, ailing as he was (he injured his

shoulder early in the season) and off the track as the team itself seemed on several Sundays, Hornung still counted up more points than anyone else on the club, enough to delight most other backs. But Paul was not delighted. Personal statistics gave him no nourishment at all, if he did not win. This wanting to win, he said once, almost spoiled the game for him. It built tension so extreme that it devoured his sleep and soured his meals.

This fierce desire of his, that expressed itself in grim effort rather than in yelling and college-type exhortation, was what made him seem like the real leader of the club. Starr called the signals and Jim Taylor gained more yards. But Paul Hornung set the pace. When Paul was off his feed, so was the club.

In 1965, they took the kicking away from Hornung and gave it to Don Chandler, secured from the New York Giants through some bit of necromancy. With this responsibility off his back, the Golden Boy came back to set new records once more. In a game against Baltimore, Hornung five times carried the ball across the goal line, to beat a record he had held himself. (If he had been kicking the extra points this year he would have broken his own record for total points in a game—thirty-three made against Baltimore in 1961.) In 1966, however, Hornung had faded beyond hope of recovery, and he scored his last touchdown for Green Bay in a game against the Chicago Bears in mid-October. He did not play again until Green Bay beat the Rams in the final game with the divisional championship already tucked away. Paul carried the ball five times in that game and averaged about five yards a carry. His average for the whole season was less than three yards, and professional ball carriers do not hold their jobs with figures like that. When his club fought Dallas for the league championship, Paul sat hunched on the sideline. At the Super Bowl, the first ever played and the only one that failed to draw a full house, Paul again sat and watched, while younger and spryer men carried the ball.

Hornung therefore left no spectacular records behind, beyond a few miraculous kicks and his five touchdowns. Still he remained one of the big names in football, partly it must be granted because of the deliberate exploitation of the reckless manner in which he indulged his taste for good drink and the tender attentions of light-hearted females. He was, he did not hesitate to assert, a "swinger"—the mid-century term for a sex athlete. He even wrote a book that pretended to retail some of his adventures in that area and thus helped set the new tone in sports literature, which taught young readers more about how high-paid athletes *spent* their salaries than how they earned them.

Looking back over his career, Paul liked to dwell upon just one feat, of the many he performed for Green Bay. That was one of the game's oddities—a field goal attempted on a "free kick" after a fair catch. Paul kicked it from fifty-two yards out and sent it right into three-point territory.

Johnny Unitas, the Modern "Maximum" Quarterback

One young man, however, who made no brags whatever on the way he spent his money—a young man who was unutterably square, in his bristle haircut and in the speeches he liked to make to groups of schoolboys about completing their education, obeying their parents and drying the orphan's tear—was quarterback John Unitas of Baltimore, a Horatio Alger type who came into professional football, on the end not of a six-figure bonus but of a sixty-cent phone call, asking him if he was still looking for work.

In 1958, if you had grabbed a football fan in the street in almost any city and asked him, before he had a chance to gather his hometown loyalty about him, who was the greatest football player alive, he'd have said John Unitas, for John, by his cool, indomitable and disciplined way had just won "the greatest football game ever played" to give the Baltimore Colts the championship. In the final game against the Giants, the first pro football game ever to be played with a sudden-death fifth "quarter," John had showed himself as the modern version of the "maximum quarterback." He did not spit fire and defiance like Bobby Layne, nor was he the hell-for-leather, let-me-do-this-my-own-way type, like the great Dutchman, Norm Van Brocklin of Los Angeles and Philadelphia. He listened respectfully to his coach and took charge on the field by his calm, authoritative manner (he would stay clear of the huddle and the gimme-the-ball pleas of his mates, make up his own mind, then step in and snap off the call). In the field of play, he was as relaxed as if he were playing touch football in a school playground. In the championship game against the Giants, he once stood still and calmly waved his chosen receiver to go deeper and deeper still before he would throw him the football. Another time, with the famous New York front four clamoring for his blood and barely held at bay by the Baltimore pass blockers, John with a cool pump-

fake froze a linebacker in place long enough to shake a receiver free and complete a crucial pass.

Unitas was everybody's idea then of the new breed of football player, mature, modest, non-swinging, and apparently content in his public pronouncements to play the part assigned him by the People Who Counted. John was not a ball carrier, although he did not fear to risk his ribs by carrying the ball if the opportunity seemed especially ripe. He was instead one of the readiest to "eat" the football when there was no place to throw it with any chance of its falling into friendly hands.

Y.A. Tittle Earned His Laurels on the Field

Unitas' rival in that championship game was an even more mature type, who had already "completed" a career on the Pacific Coast before being traded to the Giants. Counted as used up in San Francisco where a knee injury seemed to have left him immobile and off-target, after several brilliant seasons, Y. A. Tittle, the baldest man in the game, came to New York to post even greater records than he had made on the coast. He too was cool, crisp, wise to the ways of defensive backs, and gifted with that wide-ranging vision a quarterback needs to see the whole field from sideline to sideline while looking straight ahead. (Unitas, observed Benny Friedman, did not possess that gift, and "turned his head too much.")

The great Y. A., who led the Giants into several playoff games, was no ball carrier either, although he too would bang into the line or dive head first over the top if that was the only way to score. Like Charlie Conerly, his teammate and immediate predecessor at quarterback, Tittle preferred to plant himself firmly, like an outfielder making a throw, and trust in his blockers to keep him safe. (Charley Conerly would run on occasion too, but his method was to scurry through the open center and keep going until he met opposition. Then he would turn his back and try to shove his way a few feet more like a man pushing his way into a subway car.)

Y. A. Tittle was perhaps not the strongest quarterback who ever threw, although he could unleash a long bomb, but he was one of the most accurate, when he was given the protection he needed. He was no fire-eater, although he took complete charge in the huddle, and he made no efforts to set records, or even leave tracks, along the East Side of New York, where many famous New York athletes loved to prowl. He earned all his newspaper publicity on the gridiron and away from there he could have blended without effort into a crowd of commuters on a station platform.

Some said of Y. A. Tittle that he became great only because he had several of the greatest pass-blockers in the business to keep the beasts off his neck—or off his tender knee, which eventually did suffer a severe injury. But that could be said of several others who faced Y. A. in playoff games—Bart Starr of Green Bay, who was to have his own turn as top quarterback in the nation, or Bill Wade of Chicago, who beat Y. A. in the 1963 playoffs. A quarterback could not thrive in the modern pass-from-the-pocket game without strong blockers to keep him safe. But he also needed a cool head, a fast hand, a quick eye, and a store of instinctive knowledge of defenses. He also needed enough self-confidence to impart to all his mates the feeling that he knew exactly what he

was doing. Quarterbacks like Starr, and Tittle, and Unitas, and Van Brocklin, never threw passes and hoped they would complete them. They *knew* they would complete them, and did not hesitate to toss them even in mortally dangerous moments. Bart Starr once confounded the enemy completely by throwing a pass for a touchdown when he was in his own end zone and everyone *knew* he would send a back into the line looking for a little more room to operate.

Sonny Jurgensen—Living the Good Life in Football

Smartest of all the pass-throwers, and a man who never was blessed with quite the consistent protection that helped make Unitas and Tittle and Starr into champions was a happy-go-lucky type called Sonny (for Christian) Jurgensen. Sonny was six feet tall and weighed 200 pounds when he was in top condition. But he was not, as he would always be the readiest to admit, always in top condition. Sonny, a red-headed, outgoing fellow whom no one could dislike, believed in enjoying his success and popularity while they were his to enjoy. Nor did he ever, in his early seasons, it must be granted, work for the sort of coach who would scare or inspire him into giving up his most darling indulgences. As a result he used to carry through the season a small pot belly that became a sort of trademark with him, and a signal that he was, even when his club was not winning championships, ingesting his share of the things that tasted good.

Sonny for a time understudied Norm Van Brocklin, former field leader of the Los Angeles Rams, who had been talked into completing his college work a semester ahead of time so the Rams could snatch him away before any other clubs could claim him. Van Brocklin came to Philadelphia in 1958, a year after Sonny Jurgensen joined the club, and took over at once as boss quarterback. The Dutchman was not the sort of fellow to hold up as an example to the young. He was a snarling Bobby Layne type who made his own rules and called his own plays—and took no guff from coach or teammate. He was also a man who had no fear of contact and who was very likely to call his own number when the ball was within diving distance of the enemy goal line. Whether Sonny needed any lessons from Van Brocklin in making his own arrangements is of no immediate interest. But by the time the big Dutchman resigned and went growling off to coach the Vikings, insisting that he had been done out of a chance to coach the Eagles, Sonny was a polished quarterback. A sharper passer even than Van Brocklin, just as cool and as much in command on the field, Sonny may have been even smarter in diagnosing defenses and outwitting the enemy. At least he was far more willing to take orders from the coach.

Coach Nick Skorich of Philadelphia gave Sonny some kookie formations to work with, including a line-up of three receivers in single file, which he called "the stacked deck." And Sonny was far more willing than Van Brocklin had been to let somebody else run with the ball. With Sonny in charge then the Eagles showed a balanced offense, and when they took to passing they had the best arm in the league to fire the ball for them. Sonny in 1961 set a new league record for completed passes (235) and for yards gained through the air (3723). He brought the Eagles to within half a

game of a divisional championship, and lost only through some uninspired officiating that kept coaches, officials, and players shouting dirty names at each other most of the game between New York and Philadelphia. Next year, Sonny needed an operation for a shoulder injury; then when play began he tore cartilage loose in his knee. But in the second game of the season, a loss to the Giants, Sonny threw fifty-seven passes and completed thirty-three—an exhibition that not a man in the stands could remember seeing the like of anywhere before. Injuries and all, Sonny managed again to lead the league in passing yardage. But the next year a chipped bone in the shoulder kept him off the field most of the season, and when the season was over he was shipped to Washington in exchange for a tall young quarterback named Norman Snead.

In Washington, for certain, Sonny found the fleshpots all abubbling, even though there were no championships in instant view. He liked his job there, and his mates, and his surroundings. And he began to put on the sort of weight men carry about when they think more of the candle than they do of the game. So when word arrived that Vince Lombardi, that granite-fisted disciplinarian, who had been known to sweat one or two veteran players to the point of quitting, was to take charge of the Washington club, Sonny began to think of other ways of making a living. Paul Hornung, who had had his own nighttime range cut down a little by the Great Man, reassured Sonny, however. "You'll *love* Lombardi!" said Paul. And whether Sonny loved the man or not, he did hitch up with him extraordinarily well—to the point where Sonny, believing in victory once more, actually peeled off pounds of joyously acquired flesh and bade good-bye to the little lump of laundry he had carried for several seasons just over his belt.

There were, of course, through the years when these men disported themselves on the professional football fields, a score or more of passers and runners who, on one special day, or through one or two brilliant seasons, could have been matched with any of the greatest ever memorialized. There was Mel Triplett of New York, the fullback with the chuggity-chug way of galloping into a line, determined to bust it open and come out on the other side. There was Bob Hoernschmeyer of the Detroit Lions, who once took the ball on a ninety-six-yard run from scrimmage, for a touchdown against the New York Yanks. There was Alan (the Horse) Ameche, of Baltimore, who charged across the line with the score that beat the Giants in the sudden-death play-off of 1958. There was fullback Rick Casares of the Chicago Bears, who could blast his way through an opening that seemed hardly big enough for his head. There was Jim Taylor of Green Bay, who had the most miraculous balance of any runner in the game, and who always gained most of the yards the Packers took away from their foes.

There was also "little" Dick Bass of Los Angeles (in a crowd of ordinary people he would look like "big" Dick Bass, for he was five feet ten and weighed two hundred pounds). Dick was called the human manhole cover because of the way he rolled downfield, knocking over anything that tried to halt his flight. Dick ran seventy-three yards from scrimmage one day and another time he carried a punt back ninety yards to a touchdown.

The Philadelphia Eagles, to go with their "maximum" quarterbacks, had some maximum runners too, including Timmy McDonald, who was cut off the Green Bay squad after one game, then came to Philadelphia to lead the club in rushing, in kick-off returns, and in punt returns. There was Tom the Bomb Tracy, a sort of throwback to the triple-threat days, in Pittsburgh. Tom in one game against the Redskins kicked three field goals and ran twenty-eight yards to a touchdown. The Cardinals owned John David Crow, who ran as if on roller skates, never seeming to lift his feet far from the ground, yet could almost never be put down by a single tackler. And the Redskins, after George Preston Marshall had been dragged into the twentieth century, presented Bobby Mitchell, former non-paleface teammate to Jimmy Brown, and Bobby ran wild on the field in Washington.

Givers and Receivers

WHEN the American Football League was born, in 1960, the few fans who were moved to watch its play found it lacking in much of the precision and excitement that the National Football League had taught them to look for in the professional game. It looked instead rather like college football in more formal dress. There were men running with the ball who had long before sunk out of sight in the National League. There were linemen who seemed too small or too slow to last past the first cut in the other league. And the games did not seem to be played with quite the dash the older league displayed.

Even when a few ball carriers and quarterbacks who were obviously still able to earn jobs in the "big" league were lured into the AFL, fans still missed the murderous whacking of leather on leather that marked a battle among equals. Speed the new league had. It even in some respects displayed more imagination. But the thunderous defensive play was missing.

Defense by this time had earned as much devotion from the pro football fancy as had passing and running. Millions of TV viewers had shared, through means of a tiny microphone worn in his helmet, the threats, the exhortations,

253

Sam Huff, formerly of the New York Giants, was reactivated when Vince Lombardi took over the Redskins. Here he makes ready to pounce upon quarterback John Brodie of the 49ers. Note ball being snapped into Brodie's hands by center.

Gino Marchetti, Baltimore's mighty defensive end, showing some of his years, after his return to the active list following his "retirement" in 1965. Coaches, teammates, and fans urged him to return to the football wars.

the shouted (and slightly censored) defiances of Robert Lee (Sam) Huff of the New York Giants, a middle linebacker of great ferocity. Sam is not really all *that* good, said fans from Detroit and Green Bay who worshiped their own warriors, Joe Schmidt and Ray Nitschke. But Sam was good enough to stop Jim Taylor and Jimmy Brown in their tracks from time to time. He seemed to specialize in a round-the-throat tackle that caused many a ball carrier to roar in anger as Sam seemed intent on finding the twist that would remove the

head from the neck. Yet Sam had not always been the fire-breathing dragon the seasons (and the press) helped make him. When he first came to the Giants he decided that he was not going to make the club and he took off, after some long discussion, for the airport. Had the plane been on time, Sam might never have played football again. Vince Lombardi, then an assistant coach with the Giants, thought he had already talked Sam into staying but Sam had gone to the airport to "say good-bye" to Don Chandler and had then begun to suspect he was right in his first decision. So he and Don were minded to disappear when Lombardi roared up in a station wagon and "ordered" both men to stay. They stayed for more than a dozen seasons.

Huff, with his television program "The Violent World of Sam Huff," may have helped a little to turn the linebackers and front four into heroes. But the mighty deeds of the men themselves had already taught spectators to distinguish among the masked and armored gladiators to pick out their favorite monster.

As Sam Huff had his private cheering section in New York, who would scream "Huff! Huff! Huff!" when the struggle grew bitter, Gino Marchetti, the great defensive end of Baltimore, had his own rooters, who loved to chant "Gino! Gino! Gino!" in much the same manner that Roman crowds in another day had shouted "Duce! Duce! Duce!" Gino became so inspired in a game against New York that he broke his own ankle in a ferocious surge that stopped Frank Gifford short of a first down.

On team after team, the names of the "front four"—those assigned the task of dismembering the quarterback or shoving the blockers down a ball carrier's throat—became as well known as the names of the men who made the scores. And each man began to win for himself a private gallery of devotees—not so numerous nor so vocal perhaps as those who undertook to beatify certain wing-footed ball carriers, but earnest and knowledgeable and plentiful enough to impress the paymaster.

Joe Schmidt of Detroit, who was destined to become a coach, was, as a linebacker, quick, crafty, and strong. It was his assignment to hurl himself into whatever breach the enemy managed to create in the Detroit forward wall, to prevent the completion of the quick pass over the middle and to protect the "hook" zones, where foreign pass receivers would run out and hook back toward the line of scrimmage, to receive a spot pass. Keeping these zones covered, when other receivers might be bent on luring him away from them, required the wide vision of a quarterback, a thorough knowledge of the enemy behavior, and an ability almost to read the mind of a quarterback through studying his eyes and his moves. There was hardly a linebacker alive who did this job better than Joe, because not many men in football combined Joe's mental and physical ability with his playing experience. Joe came from the University of Pittsburgh in 1953 and went to work full time almost immediately for the Detroit Lions. Within three years he had been named defensive captain—a job he took on with utmost seriousness, so that he found himself the chief morale builder of the club both on and off the field.

Undoubtedly much of Joe's ability to give some sort of emotional leadership to the club derived from his doing his

Gentle Joe Schmidt of Detroit could turn himself into a raging beast on defense, once the game began.

255

own job so miraculously well. There are few harder jobs on defense than middle linebacker, for he is a constant target on every sort of play. A big tight end may be sent blasting through with no other aim in mind than blotting the middle linebacker out of the play. Often two defensive men may be awarded the job of taking him out. And on pass plays, when he is looking for the receiver who will come flying past him to hook back and stand for a second or two in the open zone to get the short pass, there may be two such men at once, sent out to encircle the middle linebacker and befuddle him utterly.

But Joe was the very best at keeping his wits and his feet in all such circumstances and quickly smashing to earth any receiver who did manage to complete a pass in his territory.

Under Joe's leadership, the Detroit Lions became the fiercest defensive club in the league, whose fans came out to watch them roll the other team's attack back upon itself. Joe especially delighted the fans because he was so strong and so unpredictable on the blitz, the sudden shooting through the line to help the front four gang up on the attacking quarterback.

Joe loved to blitz. He did it fervently and often. Yet he did not do it always, and the quarterback often found himself spending precious energy and time studying out Joe's intentions, because you never *knew* when he might decide to abandon his position and bet everything on being able to nail the passer before he could let the ball go. Many quarterbacks found it best to figure that Joe was coming through *every* time. Even then there was no assurance that any man could escape Joe's charge, for he was agile as a terrier and could fake

a defender off balance or mix it with any of them.

Joe Schmidt was named All-Pro linebacker three years in a row. In 1956 he made twice as many tackles as any man in the squad. But it was not until 1957 that he was able to help bring Detroit a championship. That was the year Bobby Layne was laid up (Tobin Rote took over as quarterback) and Joe alone had to provide the rage and the fire that Bobby had always injected into the squad. But Joe's finest afternoon probably came on a Thanksgiving in Detroit in 1962, a year when the Lions missed the title.

Detroit Crushes an Invincible Green Bay (1962)

They still had a chance for it when Green Bay showed up in Detroit that gloomy, snowy morning. (The game began at noon, and because it had no competition on TV perhaps was watched by more fans than any other regular-season game.) Joe had his club so fired up that day that they seemed almost trembling with anger—anger because they had blown a previous game to this bunch and angry because they had to win this one or miss their chance completely. Almost from the moment Green Bay laid a hand on the football, Joe had his cohorts roaring in upon them. How many times Joe Schmidt called the blitz that day there is no recalling. But he made poor Bart Starr, the Green Bay quarterback, wish he had missed the plane.

Joe had a powerful and charged-up gang under his command, including 300-pound Roger Brown, who was so fast off the mark that, in the first twenty-five yards, he could outrun any halfback the club owned. Roger, with Joe cracking the verbal whip behind him, bore down again and again upon the passer, flinging blockers aside like empty milk bottles. And often he and Joe and one or two others all had to compete for a handhold on the hapless quarterback, who felt lucky when it was over to find all his limbs still attached to his frame. One time Joe Schmidt, his hands clutching hungrily, chased poor Starr in circles through the backfield and flung him to the turf fifteen yards behind the line of scrimmage.

The sudden-death game between Baltimore and New York in 1958 was called, as has been observed, the "greatest game ever played." But surely this fearsome exhibition of defensive determination, dash, power, and unity stirred the spectators as deeply and lasted as long in their memories. Green Bay had come to town as the club certain to win the title and this pre-turkey-dinner affair had been viewed by most out-of-town sportswriters as just a sort of warm-up for Vince Lombardi's invincibles.

So when the Lion defensive club grabbed the initiative and never let it go, the sight filled all local hearts with such glad surprise that the fans just could not stop yelling. Most had been willing beforehand to settle for two touchdowns against Green Bay. As it turned out, Joe Schmidt's gangsters did not allow the *Packers* to score that many. And the defensive unit itself scored eight of Detroit's twenty-three points—six on a touchdown by defensive end Sam Williams, who scooped up the football when the defensive charge knocked it loose from Bart Starr, and two more when Roger Brown pursued Bart Starr through the end zone and captured him there, to earn two points for a safety.

The defense also blocked a field goal attempt by Green Bay and just missed turning it into a Detroit touchdown. It was such a triumph for Joe and his unit that hardly anyone afterward could recall what the Detroit offense had done. It just seemed that Joe had led charge after charge into the backfield and come back each time with a handful of Green Bay scalps.

Playing alongside Joe Schmidt that day was another one of the best at the job of stopping the enemy and taking the ball away. That was Dick "Night-Train" Lane, at that time the next-best pass intercepter in the business. (Best was Em Tunnell of New York.) Lane, six

What Night-Train Lane did best. Having timed his arrival perfectly, Lane leaps to interrupt a catch by Green Bay's Ron Kramer.

feet two and 200 pounds, was rangy, alert, and so aggressive that he kept pass receivers off balance wondering what he was going to do to them next. This psychological advantage (usually it's the defensive man who worries about the receiver's intent) often enabled Night-Train to anticipate the receiver's move and beat him to the football.

Night-Train (he won his nickname in Los Angeles from his habit of climbing up every night, on schedule, to Coach Tom Fears' room to get extra help with the intricacies of playing offensive end) got his job just as Em Tunnell had, by walking into a football office and asking for it. Lane signed up in Los Angeles but did not assure himself of the job until he had switched to the defense, where he did not have to crack his head learning pass patterns. Lane also became a sort of specialist in blocking place kicks—a cooperative job that requires expert coordination and timing to keep one protector occupied while the kick-blocker shoots in from outside. But what he did most of was grab forward passes that were meant for someone else. In one season with Los Angeles (1952) Night-Train Lane intercepted fourteen.

Many a defensive man in this era possessed, as Night-Train Lane did, all the qualities a fellow needed to play on the offense—speed, alertness, aggressiveness, ability to change direction and shift gears in the space of a wink. But many also preferred the defensive work for it meant a constant seeking after contact, and did not lay the restrictions on use of hands and arms that kept an offensive man from punishing the opponent as he might have liked to.

Emlen Tunnell of the Giants might have received passes just as ably as he intercepted them and could have carried the ball with as much authority as 90 percent of the halfbacks and fullbacks in the league. Actually, in 1952, Emlen Tunnel gained 924 yards on the ground, which was thirty yards more than had been gained by big Deacon Dan Towler of the Los Angeles Rams, league-leading ball carrier on offense.

The Pacific Coast too bragged some particularly ferocious defensive players, who helped accentuate the wide difference between the play in the two leagues. Even when the American League had captured a few ball carriers who could run as fast as anyone in the game, and some pass receivers who could pluck footballs safely from the middle of a crowd, they had no one who could match men like Leo Nomellini, the toothless terror, a wrestler turned linebacker, who caused rookie fullbacks to quail when they tried to break the San Francisco line. Or like Bob St. Clair, Leo's teammate, called "The Geek" because he ate raw meat from simple preference. St. Clair, like Roger Brown, played defensive tackle and could sometimes outrun a ball carrier, despite his being six foot nine inches tall and weighing 265 pounds.

The AFL Begins to Gain on the NFL

In the beginning, the new league, even in the matter of offensive men—who would in theory be the names that brought the crowds to the park—had to be satisfied with the other league's leavings. More than one or two passers and ball carriers who just about earned bench-room in the other league leaped into first-string jobs with the AFL. The trouble was not so much that the AFL lacked the funds to tempt the college products to join them as that most lads who looked toward a career in pro football were doubtful that the AFL was going to last. The National Football League, even if it did not offer an immediate thick-steak salary, was still the Big League, where a man, if he had the ability, could build himself a fifteen-year career, with a pension at the end of it. So the AFL collected taxi-squadders, castoffs, malcontents who had jumped the older league to play in Canada, and kids who did not get tapped in the National League draft.

Sorriest entry of all in the American League was perhaps the New York franchise—calling itself the Titans, in hopes some fans might be fond enough (and literate enough) to confuse them with the Giants. Without a strong New York franchise, no professional league could prosper. And, with the New York club hitch-hiking along from game to game, never quite sure it could meet the payroll (one week, it actually faced a players' strike because the checks had not come through), operated by an eccentric fellow who was far more of a radio personality than a businessman or a promoter, and even "coached" in some degree by the owner's wife, who would sometimes insist that a particularly "cute" ball carrier be given more opportunity—with all that load of woe on the back of what should have been its most glamorous franchise it was no wonder the new league had difficulty drawing its breath.

The AFL did have a number of lively young men on its roster, and a share of able eccentrics, who could not only play big-league football but could get their names in the papers too for their antics in their off hours. Some men who had supposedly played out the full string

in the NFL found a whole new career waiting in the other league.

George Blanda, the tireless place-kicker who had played ten seasons in the National League as quarterback with Baltimore and Chicago, found a new and apparently permanent home in the American League. He joined the Houston club in the new league in 1960, moved to Oakland, and when last seen was still wearing that uniform, and seeming in no haste to shuck it.

Tobin Rote, who had been traded off by Green Bay to Detroit in 1957, after seven seasons, put in two seasons with Detroit, was counted washed up, then joined the San Diego Chargers in the new League and in 1963 led the league by completing 179 of 286 passes, despite a passing arm tortured by frayed ligaments and bursitis. But the success of these ancients was just accepted by most fans as an indication that the AFL was a minor league where fading players would coast gradually down hill.

Many players, however, found riches awaiting them in the AFL, for some of the best-heeled franchises offered glittering bonuses to NFL stars to come play where the living was easy. So little by little the younger league, by picking off a share of the best college players and coaxing a few stars away, began to creep close to the National League in talent.

The Coming of Joe Willie Namath

The leagues officially remained bitter enemies, even to the point of avoiding off-the-gridiron association at testimonial dinners. The AFL sued the NFL (and lost) in an effort to beat back the retaliatory measures the wealthier league was taking to shut the AFL out of some cities.

It was not until Sonny Werblin took over the New York Titans (in 1963), changed their name to the Jets (to rhyme with Mets, the darlings of the younger fans), that the AFL really began to assume equal footing. Sonny was a showman who knew that what the New York franchise needed was a spectacular publicity break to bring it even with the Giants in the minds of the fans. So in 1965 he offered Joe Willie Namath, a hedge-hoggy young man from Alabama who seemed able to throw passes in his sleep, the largest bonus ever mentioned aloud since the ransom of Troy. It was "estimated" at $400,000, and fans who would never live long enough to earn such a sum, thought of it as bundles of new-printed banknotes all neatly bound and stacked on Joe's Willie dining room table.

But the bonus was much of it on a contingent basis or in the form of future benefits that could not be accurately appraised. Still it was so fat a figure that no one reading it could doubt any longer that the American League had come to stay. The brass of the old league still kept whistling, although more than one or two of them began to detect arthritic pains in their bankrolls—not for what they had spent, but for what this "war" might be going to cost them. So they continued to pretend the other league was not there and that they operated the only game in town. The New York Giants would never report the doings of the club across the river. But the Jet management blithely posted the New York Giants' score, quarter by quarter, just as if they lived in the same world.

Joe Namath received an attentive but not always a friendly press, for veteran sportswriters were always turned off by

a rookie who showed no humility—a quality Joe apparently set little store by. It was hard to make Joe out a braggart and a phony for he was obviously neither. But some people, irritated by his high-cut white shoes and his blatant self-indulgence (a llama rug in his overdecorated apartment was deep enough to conceal a nest of rattlers) picked Joe out for special dislike and came to Shea Stadium to wish him the worst luck in the world.

Alas for them, Joe Willie actually was one of the best throwers of forward passes either league had seen, even though, until they gave him someone besides well-meaning country boys to keep the enemy off him, Joe had some exceedingly bad days. He had exceptionally sharp eyes, and learned rapidly to "read" the moves and give-away postures of the defenses. He also had what is known as an exceptionally quick release. That is, once he spotted a receiver, he could put the pass in the air quicker than a man could count. This rare skill did not spare him from much punishment, for driving defenders would pound him into the turf regardless of whether he had let go of the ball or still held it. But it enabled him to complete many a pass that an ordinary quarterback would not even have been able to attempt.

Joe ran with the ball fearlessly too and sometimes with startling effect, giving evidence of becoming, in fairly short order, a "maximum" quarterback. But he was not an impregnable quarterback and soon found himself—as had many other quarterbacks—suffering from too much walloping about the knees. There were days when Joe had great difficulty moving away from the pass rush and when he could not run the ball at all.

Of course Joe Namath alone did not lift the AFL from failure to success. Moving the New York franchise to Shea Stadium, where they shared the glamor of the Mets, helped recruit a new following. (The opening game at Shea set a new attendance record for the AFL—a record that was broken in the same park a few weeks later.) The signing of a television contract, guaranteeing to each club cash enough each season at least to meet the basic running expenses, helped steady the league's framework. There had been several franchise shifts already and not every club had Shea Stadium to play in.

The creation of a pension plan made an AFL contract look just about as attractive now to a college prospect as one from the older league. And the feeling that competition for jobs was less fearsome persuaded many young men who lacked All-America status to seek their fortunes in this new football world. Then along came Joe, and provided the new league with the atmosphere of big money, Broadway glamor, and headline publicity that had always belonged to the National League alone.

Joe was teamed up with a young man who offered an illustration of another of the advantages a player might find in the American League. He was Don Maynard, lean, long-legged pass catcher from Texas, who had tried in vain to impress the New York Giants with his skills as pass-receiver and ball-carrier. His stride was too long, said one Giant coach, he runs like a college boy. (Runners who run with long strides are far more susceptible to injury, from having their weight planted too long on one foot.) He hears footsteps, said another Giant coach, meaning that Don, while awaiting a pass, was too conscious of the approach of the thundering backs, bent on ringing his bell. Consequently he fumbled too often. But in the new league, where fast-moving young men were rather thinly planted, Don had a chance to acquire the seasoning he needed to get those footsteps out of his head, and to demonstrate that one of his loping strides was equal to three of the short choppy strides of a standard-type flanker—or wide receiver, as they came to be called. Don had time too to practice the head and body fakes that help a receiver deceive the defenders, and to learn how to make those fakes without breaking stride. After a few struggling seasons Don became, with the help of Joe Namath's bull's-eye passes, the leader in yards gained through catching forward passes, his total of better than 9,000 yards putting him first among active players in both leagues.

There were those who maintained, however, that the best receiver in either league was Lance Alworth of San Diego, a free soul who earned almost as much attention with his unusual wardrobe as Joe Namath did with the outlandish furnishings of his New York apartment. Lance was a fellow who never doubted his own ability to catch a pass at any point in the game and carry it for a touchdown. In every huddle, except when his club was about to kick an extra point (and sometimes, said Lance's admirers, even then) Lance would insist to the quarterback: "I've got the up! I've got the up!" meaning that he had learned how to break free from his defender on the "up" or "fly" pattern that was meant to carry the whole length of the field.

Very often, it must be granted, the young man who liked wide-brimmed hats and flaming slacks, was right about it. He did indeed have the "up" and could take the ball for a touchdown. In seven seasons he had scored seventy-three touchdowns, only five less than Don Maynard had scored in nine. And in nine straight games in 1963, lean Lance, who seemed too frail to be a football player, took at least one pass in for a touchdown.

Still, most observers were ready to grant that the American League had not yet spawned pass-catchers who belonged on the stage with National League heroes like Don Hutson, the storied Alabama Antelope; Pete Pihos

Elroy Hirsch, who succeeded his teammate Tom Fears as top pass catcher in the league, did not often get easy ones like this. He usually took them over his head, arms fully outstretched and legs churning.

of Philadelphia; Tom Fears of Los Angeles; Raymond Berry of Baltimore; Elroy Hirsch of Los Angeles; or Bill Howton of Green Bay. Pete Pihos, who in 1955 caught sixty-two passes for 864 yards and seven touchdowns, played for the Eagles until he began to look like somebody's father. (He had caught eleven touchdown passes in 1948.) Tom Fears joined the Rams in the days when they had begun to specialize in the long, long bomb, and he hired out for his speed and agility, as well as his skill at taking footballs on the run. Tom brought Los Angeles its first championship, in 1951, when he took a long pass from Norm Van Brocklin for a seventy-three-yard touchdown play. He still holds the record (eighteen) for pass receptions in a single game.

Fears and Hirsch (called "Crazylegs" by some misguided sportswriter) were both men who were practiced in taking the football when it was ostensibly out of their reach, on their very finger-tips while trolleying at top speed down the field. Hirsch's specialty was receiving the ball right over the top of his head, without even turning his body, just grabbing it at the end of his finger-nails, like a centerfielder taking a long fly.

Raymond Berry, a wizard at faking his way past defensive backs, was the man who helped John Unitas become a maximum quarterback. In the Colts' championship seasons of 1957 and 1958, Ray led the league in catching passes and no one has yet approached him in total pass receptions—631 in his career, for a thirteen-season total of 9,275 yards. (Bill Howton, in twelve seasons, caught 503 passes for 8,459 yards.)

But there were other pass-throwers in the new league who were the equal

Dandy Don Meredith, of the Dallas Cowboys, hands off to Don Perkins during the 1966 championship game with Green Bay. Perkins seems torn between accepting the ball and getting away from Green Bay defensive tackle Ron Kostelnik.

of Joe Namath on their best days— those days often coming when their blocking was at its best, so their receivers had time to throw that extra fake at the cornerback that would set them free. George Blanda, growing old in his job and still growing smarter, owned most of the "lifetime" records, just because his football lifetime had been longer than that of any other player alive. He no longer rated as a serious threat to run more than five steps with the ball, but he knew defenses as well as his coach did, and he had a mind of his own. He could also kick field goals with all his pristine power and accuracy.

In the eyes of Paul Brown, who returned to football as coach and part owner of the new "expansion" team when the American Football League granted a franchise to Cincinnati, the best quarterback in the league was Len Dawson of Kansas City, a very non-flamboyant sort who had been doing his work with quiet efficiency from season to season. But according to Daryle Lamonica, quarterback of the Buffalo Bills, who was to become a teammate of George Blanda, the best quarterback in the league was Daryle Lamonica. Daryle was not beating his chest as he gave out this word. He was trying to state the facts as he saw them. And he had the sort of confidence a quarterback has to have to stand up and throw passes despite failure after failure.

The development of stars like this and the appearance of runners like Cookie Gilchrist of Buffalo, an uninhibited young man who had been a hero in Canada, or Clem Daniels of Oakland, and Abner Haynes of Kansas City, still did not persuade the mass of football followers that the American League was the same as the National.

And when the two leagues finally made peace and met at last in the game every fan had talked of—the Super Bowl, the World Series of Football—the superiority of the National League seemed to have been established. For Vince Lombardi led his champion Green Bay Packers to Los Angeles, where they trimmed the American League champions, the Kansas City Chiefs, so handily that Lombardi never knew a single uneasy moment and left town with a comment typical of a man to whom losers were nobodies—that it would be years before the other league caught up to his.

But the "losers' league" persisted, even though now there were sophisticates among the commentators who evaluated every American League star and record as being but relatively good. Joe Willie Namath had replaced Paul Hornung as the acknowledged King of the Swingers in the public prints, but the details of American League football games were invariably accorded secondary status on the sports pages of the big city newspapers (except in towns where the AFL had no rival). And when the Green Bay Packers again won the Tiffany trophy in the Super Bowl hardly anyone looked surprised.

The Oakland Raiders, representing the American League, acted as if they had been terrorized by Vince Lombardi's growl. Even Rodger Bird, their matchless punt-returner (he led the league that season with 612 yards worth of runbacks) clearly heard enemy foot-

The Cowboys had their first league title *won* before this happened. The Cowboy Doomsday Defense had held the Packers scoreless all through the second half. Then, with sixteen seconds left in the 1967 league championship, Coach Lombardi asked for a "wedge" play with the fullback carrying. Bart Starr called the wedge, but kept the ball. Jerry Kramer on the ground in front with his mittens on, threw the mighty block that moved Jethro Pugh just enough to allow Bart to slip across the line.

steps as he stood waiting to catch a punt at midfield, two minutes before the end of the half. He signaled for a fair catch, then foozled the catch and saw it recovered by Green Bay. In the second half, just as it had in the first Super Bowl, Green Bay did all the scoring, and won again by a wide margin. Vince Lombardi was not at all surprised.

In 1968, Joe Willie Namath had developed into a sort of caricature of the Happy (and slightly hippy) Bachelor. His amatory triumphs were catalogued almost as faithfully, if not as minutely, as his victories on the football field—just as if every young unattached professional football player did not enjoy similar successes in that pursuit. (Said one colleague wryly: "Joe gets the publicity *and* the girls.")

Joe's hair curled up under his football helmet and made him look more than ever like a hulking hedgehog, or a beaver (he was raised in Beaver Falls, Pennsylvania). He grew a variety of whiskers on his face that resembled the adornment worn by movie star Warner Oland, when he played the part of Fu Manchu. Then he shaved the whiskers off on television in exchange for a fee of $10,000. All this added to his reputation as a somewhat effete character, and the press and part of the public refused to believe he was really anything more than a kind of stuntman on the football field.

Namath and the Jets Humble the Mighty Colts

So when Joe's Jets, after almost coming out on top two years in a row, finally won the American Football League Championship, they were given practically no chance against the champions of the National League—the unbeatable Baltimore Colts, led by a resurgent quarterback named Earl Morrall, who had risen from the depths of ignominy with the Giants to take the place of great Johnny Unitas in Baltimore.

The Colts were clearly the toughest defensive team in the National League and Morrall, with 182 completions out of 317 attempts, was easily the most effective passer. Joe Namath had not come close to Morrall in effectiveness. Nor had the Jets come up with any offensive operator with the speed, ferocity, and plain unstoppability of Baltimore's tight end, John Mackey, who with an average gain of better than fourteen yards on forty-five receptions stood top among the flankers and split ends in the league. (Don Maynard, a far more frequent target, had caught only twelve more passes in his league.)

In the league play-off against the Cleveland Browns the Colt defensive unit had exhibited such ferocity that watchers were agape. Again and again the Colts seemed to pick up the Cleveland offensive line and toss it back into its own backfield. Most who saw that game gave up all hope that any such

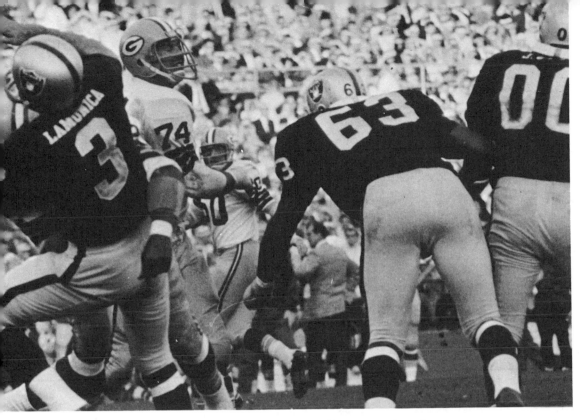

collection of gimpy-kneed minor leaguers as the Jets were supposed to be could even offer Baltimore as much of a contest as the Browns had. The men who decided on the betting odds on the game offered bettors on the Jets a seventeen-point handicap, meaning that if Baltimore failed to beat the Jets by *more* than seventeen points, then that was the same as Baltimore's losing the game.

There was just one authority who predicted with complete equanimity that the Jets would come out ahead in the score, regardless of handicap. ("I'll guarantee it!" he said.) This was Joe Namath himself, who seemed so relaxed about the prospect that ancestral voices of all sorts prophesied his doom. A man who dared brag that way would do no more than stir up the beast in the Baltimore breasts. And to give himself over to premature relaxation, as Joe seemed to be doing—that was merely consigning one's self to the pyre, where time had tossed the bones of all foolish young men who liked to light both ends of the candle at once.

But when Joe, in response to a routine question, calmly rated Earl Morrall a second-rate quarterback, below two or three of the American League passers, upright fathers hastened to stop their children's ears. It was an obscene violation of the sportsman's code to bad-mouth your opponent this way. No one but fighters who had risen unchurched out of the gutter had ever, in the history of professional contact sports, put down their prospective opponent so bluntly.

These tactless comments by Joe Willie actually seemed to increase the odds on Baltimore. It was clear to those who made a lifelong study of such matters that this sort of belittlement was exactly what the Colts needed to insure that they would be emotionally "up" for the game. But why should a professional football player about to risk teeth, ligaments, cartilage, and vertebrae in a struggle to see who would take home the $15,000-a-man first prize need an extra goad to start his ductless glands to flowing?

The fact does remain, however, that

the Colts were not "up" for the game at all. They had obviously been persuaded by Joe's crafty "psyching" to label the man "bush" and rate all his mates on the same level. They trotted on the field as if they had come to demonstrate football to the local junior high. In the early part of the game, when the Jet fullback, Matt Snell, began to burst through their line like Jimmy Brown, they would regroup with a sort of "let them have their fun" air. Even when mighty John Mackey failed to fling any linebackers around and again and again seemed to have his feet rooted in cement, the Baltimore troops showed no sense of urgency.

In the second period, Matt Snell crashed into the end zone with the football in his arms and fans at TV sets the country over goggled at each other. The Jets had scored first! And the mighty Baltimore quarterback-crushers—Bubba Smith, Billy Ray Smith, Ordell Braase,

and Fred Miller, the very men who had rocked the Cleveland forces back like duckpins—were simply not reaching Joe Namath. And Namath himself apparently had been reading the private correspondence of the Colt defensive unit, for he kept putting his receivers into empty spaces and anticipating the blitz almost unfailingly. As for Earl Morrall, he completed only six of his seventeen passes and blew one play badly when he had a receiver standing unattended and unobstructed near the goal line and instead slammed the ball into the teeth of the defense.

The first half ended with the Jets ahead 16 to 0. The Colt defense had been able to deny Matt Snell further entrance to the end zone. But Namath five times brought his mob near enough to try a field goal—and Jim Turner missed only two of them.

In the second half the Colts had obviously decided it was time to stop

Winning longhairs. Jet quarterback Joe Namath and receiver George Sauer savor satisfaction of upsetting the favored Baltimore Colts at the third Super Bowl.

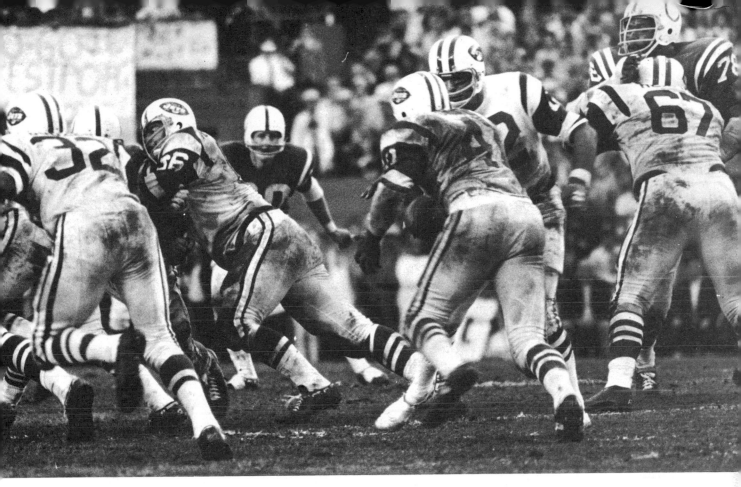

A good illustration of how the Jet offense pushed around the Colt defense at the 1969 Super Bowl. Here Namath is handing off to Matt Snell.

temporizing. They sent Johnny Unitas in to replace the man who had been *his* replacement and they fought with noticeably increased fervor. But by then the New York forces had begun to taste the corners of those $15,000 purses and they played with a desperation unmatched all season. They could not get close enough to score again but Joe Willie, with his quick jabbing passes, held possession of the ball long enough to leave the Colts with too few minutes.

Unitas finally fashioned one long drive, consuming a fat segment of time, that ended in a touchdown. But the New York defense, and particularly the defensive backs, who reacted to every Baltimore pass pattern with violent resentment, kept choking off each Baltimore advance at third down. The Colts, in the end, looked as if, with

half an afternoon more to play in, they might have pulled even. But they were granted only the usual space and that was just not long enough.

The Jets rejoiced over their victory in a manner so exuberant and even vulgar, crying and signaling that they were Number One, that some sourpuss might have grumpily told himself that they were "bush" indeed. But none of the Colts was saying that out loud. For the Baltimore club had been roundly outplayed, outguessed, outlucked, and outfought. The Jet defense had done what the mighty Baltimore defense had promised to do. And the Jet offensive line, which had been rated not even half so good as the one that worked for Cleveland, had moved those Baltimore monsters like empty crates.

It is true that the Colts suffered at

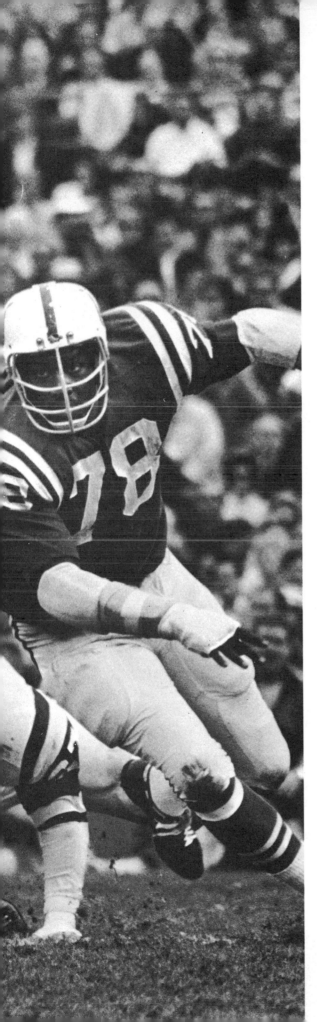

Bubba Smith (78) is about to dump Joe Namath at the 1969 Super Bowl as Namath's protector loses his footing.

least one fantastically cruel break. A "touchdown" pass bounced off the receiver's shoulder-guard to shoot backward like a rebounding tennis ball, and was handily plucked out of the air by a New York defender. But even if that pass had not been intercepted, and the next pass had scored, the Jets would still have led the way to the finish line.

This astounding upset was more than just a surprise victory. It altered the whole aspect of professional football. Now it was clear that the leagues were at last on a par. (Joe Willie Namath insisted that it would take time for the National League to catch up with his own.) Several American League club owners, who had paid staggering "admission fees" to be taken into the new combined organization, began to wonder if perhaps they should have made the National League pay *them*. Sports editors the following season offered equal treatment to the two leagues. And the TV take for the new league began to respond accordingly. Gate receipts in the AFL, however, did not rank with those in the older league, largely because there were many fields of limited capacity in the younger circuit.

The game in both leagues now looked much the same, with the same awesome whacking of leather as the ball was snapped, the same backfield formations, combining the advantages of the wingback and the T, and the same deployment of the defense. The game was the same because its teachers were the same, most of them men who had learned, in the older league, how to turn a gang of professional football players into a team.

271

What Should
I Do Now Coach?

ONE of the first things a player notices when he moves from college ball into pro football is the difference in the atmosphere of the locker room and the change in attitude of the coach. Professional football players may all have their ways of psyching themselves to attain the proper emotional pitch for a game but they scorn the sort of gang emotionalizing that sends college squads roaring in a body out of the clubhouse ready to even the score against the Yales. The cigarette smoker in a pro squad will stroll instead toward the ramp, sucking the last bit of sweetness out of the butt and hurling it away only when he is ready to trot out into view in company with all the others, calm as a cornet player in the band.

As for the pro coach, he would be deemed tottering on the brink of senility if he went in for the sort of phony self-dramatization that many college coaches are given to—the fist through the blackboard, the fake-spontaneous knocking over of a stack of equipment.

Yet there is no blinking the fact that the professional player, cool as he may be, and the professional coach, icy-miened and calculating as he may appear, still deal in emotion, and, as the most perceptive of them will readily

273

One of Vince Lombardi's favorite deals in training camp was riding the blocking machine.

admit, emotion of the "squarest" derivation. The most successful of the coaches are those who are able to instill this emotion most readily. And a few coaches attain success because the club has a player who himself is able to prompt it.

Yet successful coaches are of every temperament—moody and remote; grim and iron-willed; angry and vociferous; firm and self-effacing. Try to create a composite of the men who have made a habit of creating winning clubs and you will come up with a creature as incongruous as the animals in a children's do-it-yourself cardboard zoo. Yet essentially they all manage to sell their charges, by precept or by example, the same packet of emotions. Occasionally it may be the tight loyalty of any fighting unit in the face of a common enemy—the common enemy sometimes being the coach himself. But usually it is the hard-to-articulate conviction that the whole organization is a family unit. Hardly any man will say as much out loud, but what inspires a man to exceed himself on the field in the press of battle is this feeling that we are all in the struggle together and I must not be the one that betrays my brothers into the hands of the enemy.

While all coaches, or nearly all, will still lead their squads in some sort of prayer, hardly any (other than Tom Landry) managed it with quite the sincerity of Vince Lombardi who would openly urge upon all his charges loyalty to church as well as team and family. Nor does any big-time coach have the face to adjure his players that they "love each other," as Lombardi was wont to do. With his passing, some of the naivete and unabashed squareness may have left the locker-room for keeps, just as it has vanished from the culture of the young

who are engaged in more sophisticated pursuits.

Of course some of the Boy Scout atmosphere that has persisted in football locker rooms has always been mere facade, or a public relations device like the open-air religion of the Centre College football squad in the 1920's, the famous "praying Colonels," whose coach, tough Charlie Moran, was reputed to have growled at them one time in a hotel lobby: "Here come the sports writers! Down on your knees!" But most coaches are fairly solemn about the standard pre-game prayer (in which God's help is invoked to keep even the enemy from injury), even though an increasing percentage of the troops hardly bothers to do more than mumble the final Amen.

What Lombardi may have bequeathed to the game is more his devotion to "execution" than to the Victorian virtues. For Vince, even though he worked harder at keeping his practices secret than some coaches do, never bothered to go in for complicated deceptions or trick formations on the field of play. Tom Landry could have his sudden shifts and Hank Stram his power I. But Lombardi always felt that proper execution of all assignments could make a play work even if the opponents had a diagram of it in their hands. The togetherness he cultivated off the field he whipped into his blockers in practice, so their charge was as unified as the cavorting of a Busby Berkeley chorus line.

Other coaches may have worked even harder at promoting the "togetherness" off the field. Lombardi did sometimes, it was said, play favorites in the application of discipline, while other coaches have made absolute fairness a religion.

There Can Be No Favorites in the Pro Game

This element of "playing fair" apparently has much to do with the development of the group loyalty that is required. The one thing that almost all successful coaches do own in common is a refusal to play favorites. Some brilliant tacticians and traders, who will get by for a while on the ingenuity of their attacks and defenses and their ability to collect large helpings of talent, will fail in the end because they let themselves become "one of the boys." And once a man becomes "one of the boys" on a club he will have both friends and enemies. The players who disappoint him will become enemies. He will drop them from his list of intimates and ignore them at game time. Conversely, to hold on to his friends, he will have to put them in the line-up when there might well be, on any single Sunday, a better prepared or better conditioned or more talented hand on the sidelines. Under this sort of regimen, cliques are fashioned and the "family" is just a collection of strong, able young men intent on "doing their jobs."

This would be well enough if a football game were a set of eleven individual encounters, like so many prize fights. Then mere professional pride and hope of profit and preferment would suffice to keep a man trying his best. But a football game often requires sacrifice of individual glory, publicity, and personal accomplishment for the sake of the club. The man who is not ready to hurl his own body anonymously into the path of a tackler, or toss the ball off to a teammate when some crisis requires it, will not long hold a place on a winning football team. Football also requires a degree of unity of effort unknown in other team sports. When an offensive line charges it must do so, as Vince Lombardi would say when he was in charge, not in random order

like a bunch of typewriter keys, but "Together! Together! Together!"

Paul Brown, who has coached more championship football clubs than any man alive, has but one type of player he says he will not tolerate. That, he says, is a "selfish player." But, not being fanatic, he has been known even to keep a "selfish player" on his club (and work his tail off), if the man owns an extraordinary talent that can help win ball games. But generally he shuns such fellows, and he rates as selfish the man who forgets the team in his concern for himself — the man who gripes that he does not get the ball often enough, or gets it too often, the man who will not block to protect a teammate, the man who will not accommodate to a shift in position for the good of the team, the man who tries to treasure his own game wisdom, lest some rival beat him out of his job.

Paul himself offered the league an example of what he meant by being unselfish when he gave up his coaching job in 1976 to let his chief assistant, Bill Johnson, take over. Bill, who had been an assistant coach for twenty years in the National Football League, was ripe to be plucked away by another club to become head coach. No one ever loved the job of coaching more than Paul did. ("It saved my life," he once said, meaning that, after the loss of his wife, only the daily satisfactions of coaching football kept him from sinking into despair.) But Paul knew the Cincinnati club could not get along without Bill, so he took himself upstairs and off the sidelines for good.

The Paul Brown system, however, under which Bill Johnson was raised for some seven years, will probably endure, with no screaming from the sidelines, no wild scolding of erring ballplayers, no "slaughterizing" (Paul Brown's word) of the players in practice. Nor will any private

1. Coach Don Shula (left) of the Miami Dolphins, owner of the most aggressive chin in pro football, shares some gloom on the sidelines with his quarterback, Bob Griese (right).

2. Chuck Number Three — Knox of the Los Angeles Rams — like most professional coaches, takes a solemn view of the proceedings on the field.

3. Chuck Noll, Pittsburgh coach, one of three "Chucks" who were coaching pro football clubs in 1976, tries to influence the play from the sidelines, while wide receiver Lynn Swann makes ready to move in.

4. Unhappiest Coach of the Year was Tampa coach John McKay (left) whose Buccaneers made it through the season of 1976 without a victory.

5. Bud Grant, coach of the Minnesota Vikings, and Fran Tarkenton, his veteran quarterback, found no joy in the closing moments of Super Bowl XI.

6. Papa Bear Halas, in a prayerful attitude, seems to repress his disgust at what he has just beheld on the field.

7. Three Cheers for the Redskins! A typical scene in the Washington Redskin locker room as coach George Allen leads his club (or part of it) in anticipating victory.

8. Another head coach named Chuck, Chuck Fairbanks of the New England Patriots — intense, aggressive, and completely involved in the play — cheers on his club at Buffalo.

9. Winning coach Hank Stram exhibits his astonishment at an official decision during the 1970 Super Bowl, as an assistant endeavors to snatch him back before a penalty flag is thrown.

10. Football's worried man is Don Coryell of the St. Louis Cardinals. No man puts more heart and soul into the job than Don does. But, like Bud Grant, he is blessed with the ability to put football out of his mind when it is time to go fishing.

prejudice ever intrude itself on the handling of Cincinnati ballplayers, as long as Paul Brown's mild eye looks down from the General Manager's window. A ballplayer may be black or white, veteran or rookie, square or hippie, swinger or teetotaler; he will still be held to the same rules, judged by the same standards, penalized at the same rate for infractions, and rewarded the same for accomplishments.

The very archetype of the football coach was once thought to be Vince Lombardi, a fiercely egotistical man who was almost as successful as Paul Brown in devising ways to win football games and building clubs that could execute his schemes. Vince, who died of cancer at the very height of his career — after he had walked off his job in Green Bay to try to repeat in Washington his miracle of turning a confirmed loser into a winner — relished the role of petty tyrant and Sport's Angry Man. (Some observers insisted that his fits of rage and his howls of indignation were usually staged only when sports writers were on hand to celebrate them.) A stranger stopping to observe a Lombardi practice would ask himself how in hell these hulking men in football armor could retain any pride at all after the kindergarten scolding the coach would pour on their heads.

"Look at that ball!" Lombardi would scream, his fists half-raised, tight-clenched and trembling. "Look — at — that — BALL! Where the hell were *you* looking!?"

Or he might yell to a struggling quarterback, loudly enough for people across the field to hear:

"You throw like a girl! Exactly like a damn GIRL! If you don't stop aiming that ball and start *throwing* it, you won't be here much longer!"

Or to a towering lineman who failed to make contact on a block, he would bellow:

"What a fine performance! Right into the ground! What a hell of a fine spectacle! Get out of here! Take a lap! And RUN!"

Some players, when Lombardi first took over at Green Bay, did walk right off the practice field never to return after a dose of the Lombardi hiding. But most of Lombardi's players accepted this abuse as hulking boys would bow under a deserved scolding from a diminutive parent. For most of the players did respect Lombardi as properly raised young ones respected their parents. They knew he played no favorites, that he would order a seven-year veteran to "Take a lap!" as quickly as he would heap scorn on the head of a frightened free agent. "He treated us all alike," said one Green Bay graduate, "like dogs."

There were many players who truly loved Lombardi, however, and a few who obeyed his commandments almost worshipfully; his knowledge of the game and his coaching skills could not be denied, and he led a good many half-worn out ballplayers right into the Promised Land of glittering purses and six-figure salaries.

Different from Lombardi in nearly every way — except for his fanatic devotion to victory — is George Allen, who took over the Redskins after Lombardi's death. George Allen never screamed at anyone in his life, or if he did none of his public was on hand to hear it. George's way of "motivating" players is to sit face to face with them and paint pictures of the glorious future that stares them in the face — if only they can develop the hunger for it. He will seize a man unexpectedly by the elbow and ask him in a private tone: "Are you hungry?" Once he bragged that a new player he had just traded for, and whom he had subjected to his "motivation" treatment had called him at home ("I don't know how he got my private number!") to say:

"Coach, I'm hungry!"

On the practice field it would be difficult to sort George from his assistants. Usually they do the yelling and he just stands quietly, timing the "hang" of a punt with his stopwatch, or appraising the success of some defensive maneuver. Even at a game, sideline visitors occasionally ask "Which one is the coach?" for Allen neither struts like Vince Lombardi, nor rages along the sideline like George Halas and Curly Lambeau. Instead, he comports himself like a cheerleader, rushing to greet the returning heroes, slapping fannies, offering handshakes, and comforting the wayward. Occasionally in the locker room or on the practice field when the whole squad has gathered, he will cry out: "Three cheers for the Redskins!" and most of his weary warriors will dutifully give tongue.

Allen looks less like a football coach than nearly any one of his colleagues. He could pass for the ambitious assistant manager of a thriving department store. He does not dress in the small-town "men's store" style of Tom Landry, nor with the supertailored and impeccably "in" look of Hank Stram. At a game he is usually dressed neatly and expensively, with just a hint of disarray — perhaps a drifting necktie. At a summer practice session, he may look as if he just got out of bed. His lack of affectation, is deceptive, however, for George is a complex man, with a raging ambition that will probably never be sated. Despite his occasionally tousled appearance and apparent disregard for the way he looks, George does indeed care about his public image. Some days he portrays himself as an abstemious man who never touches more than "a little blackberry brandy." But anyone who sits with him in the evening may discover that the "blackberry brandy" looks remarkably like good Scotch and soda. His career has shown a steady and determined rise from fairly stringent times, when a $12,000 house seemed more than he could afford and when he rode a bicycle to his job at a small freshwater college (and dreamed of some day coaching at Harvard), to his current state of chauffeured and swimming-pooled elegance, with an expense account that has no describable limit. Along the way, Allen has left some disgruntled, even angry employers, including George Halas, who took Allen to court and won for walking out of a contract, and the late owner of the Los Angeles Rams, whom George privately accused of wanting the team to get beaten, so George might be diminished thereby. But George's clubs are not too often beaten. Indeed in 1977 he was still the only pro coach who had never posted a losing season. And he likes to mention the fact that wherever he has been head coach in the pros (Los Angeles and Washington) his club has *always* won its opening game.

Despite the mildness of his manner, George Allen is perhaps the most devotedly "physical" of all the pro coaches. While every coach urges his charges to violence, George has been accused of urging them a few steps beyond. As long as it was legal (and, according to a few of his rivals, even after it wasn't) George's troops specialized in the crackback block, a form of clipping on the scrimmage line that can render a linebacker's knee ligaments to Jello. He has also been charged with inventing what some opponents have named the "Redskin tackle" — a grab and hold from the rear to keep the ball-carrier on his feet (and so not immediately "down" and not eligible yet for a play-killing whistle) while a second "tackler" approaches from the front and applies the heels of both hands with sudden extreme prejudice to the underportion of the ballcarrier's chin, hoping thus to stun him and cause him to loosen his grip on the ball.

But whether that was George's invention or just the inspiration in the dark soul of one of his "physical" defense men no one dares say. All George will admit is that his club's great good fortune in forcing "turnovers" on the field of play is not all good luck. "We have drills for that!" he avers. It is true that George has been occasionally heard to "predict" that an quarterback might get hurt in an upcoming game with his Redskins.

George's true peculiarity has been his scorn for the draft and his conviction that experience is more worth than Norman blood, a bright college record, and panting desire. "A rookie," George says, "can hurt you fifty ways." And while he names "speed and size" as the qualities he most seeks in a ballplayer, he has filled his roster of other coaches' cast-offs with veterans he has lured away from Los Angeles and with venerable free agents whose salary demands have caused other owners to rebel. He has also, almost as a matter of pride, recruited a few of the game's noted misfits and set out with money and tender treatment, to motivate them back to stardom. The Redskins, confessing no other parent than a charitable trust set up under the will of the late George Preston Marshall, were under no compulsion to show a profit and could let the players have *all* the money left over from the operating costs, if George should so will it.

"George Allen *bribes* his players!" some jealous rivals have complained. But bribery in the form of increased salaries and well-earned bonuses are deemed immoral only in the upstairs offices of a few of the old-style owners. George for his part makes no secret of his scorn for a penny-wise policy that pits the interest of the owner against the good of the game. He has long favored, as most other coaches have, the creation of a permanent staff of full-time officials, who would be trained and not need to hasten back to a full-time job after picking up their yellow flags. "We spend millions for lawyers," says George, "and still can't afford full-time officials."

George was accused by his former boss, George Halas, of "deceit and chicanery" after George deserted his post as Halas' defensive coach in Chicago to take the top job in Los Angeles. Deceit and chicanery, of course, have long been important attributes of football, since long before the days when Pop Warner had fake footballs sewn on every jersey, so the defense could not immediately sort the ball-carrier out from the pack. But Halas was not referring to mere deception on the playing field. He meant that George was out to seize any advantage over an adversary, or all his adversaries, at any time of day, without too much regard for what the rules required.

Once, after game films had revealed that the center on the current opponent habitually lifted the football off the turf while positioning it to get a proper grip, George asked the referee in advance of the game if his defensive linemen would be allowed, when the center made this move, to slap the ball free and capture it. Absolutely not, said the official. If you do it will cost you.

So did George abandon this maneuver? Of course not. At the first opportunity, a Redskin defensive lineman slapped the ball loose from the enemy center's hands and fell upon it, claiming it for his own. Other officials promptly signaled that the ball now belonged to the Redskins. The referee, who may have harbored his own suspicions of George Allen, had watched the whole performance and promptly threw a flag, penalized the Redskins for encroachment, and gave the ball back to the foe.

Rivals have accused George of trading off draft choices he *knew* he did not own (he was disciplined for this once by the league and insisted he had committed the sin through inadvertence). Players have complained that they have yielded to some blandishment by George only to discover that the reward he had promised them had been promised to one or two others as well and someone else had got it first. But, as a former Redskin employe declared: "Right and wrong are for other people. George Allen just cares about winning."

Some players have shown a willingness to return to the game, despite advancing years and business obligations, just to repay George for some earlier show of loyalty and generosity. Most of his players are sufficiently impressed by George's own willingness to empty his own veins to bring victory to the ball club that they often play in higher gear than outside observers had thought them capable of. How could a player bear to see George so obviously cultivating a set of ulcers, with his limitless hours (he gets to his desk about eight in the morning and is often there past midnight), his endless fretting over detail, his continual shopping about the league (by telephone) to add strength to his roster, and not feel himself prodded to make a double effort on his own?

While Lombardi is the man accused of having coined the adolescent-type slogan: "Winning is the only thing!" George Allen is perhaps the one coach who so consistently divides the world into "winners" and "losers" that some folk occasionally question his sanity. He may even take a dislike to a training ground because "its trees seem like losers," or he may sententiously compare winning a football game to bringing a new life into the world. But one suspects that George, for all his apparent simplicity, is almost always on stage, "building the image" or at the very least conducting a private PR campaign that will substantiate and enhance the George Allen legend.

Allen was one of the first coaches to focus coaching efforts on the specialty teams — the suicide squads of kick-off and kick-return yeomen that were sometimes just places to put strong and willing guys who were not quite smart enough to learn offense and defense. On George's clubs there are men who devotedly practice ways of blocking kicks and shaking opponents loose from the football. While George never has been the big winner that he has claimed to be, and has often failed in rehabilitating the cast-offs of other clubs, his teams do recover an inordinate number of fumbles and win close games now and then by blocking a crucial kick. They are *always* in contention and always draw top audiences on TV.

A more successful coach than Allen, as far as winning championships is concerned, and one even farther removed from the Lombardi model, is Tom Landry, the only coach the Dallas Cowboys have ever had. Unlike Allen, Tom seems to give little thought to his public image. For years, observers used to make fun of Tom's "thirty-five dollar raincoat" and the felt hat that had gone out of style about when the boys came home from the Korean war. Nowadays Tom is a bit more with it when it comes to the gear he sports on the sideline, even though his glossy new coat may look like something his wife picked out. Tom has never been seen acting the part of cheerleader on the sidelines, George Allen-style. When his club achieves a score or intercepts a pass or accomplishes some other victory on the field, Tom usually expresses his approval by chastely beating his palms together just under his chin, like a preacher awarding the attendance prize at Sunday school. Indeed, Tom is about as close to being a preacher as a layman can expect — a "born-again" Christian who gives a considerable portion of his time to proselytizing for his faith.

But above all Tom Landry is a thinker, possibly the deepest and the most painstaking, as well as the most systematized planner in the league. The ingenuity of his offenses and the methods he uses to instill "responsibility" rather than mere "reaction" into his defense have earned the respect of most of his rivals. While George Allen teaches his defense to "play for the pass and react to the run," Tom believes a defensive man should stand guard over his assigned area, no matter which direction the immediate flow of the play may take. It requires much patience and long practice to keep a charged-up lineman from hastening to the spot where the action seems to be headed. But Tom is convinced his method is the only answer to the run-to-daylight design of Lombardi-style offenses. Tom's defense leaves no daylight anywhere, unless the offensive linemen are tough enough to make some. And Tom has the patience (it sometimes takes three seasons) to raise up guards and tackles who will hold the fort no matter how strong the temptation to hurry down to the plain and join the free-for-all.

Landry runs a well-organized but disciplined and relatively quiet practice, with men moving swiftly from one drill to another and none idling on the sidelines or strolling to the next assignment. Discipline is tight and workouts demanding. (When his sweating crew, agonizing in a bright California sun, begged that they might be allowed to do the final wind-sprints without helmets, Tom called out in clear and measured tones: "Do they let you take your helmets off in the last two minutes of a ball-game?")

Perhaps because of Tom's commitment to religion, he seems the most tolerant of all his colleagues. A football coach is, after all, usually the master pattern of the Square and a Defender of the Establishment. George Allen paid homage to Nixon's "persistence and determination." Paul Brown expressed open scorn of "hippies and long-haired kooks." But Tom Landry will say of youthful dropouts only that "they are pointing out to us the ills of our society."

Although Tom Landry may no longer be the worst dressed of all professional coaches (John Madden stalks the sidelines looking like a Little League parent in his working clothes and Don Coryell of St. Louis pleads guilty to owning "only two suits and a wild-looking tuxedo someone gave me"), there is not much question about who is the best-dressed. That is, and probably always will be, Hank Stram, formerly of Kansas City and now of the New Orleans Saints. Hank's father was a tailor who instilled in young Hank a love of handsome clothes. The red vest Hank Stram wears on the sidelines during games is famous throughout the land — or that part of it that watches Sunday afternoon and Monday night televised games. But even on the field in summer practice, Hank looks as if he had been lifted, all shaven, shorn, brushed, creased and pipe-clayed, by gloved hands out of a store window. He once was accused of carrying four suitcases to New York for a two-day stay.

But Hank is no dilettante in football. He is an innovator of unusual originality who is often two jumps ahead of the pack, and he is a shrewd appraiser of talent. His "power I" offense, with a variation he called the "cock-I" that put the tight end in the backfield, helped him win Super Bowl IV, played in New Orleans on January 11, 1970. Soon thereafter, when the game's wiseacres were still warning that "quarterbacks should run only in self defense," and when Bert Jones and Steve Grogan were just names for somebody's children, Hank predicted that quarterbacks were going to have to move to outdo the new defenses. (In 1976, buried in New Orleans with a club that was never in contention, Hank predicted that quarterbacks would have to rejoin the offense in carrying the ball consistently on plays designed to turn them loose.) Hank always seems to have some new offensive formation hidden under his sleek brown hair (he seldom wears a hat) and once surprised the opposition by going back to the "old-fashioned" T formation, familiar to grandpa in the 1920's. Like George Allen and Tom Landry, Hank Stram works with relative quiet at practice. He too avoids "slaughterizing" his charges in practice scrimmages and usually confines his exhortations to a somewhat plaintive "What's the matter?" or "Don't you want to win?" He has been known to fret unduly over whether his players like him or not, but when it comes time to yell at the team a little he takes them off to a corner and yells

Quite the opposite in manner and appearance from Hank Stram is one cock-of-the-walk who looked, in the mid-1970's, as if he might keep on winning football games until the Tiffany silver football (now called the Lombardi trophy) was worn down to a banana. That is Don Shula of the Miami Dolphins, originally a collection of left-overs and untried draftees such as George Allen would have traded six-for-one. An eternally aggressive man to whom not even a touchdown play ever seems to give full satisfaction, Don managed to imbue his club with his own aggressiveness, so that they took the field ready to clobber even the clubs that were supposed to push them over. George Allen believes that he gets his club "up" by the slogans he tacks up in the locker room, such as "This is a playoff game!" when it is simply the season opener. Shula is a bit too sophisticated to imagine he can stir the blood of a veteran

Most of the penalties in the 1976 playoff between Oakland and New England were called against Oakland. Here coach John Madden seems about ready to bite a chunk out of an official.

pro by any such adolescent appeals as that. But he does manage to transfer to his charges a good dose of his own seething aggressiveness before every game, "critical" or not. In that way he once won every game in one season, plus all the playoffs and the Super Bowl, a record that may live as long as the Republic stands — seventeen consecutive victories. Indeed Don Shula's Miami Dolphins might have continued forever to win playoffs and Super Bowls had not a gathering of wealthy men with stars in their eyes put together a new professional football league — the World Football League — and by waving three million dollars at them, lured away the very heart of Shula's club: Csonka and Kiick, his intrepid ball-carriers, and Paul Warfield, his magical pass receiver (11 touchdown receptions in one season) leaving Miami, or at least Don Shula, desolate. The World Football League managed no more than half a dozen deep breaths before it expired from starvation. But Csohka and Kiick and Warfield hung on to their six-figure bonuses and when they returned to the fold they made separate deals with clubs in differing climes.

Don Shula however did not pine away. Taking what fate and the college draft had left him, he plugged up the holes the World Football League had shot in his line-up and kept his Dolphins in contention. In 1974, without their wayward stars, Shula's Dolphins still came within two points of winning their fourth straight divisional championship.

It was not that Shula owned any hypnotic powers (although he did, in 1976, talk linebacker Nick Buoniconti into giving up his law practice and returning to thrust his 35-year-old carcass into the breach) nor was he possessed of any more than normal acuity at recruiting. When he came down from Baltimore, trailing a lot of hard

feelings on the part of the Baltimore ownership, Shula found his champions-to-be almost all in the corral. Buoniconti was there, deemed a little too small to be an all-pro linebacker. Csonka and Kiick had not yet earned their Butch Cassidy and the Sundance Kid nicknames but they were ready to go. So was Bob Griese, just a run-of-the-mill quarterback in that day. As for Paul Warfield, he was immediately captured by Joe Thomas, the general manager, who had already put one championship club together in Minnesota and would soon move on to Baltimore to build another.

What Shula did was what Lombardi was noted for — driving his men until they were ready to drop, then rewarding them with victories. Like Lombardi, Shula, who wears the most prominent chin in football, was stingy with praise and lavish with sarcasm, usually delivered in a bellow. Some observers did say that Don was determined to make up for his holding too loose a rein on his Baltimore Colts when he brought them to Miami in 1969 to knock over the upstart Jets in Super Bowl III, only to see his darlings everlastingly humiliated at Joe Namath's hands. Don, that time, had allowed his club to make a holiday of their Miami trip, to bring wives and little ones along — or to find agreeable substitutes and to savor the sun and the neon for which the resort was famous.

Never again, Don must have promised himself. The following '70 season when he was head man at Miami and the players had all stayed away from training camp until the first exhibition game was just a few days off, Don Shula set them all to practicing, not twice a day, but *four times!* A fast workout at seven in the morning, when most of the men still had sleep in their eyes. A drill at ten o'clock, when breakfast had hardly time to settle. Another practice at three in the afternoon, when the summer sun was at its most brutal. And a final workout at seven P.M., when the fun was supposed to begin. Two workouts a day, to a pro football player, was often a living hell in summer. But four! It nearly drove the men to mutiny. But then they started to win game after game, to *feel* like champions, and to rejoice in their might.

Don himself is not much given to rejoicing. Even when his club beat Baltimore in 1971, on their way to the Super Bowl, and the players awarded the game ball to Shula, he turned it down. "I want the Super Bowl ball," he told them. He did not get it that time but he did the very next try, and for the two Super Bowls after that.

Even after the sweetest victories, it is doubtful that Don ever led his hearties in delivering "Three cheers for the Dolphins!" Don usually greets a touchdown, not with shouts and waving of the arms but with a sort of "That's more like it!" or "It's about time!" expression. Not that he holds his tongue or even his temper on the sideline. But he is more likely to be heard above the tumult when he stamps up to the edge of the playing field to explain to an official in a well-modulated roar: "That was the most unbelievable goddam call!"

Another coach who "turned a team around" in the manner of Lombardi and Shula, but without quite so much scolding and bombast, was gentle Don Coryell of the St. Louis Cardinals, one of the former college coaches who began to move into the National League in the 1970's. Don did not strut, nor jut out his chin, shout abuse at officials, nor sweat his employes through four daily sessions of practice. But he *did* yell at them when he thought they needed it. "I respect my players," Don says. "But I don't always treat them with respect."

Above all, Don Coryell seeks ballplayers who want to play ball. Men who are bored with the whole scene, who count on great natural gifts to compensate for a lack of enthusiasm, who must be goaded and scolded and penalized into putting out at practice and in games are not welcome in Don's backyard.

"If I have to keep kicking a guy in the tail to make him play football," Don vows, "I won't have him on the squad. I'll take a man with less ability who really wants to play." Maybe, he allows, such a system will mean fewer unbeaten seasons, fewer victories, even a little less money in the till. "But I'll live longer," says Don.

Like other coaches who came out of the colleges straight into a top job with the pros without apprenticeship, Don is appalled at needless violence. Violence in the course of play — "legitimate violence" — causes him to rejoice. But deliberate attempts to cripple a quarterback or calculated blows to the head that are meant to intimidate or incapacitate some player far removed from the play, stunts such as the "Redskin tackle" that are intended to stun a ball-carrier rather than bring him to the ground — these cause Don's anger to smoke. The only proper cure for players who perform such misdeeds, in Don Coryell's opinion, is immediate suspension without pay.

In this, Don has the solemn concurrence of Chuck Fairbanks, rugged coach of the New England Patriots, who also lacks pro background. Chuck too likes his club to play rough, to hit hard, to run hard, and to tackle hard. He wants tough competitors on his squad, men who are determined to win, as he is. But winning does not count, in Chuck's record book, if it is not done within the rules. Acknowledging that the real source of much of this unwarranted violence is the men who direct the football teams, Chuck feels that frequent sidelining of a coach's pet rowdies will soon awaken him to the fact that he is trying to play with only part of his squad. And *that*, says Chuck, will put an end to the practice.

It took Chuck Fairbanks a little longer to turn his club around than it took some of the others. But when he finally found the line-up that suited him, featuring a new quarterback who had not been rated the equal of departing Jim Plunkett, Chuck and his boys began to win everything in sight.

Chuck has a philosophy of coaching that is distinctively his own: he is always geared for the run, offensively and defensively. Even when he faces a club that passes seventy-five percent of the time, Chuck's defense concerns itself first with eliminating that twenty-five percent devoted to the running game. With the other guys stalled on the ground, Chuck figures he can then begin to adjust and vary his pass coverage and pass rush to give the enemy troops far more than they can handle.

Offensively, the Patriots are a running team first of all. With quarterback Steve Grogan, who is a swift and aggressive ball-carrier, they can afford to add plays to their plan in which the quarterback carries the ball by design, and not from desperation. Chuck Fairbanks does not subscribe to the theory that letting the quarterback run with the ball is a form of suicide. He believes, as some others do, that a quarterback set to pass is every bit as vulnerable as a quarterback who is carrying the ball. He may even be more vulnerable, for a ball-carrier is aware of where the assault is coming from and is ready for it. A passer may often suffer a blindside blow that comes without warning. It is a fact, when you come to think of it, that the most notorious "scrambler" in the game, Fran Tarkenton, is also the quarterback who has never been totaled by an injury.

So all of Chuck's backfield men may run with the ball and run as long as the bad guys let them. Then, when the enemy has been shaken by the run, the airstrikes come with double the effectiveness. Grogan, fortunately, besides being as elusive as a wild pig when he is carrying the ball, can set up quickly, pass a long, long way, hit a bird in flight with a football (and hit him in either eye), and read defenses in his sleep. So Chuck's offense is planned, as is that of any able coach, to make best use of the personnel that the gods, or the College Draft, have granted him. Chuck is a great man for selecting his warriors, not entirely by what great deeds they are capable of, but for how they will fit in with the rest of his forces. He will not scorn a man of great talent just because his motivation may be lacking. Somewhere in the lineup Chuck will plan to have a man who is strong on motivating all his mates — and that may be just the man to goose the potential superstar into greatness.

While his assistants may be touting this college player or that for his speed, productivity, his intelligence, his strength, and his glittering statistics, Chuck Fairbanks, who will cast the deciding vote in every case, will be asking himself how the guy is going to fit into the general architecture. Will he be one too many great-motivation moderate-talent foot soldiers? Will he be too possessed of his own greatness to put team victory ahead of his own headlines? Will he carry a loser's attitude into the locker room?

For that matter, Chuck will concern himself not merely with the atmosphere of the locker room but with the tone of the whole operation. Everybody, from ticket-seller to trainer, if he wants to hold a job with the Patriots, must carry a positive attitude to work, so that the whole plant, off-season or on-season, will exude the heady fragrance of Championship.

The champions in 1977, however, were the club that, according to everybody in

New England, "stole" the title from the Patriots in a game that was not settled until the final gun had already been cocked. The coach of that club, the Oakland Raiders, was John Madden, surely the most excitable and demonstrative and most down-to-earth coach since the days of Curly Lambeau. Madden had worked long in the shadow of his boss, Al Davis, who has been credited with being the "real" coach of this gang of highly motivated blackhats, many previously owned, some cast off, some superannuated, but all thoroughly revivified and all bent on thwarting the jinx that had dogged them season after season. But anyone who wore the Oakland colors knew that as smart a strategist and appraiser of talent as Davis was, it was big John himself, overweight, disheveled, plain-spoken, crafty and tough, who really kept his charges juiced up close to the point of explosion, who sustained them in defeat, defended them from contrary officials, cooked up their strategy, goaded them over the goal line, and rejoiced with them in victory.

Like Lambeau, and like George Halas, John Madden made a spectacle of himself on the sidelines and occasionally even dared step over the sidelines to offer some constructive criticism to the referee. John gave no thought to his "public image." What you saw was John himself. And John apparently gave no thought to whether or not he was arrayed in his Sunday best when the TV camera's red eye was upon him. In his beltless slacks and dark blue shirt, he looked far less like a tailor's model than he did like a beer-drinking Little League parent striving, until his veins stood out, to urge his only son into transports of accomplishment. As a matter of fact, Billy Carter, the President's brother, who had bet a small bundle on the Vikings in the 1977 Super Bowl, bade his bet good-bye when

he got a look at John Madden and learned that John, like Billy, was a man who took beer with a beer chaser.

The other coach in Super Bowl XI was John's exact opposite — Bud Grant, a man who was reputed never to smile, just because he had never been caught at it by a sideline photographer. Called a stoneface, and a man without emotions, Bud Grant was no such thing. Indeed, his supposedly expressionless face often bore the faintest foreshadowings of a smile, a sort of Mona Lisa expression, as if Bud was savoring a private joke, and in private life he loves jokes. What Bud never did much of was build an image for himself, court publicity, or win extra ink for his sideline or off-the-field antics. Fans may have been turned off by his calm acceptance of defeat — as calm as his reaction to victory. Once he was even heard to utter the ultimate heresy — that it wasn't so bad to come in second. When he lost a divisional championship because an enemy player gave Bud's man an illegal, but undetected, nudge that enabled the enemy to complete the pass that won the championship, Bud did not run raging onto the field. Possibly he recalled a divisional title he took from Los Angeles in 1969 when an official miscalled an out-of-bounds pass. Or perhaps he had just made up his mind never to wince or cry aloud in public.

Bud admires a man who will not give the enemy the satisfaction of seeing him admit to pain or despair. If he has any act at all it is his affected detachment, as if he left his job in the locker room whenever he went home. (He won't "talk about football" when he is on vacation.) But no man who was deliberately working with a short shovel could ever get the results Bud Grant does. His teams are always hard hitting, well-drilled and intensely motivated. His apparent satisfaction with second place is not satisfaction at all. He is just too weathered by experience in professional sports — playing professional basketball, baseball and football, and coaching in the Canadian League — to dissolve into panic when he misses a championship — even the third or fourth time in a row. When a more "public" man might set out to shake up his roster, seek some spectacular trade, or otherwise flagellate himself where everybody could watch, Bud just returns to the shop and starts putting the pieces back together.

The fact that Bud's teams have come to the Super Bowl four times — more often than any other club in the league — and lost every time has earned him the label of "loser." But no loser ever got his club into the Super Bowl even once. It may well be that a club that gets there, with almost the same line-up, too many times too soon loses an edge to the club that is still on fire from the thrill of getting there at all. (One aging Viking veteran was heard to mutter that, while the first two trips to the fabled Championship game were exciting enough, the name for a third trip was "boredom."

Still, had some more flamboyant figure, or someone more given to expounding his theories for winning, or for living, or for inspiring ballplayers to pour out their blood, compiled the record Bud Grant has (four Super Bowls, eight divisional championships) there would have been volumes of prose about him and bulging books with his by-line.

Not all pro football coaches hold equal responsibility for building their clubs and turning them into winners. While George Allen may check over the final roster cuts, sit in judgment over the draft selections, and meet with free agents all over the land, Ted Marchibroda of Baltimore sticks to coaching and John Madden of Oakland lets Al Davis do the detective work.

Supplying the meat for Ted Marchibro-da's roster — until the end of 1976, when he moved on to San Francisco, seeking to make new miracles — was Joe Thomas, a man given to snap judgments and to supreme confidence in his own ability to pick a future star performer out of a crowd. No protests in the press nor howls from the grandstand ever caused Joe to back away from a choice, while his success in building winners at Minnesota, Miami, and Baltimore has confirmed Joe in his headstrong ways. While Al Davis has been accused of tiptoeing about CIA-style to learn enemy secrets and beat enemy scouts to the drawing of a contract, Joe Thomas has sometimes laid about him with a meat-ax.

When he takes over a losing team, Joe's first thought seems to be to chop away the underbrush of tired veterans and give the new growth a chance to flourish. He believes devoutly in youth — mainly because it lasts longer and keeps getting better — and he almost always tries to find a young quarterback to grow up with his team. As for sentimental attachments to by-gone heroes, Joe has no room for them in his heart. Like so many other champion sports-flesh traders — men like Branch Rickey, Connie Mack, and George Weiss — Joe knows that there is a point in every veteran's career when he is still worth something on the counter, yet has not enough left to build a future on. And that is the point when Joe will swap him off.

Despite an uproar hardly matched since the U.S. Navy tried to sink *Old Ironsides,* Joe traded off Baltimore's Johnny Unitas, once acknowledged the greatest quarterback who ever lived. But there is not a sane person in Baltimore today who would take Johnny back and let go of Bert Jones. When Joe was in Minnesota he recovered eternally youthful Fran Tarkenton from the New York Giants, who never had been able to figure out what to do with him. Fran,

Chuck Muncie of the New Orleans Saints, one of Hank Stram's pet rookie ball-carriers, looks a little like a mama'a boy in his eyeglasses and short pants. But it takes three Houston Oilers to stop him in a game in New Orleans in 1976. Chuck, the only ball-carrier in the league who wears glasses on the field, is thinking of switching to contacts for 1977.

back in friendly territory, set steadily to work wiping quarterback records off the books. If rookies hurt you, as George Allen holds, that is because you did not select them with sufficient care, says Thomas. He wants four or five rookies on any team he operates. "They're good for morale!" he insists, meaning, of course, that a few hungry rookies panting for a place in the lineup will insure the veterans give their all.

As for defense, Joe Thomas looks first for linemen — the three or four in front — because they can keep the offense in trouble "all afternoon" if they're good enough. According to Joe, the knack of picking football players is like that for appraising horseflesh — a sixth sense, a gift that can't be acquired through study. When he moved out of Baltimore to take over the San Francisco 49ers, he could look back and note that, of the 22 starting steeds in the Baltimore stable, he had selected sixteen. Should anyone ask him how he does it, and what criteria he goes by, he says it's "character" — not the "size and speed" George Allen looks for, not the "talent" Chuck Fairbanks favors, not even the "desire" that appeals to Don Coryell. Just "character" — whatever that may mean. Probably it's just what strikes Joe's fancy, like the contours of a racehorse, or the way he comports himself in the starting gate.

The Football Establishment

PRO FOOTBALL may have learned to prosper from studying all the methods professional baseball has devised for destroying itself. Or it may simply have been singularly blessed in finding for its first "commissioner" (pro football never pretended that *its* commissioner was ordained by God) a man as shrewd as Bert Bell. Bell took note of the fact that the separate franchises in pro football, while competing for the same prize, were not necessarily bent on cutting up the same dollar, and so needed to sustain each other rather than permit the strong to breakfast on the weak.

In professional baseball, each club from the beginning had made its own deal on broadcast rights — once it had become clear that fans who listened to the radio were not really "stealing" the game from its proprietors. (Charles Comiskey of the Chicago White Sox, who adored a dollar more fervently than any of his contemporaries, once refused to let telegraphers send the news of the game to the world outside the fences.) Radio broadcasts helped spread interest in the doings of the local ballclub, enabled housewives to stay with the game inning by inning and so actually developed new fans and drew people into the park from far away. But TV was a different deal. That moved the action right out to where the fan could sit in his socks

Everybody thought he had the ball on this pass, but it wound up that nobody had. Fran Tarkenton of the Minnesota Vikings threw it to wide receiver Sammie White (85, in dark jersey) in Super Bowl XI. Cornerback Alonzo Thomas (26, in white) of the Oakland Raiders set out to nestle it to his own chest, and safety Jack Tatum made a dive for it. It fell incomplete.

and watch it. As a result gate receipts in the home cities were seriously eroded, even washed out altogether at times in parks where baseball of a lesser quality was played.

Bert Bell, however, immediately on negotiating the first TV contracts for pro football, proposed a blackout of the entire area where the home club's fans grew. As a result the home fans had to pay their way into the home stadium or not see the game at all. Yet when the team was away they could still strain, sweat, and agonize over the action and keep their appetites for victory aroused.

In addition, instead of allowing contenders for the championship to make private deals for the TV broadcasts with resulting impoverishment of the feebler franchises, Bell used the TV money to sustain the whole league, dividing it up on an even basis among all the clubs. And so pro football, once the rich blood of sponsored TV began to flow through its veins, grew into one of the wealthiest entertainment enterprises in the land. Even some of the chronic losers among the franchises began to sell out their entire seating capacity on a season basis.

Naturally, there followed the accretion of a few thousand unhappy fans in every city who could not afford, or never got around in time to buy a whole block of seats out of one paycheck. Over the seasons, their unhappiness gradually penetrated the hide of their congressmen, who began a movement to legislate against such abuse of the underprivileged. Pro football never having achieved the immunity that professional baseball enjoyed from any hindrance by the anti-trust laws, it soon came to pass that football clubs were forbidden to black out the home territory if the park was sold out. (The New York Giants suffered the ultimate indignity in 1976 when the TV sponsor, despite the fact that Giants games were *always* sold out, once chose to show the New York fans the Washington Redskins game instead.) Pro football profited by another of professional baseball's mistakes when its ruling hierarchy decreed that no football franchise could be owned by a corporation engaged in interstate commerce. This was supposed to protect it from unwholesome interference by the Supreme Court and other unfriendly bodies. Professional baseball, of course, secure in its position as the National Game, and immune from oversight as long as it had heroes it could send down to overawe Congress with, had been selling pieces of itself to various conglomerates for years until even the most unschooled fan could detect tracings of a possible conspiracy in restraint of trade. The New York Yankees for a time belonged to a "communications" conglomerate while the St. Louis Cardinals (baseball) provided just a scanty few lines in the annual report of the Anheuser-Busch corporation.

Also missing from the central offices of pro football is much of the air of sanctimoniousness with which Organized Baseball has been so redolent. (Baseball once had a Commissioner who refused to be quoted on what comic strip he preferred.) The Commissioner of Pro Football is a sort of super-clubowner, a business man and public relations specialist who makes no pretense of being the Lord High Executioner or the Dispenser of Divine Justice, or even the Ultimate Arbiter between Public Need and Private Greed. His job is to keep the operation running smoothly, maximize profits, minimize public discontent, discipline the disorderly, and oversee the inner health of the game.

Largely because of his diligence, pro football has kept its skirts notably clean. A few of its golden stars have been rusticated for admitted involvement with gamblers and there have been some faint whispers of "fix." There have been occasional noisome outbreaks of drug abuse, to which pro football, with its long-time dependence on medications that will inhibit pain and repress the symptoms of fatigue, has been particularly susceptible. But never has there been any such shattering scandal as the great baseball Black Sox uproar of 1920, nor will there ever be if the current system of oversight prevails. Investigators hired by pro football to root out evil are real investigators, with training in the work of running down bad guys and thwarting their misdeeds. They are not, as in organized baseball, mere part-time gumshoes or favorite nephews of some kindly uncle who are chiefly concerned with keeping the dirt under the rug.

The relationship between club and clubhouse in pro football has been generally better too, although not because pro football has offered its hired hands a better deal. Since the coming of Marvin Miller to the Major League Baseball Players' Association, organized baseball has done better on minimum salaries, on pensions, and on players' rights. Pro football clubs, however, are often owned by wealthy men who find it enhances their image to be seen occasionally in public with famous football players, who are generally more imposing creatures than baseball players are. A second baseman may be a squat, scrubby, or even bandy-legged lad who, out of uniform, looks not much different from a railroad ticket-taker. But most pro football players are outsize people who will even dominate a crowded hotel lobby. A man who is only five foot eleven and weighs but 190 pounds is a "little fellow" in pro football, where even quarterbacks, who used to be watch-charm size, are often six feet four inches high and weigh 240 pounds in their

sweat socks. As a result, there is frequently a kindlier feeling toward the help on the part of management and football players themselves frequently feel themselves "closer" to their own club owners for instance than to their fellow sufferers on other clubs.

Because of this, and other factors such as the general pro-establishment orientation of college-trained players (at least, the white ones) the Football Players' Association came very close to expiring. A "strike" they called in 1975 closed the training camps for a time but petered out because so many of the star players, self-righteously proclaiming their duty to their own careers, violated the picket line. (When the baseball players called a strike, among the first to pledge their sacred salaries to the support of the lesser players were Mays and Mantle and other big-money players, to whom the rise in the minimum salary that the union was seeking would not have been worth ten cents.) After that, the football players played on without a union contract, with many players holding back their dues and many others simply signing out of the Association altogether.

So the League, which had absorbed the competing American Football League and so put an end to the salary wars, continued to apply the Rozelle rule that had almost exactly the effect in football as the onerous "reserve rule" had upon professional baseball players — giving them a choice of playing for the club that "owned" them or not playing at all. (The Rozelle rule practically nullified the right of a football player to "play out his option" and become a free agent. It gave Commissioner Rozelle the right, when an "option" player signed with a new club, to decide arbitrarily what the compensation to the original club should be — provided the two clubs could not agree. As a result very few clubs would even talk money to an option player for fear of what they might have to give up to get him.)

What the pro football brass forgot was the vulnerability of such restraints to action by the federal courts. Baseball may have been a "peculiar institution" but football was not. And when the football owners came to court they came in second. The first test they lost was the test of the Rozelle rule itself when Joe Kapp, Minnesota hero of the 1969 playoffs, brought suit because he had been deprived of a chance to sell his services to the highest bidder. In 1975, Federal Judge William Swigert, ruling on the Kapp case, declared that the standard player contract of the National Football League was just plain illegal. Later in the year, another federal judge, Earl Larson, ruled the Rozelle rule out of bounds too. In 1976 came the final blow when Yazoo Smith, a rookie Redskin defensive back from Oregon, won his damage suit against the League. Smith, chosen by the Redskins in the "college draft" (which gave each club exclusive rights to the players it "drafted") made the team his first year. But in the final game of the season he was accidentally kicked in the head by a teammate and suffered a broken neck that finished him as a football player. In his suit he asked for triple damages on the ground that the draft, by restricting his bargaining power and leaving him no choice but to sign with the Redskins or not play pro football at all, had prevented him from getting a contract that would have protected him against the results of permanent injury.

Federal Judge William D. Bryant, in his decision granting Smith more than a quarter-million dollars in damages, described the college draft as just what it was, "a group boycott in its most pernicious form," and urged that the League take im-

mediate steps to modify it. The judge even told the League how it could be done — by allowing three teams rather than just one to have the right to negotiate with a player.

With all their "rights" shot out from under them this way, the National Football League decided that it might be best after all to bargain with the Players' Association on all these matters they had earlier declared were non-negotiable. After weeks of bitter and seemingly aimless argument, the chief negotiators, almost by accident, sat down for dinner together one night and discovered they could settle everything in an amicable way. As a result the college draft was radically modified, giving all prospects the chance to become free agents eventually; the Rozelle rule was diluted beyond recognition, setting specific recompense for a club that lost a player who had played out his option; a dues check-off was granted that assured the continued vigor of the Players' Association; and all recriminations came to an end in a wash of goodwill.

There had been no goodwill wasted in the coming to an end of what seemed for a while like a murderous threat to the health and welfare of the club owners in the National League. The World Football League, born in a very sunburst of gold, or at least of million-dollar checks and guarantees of more, looked for a time as if it might riddle the rosters of the National League, practically wipe out the college draft, send players' salaries into permanent orbit and even woo away fans by the cityful. The very spearhead of the champion Miami Dolphin offense — ball-carriers Jim Kiick and Larry Csonka, and wide receiver Paul Warfield — fled to the arms of the new league in return for a money-in-the-bank deal with millionaire John Bassett that made each man independently wealthy for life. It also required them to play football for the Memphis Southmen, a team that had yet to draw a breath.

The new league had the sort of dream contract for players that amateur businessmen often imagine will give them the pick of the creative crop — a plan to cut all the players in on the gate receipts. Gate receipts, however, were what the new league had the least of. It invented some lovely names for its ball clubs — the Thunder, the Bell, the Fire, the Steamer, the Grizzlies, the Vulcans, and the Wings. But by the time its promoters decided they could afford no more, attendance had shrunk to less than 14,000 per game, on average. They needed more than twice that many to make the deal work. Lack of places to play, lack of interest on the part of TV sponsors, and failure to awaken any loyalty among the citizens in the cities they chose to settle in combined to sink their ship. Chris Hemmeter, a businessman from Hawaii who had tried to keep the craft afloat through its final season, also had hard words for "media skepticism," meaning the doubts most sports writers had that there was money enough in the world to finance so lavish a production as the World Football League had tried to put together.

The previous rivalry, with the American Football League, had settled into a sort of armed truce by the late sixties, with some National League clubs still refusing to post on their scoreboard the scores of games in the other league. But when the new decade began, the two leagues had merged into one, with teams divided between two "conferences" so that the rivalry could be perpetuated in the Super Bowl. Even this rivalry had been greeted, when it began, by a good deal of "media skepticism" that soon vanished when it became clear that, contrary to prediction, there was still no "saturation" of either the air waves or the

sports columns and that there were still fans enough to fill all the new football parks well beyond their capacity. (When the New York Giants finally agreed to meet the New York Jets in a pre-season game for the "city championship," such an eruption of fans ensued that traffic between New York and New Haven, where the game was to be played, resembled the wartime evacuation of Paris, with buses, trains and private cars all trying to shove their way, it seemed, through one narrow pass already jammed wall-to-wall with pedestrians. Ticket-scalpers at the game nearly outnumbered the early arrivals and all, one concludes, returned rich.

There had to be some tinkering with the rules so that the two leagues could live in peace together (the American League had allowed a two-point conversion if the offensive team chose a pass or running play instead of the standard kick) and there was some squawking to begin with when it was indicated that the "new" members of the league would all be segregated in the American Conference. "Nothing doing!" said Paul Brown, who had come out of retirement to take over the Cincinnati franchise in the American League. "We paid these exorbitant sums to become *members* of the National League and we won't agree to anything less!" Whereupon the Commissioner wrenched three franchises — Baltimore, Pittsburgh, and Cleveland — out of the old league and set them in the new where, after some mild fretting, they took root and flourished. Indeed the Pittsburgh club, which had ended its stay in the Century Division of the old league with one victory against thirteen losses, soon grew into a veritable dragon in its new surroundings, winning its divisional championship four times in the first six seasons of play.

Two-Point Conversion

THE HUMAN knee, which some authorities like to say was never meant to be used for walking erect on two legs, has long proved the most vulnerable joint in a football player's body. People who like to make wild estimates say that there are some 50,000 operations each season on football players of every level of skill who have had their knee ligaments torn. Quarterbacks, who for a long time habitually planted their feet and threw passes from a stiff-legged position, have suffered the most; many of them wear two or three long surgical scars to mark the spots where doctors have gone in to repair the ligaments or remove the damaged cartilage. Joe Namath, after a de-cade of being brutalized by pass-rushers who sought to bring him down before he could pass, or punish him for daring to, has hardly any cushioning left to keep his knee joints from grinding like a pair of ungreased cam-shafts when he moves. He gets by of course on his ability to read defenses with half an eye, his lightning-swift release of the football and his willingness to risk whatever additional punishment his job may require of him. He and Jim Hart of St. Louis both wear knee-braces.

But many a less gifted quarterback has gone limping off the stage on gimpy knees long before the rest of his body had begun to show wear. A few great ball-carriers,

The league's most valuable player in 1976 was George Foreman (44) of the Minnesota Vikings, shown here in a game at Green Bay when nearly half the Packer team seems intent on taking the ball away from him. Foreman is known as a fumbler. But he also catches passes, runs for long gains, and makes touchdowns.

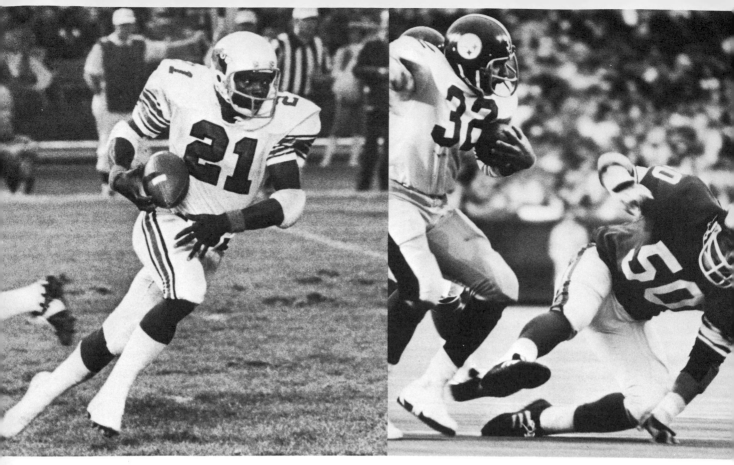

Left:
Terry Metcalf of the St. Louis Cardinals, the team's top touchdown-maker, might have been even better if he had learned to squeeze the football. Here he carries the ball against the Washington Redskins, using just his fingertips to maintain control.

Right:
Franco Harris, whose ''immaculate reception'' of a seemingly busted pass won the Pittsburgh Steelers the division title from the Oakland Raiders in 1972, did most of the work in getting them into Super Bowl IX by rushing for 152 yards. He then set a record in the Super Bowl by rushing for 158 yards in thirty-four carries. Here he eludes Minnesota linebacker Jeff Siemon, as he hugs the ball tight.

notably Gale Sayers of Chicago, have had their careers ended abruptly by knee surgery when they might have had half a dozen seasons of glory ahead. Gale Sayers indeed looked like the runner of the future when he started carrying the ball for the luckless Chicago Bears, and making more touchdowns than any man before him had ever managed (22 in a single season, 1965, a record broken 10 years later by O. J. Simpson, who made 23).

Sayers was neither as big nor as strong as Jimmy Brown, who sometimes would break out of a gang tackle by sheer power.

Sayers' specialty was avoiding tackles, or slithering away from them as Red Grange had done. Gale seemed to own not only amazing peripheral vision, so that he could pick up the approach of a tackler from almost any angle, but equally remarkable reflexes that enabled him to cut and change direction quicker than thought, as a tarantula will sometimes jump to safety almost before you aim the blow.

Because he was unable to jump two ways at once, however, Gale Sayers' career came to an end in a 1968 game with the San Francisco 49ers. Sayers, running an end sweep, had planted his right foot hard in the sod to make the sudden cut that would take him away from the looming defensive tackle when the cornerback, Kermit Alexander, threw his body across Sayers' legs. Sayers' cleats were dug so deep that the foot would not pull out of the sod and the leg gave way, putting Gale out of action for the season. He came back next season, after a whole winter of grimly exercising the damaged knee, and seemed for a time as swift and elusive as ever. But the knee gave way again and after a good deal of stopping and starting, gloomy talk of retirement and even a few muttered threats of lawsuits, Gale did indeed retire and no one will ever know what greater glory might have been his if the knee had held up.

The Offense of the Seventies

The 1970's, however, turned out to be the decade of the runner. In the 1940's and 1950's the pass had been nearly the whole offense in pro football, with some clubs occasionally throwing a pass on every down, to travel the whole length of the field. These were the days when a few curmudgeon sportswriters refused even to attend the pro games. It was nothing but basketball, they averred, in different uniforms.

After his Kansas City Chiefs had won Super Bowl IV, Hank Stram was so undone by emotion that he rashly declared that he had evolved the "offense of the seventies." After he had taken time to look back on his triumph more calmly, he granted that he had simply developed an offense that worked best for him, being suited to the personnel he managed at the time. (Hank was sometimes accused by admiring rivals of engaging in a sort of con game, pretending for instance that there was some special magic in a backfield of undersize ball-carriers, when in fact he had just found himself stuck with such an array.) But Hank, it turned out, was right about one

thing — he did predict that the new offenses would have to run more and that the quarterback especially would have to move.

Move is what the quarterbacks did. At first the few signal-callers who made a specialty of running — men like Greg Landry of Detroit and Bobby Douglas of Chicago (not to mention that incurable scrambler, Fran Tarkenton) were deemed freakish, perhaps undisciplined, or maybe even a little short of sense. No coach designed an offense in which the quarterback was ever more than a desperation ball-carrier — usually on a keeper play, when less than a yard was needed. When quarterbacks did run it was to foil a pass defense that had covered all their receivers, or to escape a blitz that had scared them out of the pocket. Coaches, players, and commentators still agreed that a running quarterback was courting destruction. As for Tarkenton, who had never been put out of commission despite his penchant for running off with the ball — well, he would never win a championship. No scrambler ever had!

This conventional wisdom began to give way with the development of the zone defense and the consequent choking off of the "bomb" — the long, long pass that always brought the fans to their feet and sometimes brought the enemy goal line fifty or sixty yards closer. The zone defenses nearly always managed to keep a man between a deep receiver and the goal line, so that it was no longer simply a foot-race between receiver and defender in the deep reaches of the field. Now a man who might fake out a defender on the way downfield would find himself "ridden" to the boundary of a zone by one man and picked up there by another. One of the first results of the choking off of deep offensive thrusts was to increase the number of field-goal attempts. Indeed, many pro football players used to describe

Hank Stram's "secret" as "a tough defense and a Norwegian field-goal kicker." (Hank's field goal specialist at Kansas City was Jan Stenerud, who first saw dawn in Fetsund, Norway.)

Inasmuch as pro football fans did not pay seven, eight, and nine dollars a seat to watch low-scoring ballgames or spend their enthusiasm three points at a time, the architects of the game began to look rather solemnly into the future. They first tried to loosen up the zones a little by shifting the hash-marks where the ball was to be put in play when it wound up too close to the sidelines. The basic theory of the zone defense, obviously, was to divide up the field, lengthwise and crosswise, into zones of responsibility, with cornerbacks, linebackers, and safeties each assigned to a territory where he was to pick up any eligible intruder and stay with him until he could be given into the care of a man in an adjoining zone.

Widening the side zones by shifting the hash-marks may have helped the offense a little. But defensive geniuses like Paul Brown and George Allen soon began to give the offense fits again by combining zone defense with old-fashioned man-to-man coverage or by camouflaging it with *apparent* man-to-man coverage that turned out to be zone coverage after all. The offense was further handicapped by a stricter rule covering intentional grounding of a pass. Of course, such malfeasance had always been against the rules but officials had grown so lax in enforcing it that quarterbacks would sometimes, when no receiver was open, or when they merely wanted to stop the clock with an incompletion, turn and flip the ball over the sideline with no potential receiver within a city block. Strict enforcement put an end to all this and sometimes brought penalties when a quarterback had honestly *tried* to reach a receiver but

had not convinced the official of the pureheartedness of his intentions. As a result the passing game received another halter.

Of course the zone defense could sometimes be beaten by a receiver with acceleration enough to run right through it. But wingfooted receivers did not grow more than one or two to the acre, so the bombs flew less and less often as more and more teams began to comb the playing fields of Norway, or somewhere, to find an easier way of getting the ball over the goal line. But the field goal was made a little less tempting by a new rule that gave a missed field goal back to the defending team at the scrimmage line from which the kick had been snapped — unless that was inside the twenty-yard line.

So eventually the emphasis shifted more than ever to the running game and great runners of the Hugh McElhenny, Joe Perry, Jimmy Brown, and Gale Sayers type began to pop up in every garden. There were mightly fullbacks who could blast through the middle like a one-man flying wedge, runners who could dodge around tacklers or run over them, and other ball-carriers who could slip and shift and cut, then outrun every man on the field. And club owners, instead of shoving and elbowing and gouging each other to be the first to lay hands on a "maximum" quarterback began to think first of offensive linemen who could open up the middle and ball-carriers who could run through the holes they created. And the maximum quarterback now became one who carried the ball by design and knew how to take care of himself when he got beyond the line of scrimmage.

O. J. — Best Ball-Carrier in the Game

Of the great new runners who matured in the 1970's the greatest of all was Orestes J. Simpson, called "O. J." and "The Juice," a big man (six foot two, 212 pounds) but one who looked actually slender beside Jim Brown. O. J. became not only the best ball-carrier in the game but on the basis of all the many things he could do with his muscles, perhaps the greatest athlete. He also seemed destined to become the richest, because of his gifts in so many other departments, and his stubbornness in sticking to his resolve to be properly compensated for the sacrifices football required of him.

O. J. played in Buffalo, New York, which was perhaps the very last place he would have chosen. But when Simpson came into the game, college players were "drafted" and they had no choice of playing field. O. J. didn't like cold weather, and Buffalo was one of the coldest spots in the world at times, or seemed so when the wind was off the lake. O. J. was hoping for a team had a chance for the Super Bowl. Buffalo seemed sometimes to be lucky to hold on to a franchise. O. J. wanted a job where he could be close to his family. They were in California and his wife cared even less for cold weather than O. J. did.

There were other drawbacks. The clustering experts mostly agreed that O. J. was not going to make the splash in the pros that he had made at the University of Southern California because he had brought some "bad habits" with him. Chief among them, they said, was his way of jitterbugging while waiting for a hole to open (what Vince Lombardi called "doing all that stuff behind the line"). In the pros, a ball-carrier has to get off the mark in a hurry and get to the scrimmage line before it gets to him or he is a very dead duck. But O. J. shook off this fault quickly. He was a highly "coachable" athlete, eager to improve, full of desire, and perhaps the easiest man on the whole squad to get along with — the politest anyway, and the most thoughtful. (If he blew up at a teammate, he very soon apologized.)

The Buffalo club had "earned" the right to draft O. J. by winning only one game in 1968 (they had won four in 1967). Even with O. J. to help them, they had won only four games out of fourteen in 1969, the last year the American League existed as a separate entity. In their first *two* seasons in the National League the Bills won only four games altogether. By 1974, however, they climbed high enough to make the playoffs (in which they lost to Pittsburgh). In 1976, they did not climb that high, but O. J., after first declaring he would never play for Buffalo again, joined up late and posted one of the finest seasons of his career. He also had signed the juiciest contract of his career — for well over a million dollars (but "substantially less than two and a half million") for three years of service. Whether his new position in the world made any cracks in his temper it is hard to say, but he did in 1976 slightly impair his cool-and-collected image by throwing half a dozen punches at Mel Lunsford, defensive end for New England, who had, Simpson felt, roughed him up needlessly. For the first time in his pro career, O. J. was ejected from a game.

When the 1976 season was over, O. J. had gained altogether 1,503 yards by rushing, placing himself second in career total of 9,626 yards only to Jim Brown, whose career total of 12,312 yards seems at least within reach of O. J. if, as they say in Dixie, God is willing and the creek don't rise.

A Little Bundle from Heaven

The Chicago Bears, in the seventies, were blessed with a little bundle from heaven named Walter Payton, a running back who looked like Gale Sayers all over again — perhaps even better. Payton did not actually run like Sayers, who was faster, lighter and more elusive. Sayers made his great gains in the open field, where his ability to change direction, almost by instinct, enabled him to slip away from tacklers who thought they had captured him. Payton behaved more like a fullback. He did not hesitate to run right over a tackler, if there was no daylight in view and he was built solidly enough (five feet ten and 210 pounds, with a great deal of his weight in his thighs) to make a tackler wish he had not gotten in his way. Payton was somewhat like Larry Brown of the Redskins, who would bang into opponents and try to fight his way through a mob, churning, struggling, twisting until he was pounded into the turf. That sort of running invites contusions, sprains, and fractures by the barrelful. Larry Brown soon collected enough to last him to his grave. Payton, in his rookie year (1975) suffered injuries in nearly every joint. But Payton was constructed more snugly than Brown was and was not so susceptible to being pulled apart at the joints. Indeed there was muscle enough in his two legs to outfit two or three grown men. But he could duck away from a tackle when he saw the chance, and often did so, halfback style.

In his second year, Payton began to learn how to run in the pro fashion (at Jackson State he did everything, even kick and return kicks) and passed the 1000-yard mark before the season was over. That accomplishment set off a joyous celebration in the Bears' locker room, for Payton was perhaps the most beloved ballplayer the Chicago club had ever owned. His teammates named him "Sweetness" — a nickname that would have caused an old-time pro to punch somebody in the head — and they meant it. Payton himself liked the nickname and never failed to remind interviewers that that was what he was called — Sweetness, for his sweet style of making gains and for his gentle, friendly, and unassuming nature.

One of the few things that irritated Payton was being compared to Gale Sayers — or to any other runner. "My style is unique," he said. His coaches agreed. Jack Pardee, head coach of the Bears, was convinced, before the 1976 season was over, that Payton had "skills he's never even used. He's just scratched the surface of his true ability."

While Payton, if he can stay alive and unbroken, seems the ball-carrier most likely to succeed Jim Brown and O. J. Simpson, other clubs had backfield men who knew how to take the ball downfield without throwing it. St. Louis owned Terry Metcalf, a cocky, merry, and light-footed young man who was deemed too light to play the pro game. Indeed, in his pads and uniform, he seemed to strut about on legs no heftier than a rooster's. But he was tough as could be and moved like a roadrunner once he got past the scrimmage line. Because of his ability to cut and dodge away from tacklers and to accelerate in half a breath, Metcalf was used as a punt-return man as well as a running back. In a game against New England in 1976 when he scored three touchdowns, he earned one with a sixty-nine-yard return of a punt. Metcalf wryly observed that his versatility had brought him an unlooked-for distinction. "Now they try to put a little extra forearm into those hits," he said. "That's what you get for being a celebrity."

Like most running backs in these days of zone defense, Terry is used often as a receiver, for he is fast enough to go on the fly pattern and run right through the zones, leaving a clutch of defense men panting behind him. But ablest of all ball-carriers on pass reception is probably Chuck Foreman of Minnesota, another thousand-yard ball-carrier who is also his club's leading pass-catcher and usually runs far ahead of all his teammates in scoring. A relatively slender man (six foot two and just over 200 pounds), Chuck in 1975 made twenty-two touchdowns and stood second in the league in rushing yardage. He was also the league's top pass receiver. But he also led, alas, in fumbles — a weakness that had plagued him since his days at the University of Miami. In the playoff with Dallas in 1974, Chuck fumbled twice, but the Steelers still managed to win the game. In 1975, however, in the Super Bowl, with his club having been limited to eleven yards rushing in the first half, Chuck had a chance to score. A pass interference call had given the Vikings the ball on the five-yard line of the Pittsburgh Steelers. The turf was slippery that January day, so Chuck was sent straight through the line. He burst through and could have put his team back in the game, except that, the officials, on checking Foreman's belongings after he was downed, discovered he had not brought along a football. That lay back near where Chuck started, in the possession of Mean Joe Greene, the Pittsburgh defensive tackle.

Nevertheless, Chuck's bosses were ready to forgive him for letting go of the ball now and then, as long as he shoved it across the goal line with such consistency. A man who could come out of the backfield and wreck the zone defense by tucking away forward passes as often as Chuck did could be allowed a few extra fumbles.

Besides, there were other backs in the league, Terry Metcalf for instance, who were subject to occasional spells of giving up the football before they finished taking it where they wanted it to go. It just seemed that nobody, except perhaps George Allen, could coach agaist fumbles. Sometimes it appeared that most of the running backs in the league had been taught to carry the ball in one hand far away from the body, as if they were wading ashore from a shipwreck trying to keep their rolled-up Sunday pants from getting wet.

A relatively unsung speedster with the San Francisco 49ers fumbled the ball only once in 1975, however, and that time he recovered the ball all by himself. That was Delvin Williams, a solid young six-footer from Texas who averaged a gain of more than five yards on every carry. Williams, strong, elusive, and given to protesting wildly against any effort to throw him to the ground, developed a private cheering section in San Francisco that saw in him a successor to the great California runners of the pre-Super Bowl days.

There was indeed hardly a club in the league that did not own a man who could duck and dodge his way through a broken field on occasion like some of the college heroes of old. Even the hapless New York Giants, whose fans in 1976 grew hoarse from booing their efforts, discovered a husky lad named Doug Kotar who could break tackles and slip away from pursuers often enough to change the boos into cheers for minutes at a time. Doug was no great shakes as a pass receiver, nor was the Giant quarterback, Craig Morton, ever mentioned as a rival in sharpness and skill to Joe Namath, for instance. Doug hardly threatened the thousand-yard mark, which no Giant runner since Ron Johnson, in 1972, had ever approached (Doug's goal would be more like five-hundred yards). But he could get away often enough for a run of fifteen or twenty yards to keep the flame of hope still flickering in the hearts of the faithful.

In New Orleans, where disaster followed disaster as coach Hank Stram struggled to discover the system that would fit his discrepant personnel, two large young running backs surfaced who looked as if they might some day, if Hank could put a team in front of them, win fame in tandem, as Csonka

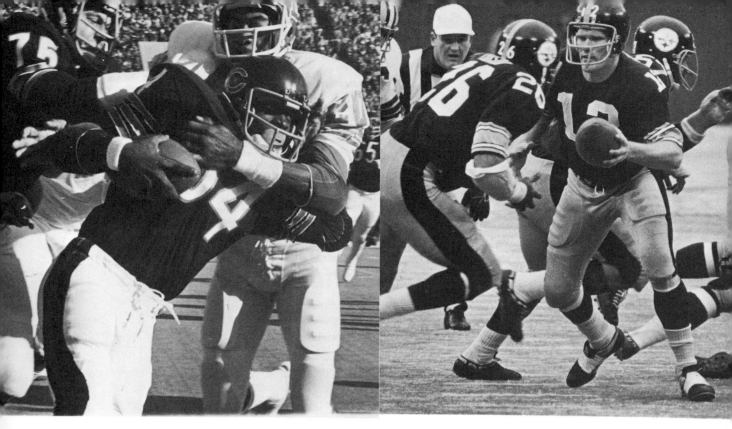

Chicago's new running star, Walter Payton, called "Sweetness" by his teammates, still keeps his eyes on the goal as he struggles out of the grasp of Louis Wright, Denver Bronco cornerback. Chicago tackle, Jeff Sevy, is trying to spring Payton free.

and Kiick had done when the decade was young. Chuck Muncie and Tony Galbreath, both over six feet and weighing 230 or better, and both as swift and hard to contain as polo ponies, almost every week lifted the hearts of fans and coach with runs that even O. J. Simpson might have bragged on.

The New Passers — Sure of Foot

The ball-carriers who really put roses back into the cheeks of club treasurers, however, were the young quarterbacks who began to act as if they had been raised to be ball-carriers. Bert Jones of Baltimore and Steve Grogan of New England carried the ball into enemy territory, not as a means of escaping a pass-rush or simply to take sudden advantage of an unforeseen gap in the defense, but with malice aforethought. Both being tall, generously muscled, and quick, they had no fear of meeting enemy linebackers in broad daylight or in the dark, no urge to slow down to lessen the force of

a collision with a tackler, no wish to curl into the fetal position to absorb, without injury, the impact of falling bodies. Often when they sprinted away with the ball it was part of a play specifically designed to give them that role. As a result, the "keys" the defensive backfield often used to decipher the upcoming plays were sometimes rendered indecipherable. It had been gospel that when the quarterback broke out of the pocket with the ball still in his possession it was an act of desperation — either a play had been busted or he needed more time than customary to find a man ready to receive the pass. Consequently, blocking assignments were in disarray and everybody up front could zero in on the hapless quarterback.

But with Jones, and especially with Grogan taking the ball, the running back and fullback, instead of deploying to receive a pass, or one to block for the other, might both, along with a pulling guard, be mov-

Another quarterback who loves to run — when the coach will let him — is rugged Terry Bradshaw of the Pittsburgh Steelers who, at six foot three and 210 pounds, is sometimes the biggest man in his own backfield.

ing out to block for the quarterback, creating a phalanx no plan had been made to cope with. Both Jones and Grogan knew how to run — whole foot on the ground to provide secure balance and drive, prepared to change direction sharply, once the line of scrimmage had been passed, ready to cut inside or outside a blocker, depending on how the defense had reacted.

Grogan, in 1975, had been just a questionable replacement for Jim Plunkett and a college has-been who had a permanent back injury, passed up by everyone else in the draft. But he had always had the confidence of his coach, Chuck Fairbanks. When Plunkett, after threatening to play out his option, was traded to San Francisco, big Steve was offered a five-year contract. By that time he had convinced everyone he could play — even Dick Shiner, the quarterback who thought *he* would replace Jim Plunkett if anyone did. After Grogan, starting the game against the Buffalo Bills in 1975, had gained 365 yards in the air, Dick Shiner retired.

Steve did not convince everyone right away that he was the man to turn the hapless New England team into a winner. In losing to the Detroit Lions, after beating Pittsburgh and Miami, Grogan threw five interceptions. There were those who muttered immediately that this was about what they could expect from a quarterback who had so little sense that he would call plays in which *he* was the ball-carrier. But Steve had qualities spectators could not see. His teammates insisted that his eyes actually caught fire when a game began. He gave pep talks in the huddle and said prayers on the sideline — once "praying" a sure field goal by Roy Gerela of Pittsburgh right out of line to save a Patriot victory. Despite a pleasant, almost retiring manner, Grogan turned out to be as tough as a lineman once the action started. He was said to have challenged even Mean Joe Greene to single combat.

And he could *run* — and would run under almost any circumstances. By the time the 1976 season was half over, he had gained an average of eight yards a carry and had already posted twelve career touchdowns. But his running did not diminish his skill at passing. In beating the champion Steelers in Pittsburgh in 1976, Grogan, after a feeble first half, threw six completions in nine attempts in the second half, including touchdown passes of thirty-eight and fifty-eight yards to Russ Francis and Darryl Stingley. (He also made a touchdown of his own on a six-yard run.)

Grogan very nearly took the Patriots into the 1977 Super Bowl and might have if he had not run up against the Snake — Ken Stabler, the left-handed quarterback of the Oakland Raiders, who was rated by almost every rival coach as the best in the league. Stabler was also a man who would run with the ball when need be, but he had slowed down a half step or more in this, his eighth season in the pros. His really extraordinary talent was his ability to spin those long passes right through a doughnut hole, again and again. He won the playoff with New England by a breathtaking march downfield in the final minutes, passing the ball almost without letup until he connected with one or the other of his antelope-legged receivers — Fred Biletnikoff and Cliff Branch. Although neither possessed unusual height, both, and particularly Biletnikoff, seemed infused with a demonic ability to find little openings in the defense just big enough to slide a football through.

The really vital gain, however, was made by a pass that was never completed, that was actually tipped as it left Stabler's hand. Ray Hamilton, the New England defensive tackle, 245 pounds of meat and muscle, descended upon Stabler after he had let the pass go, flicked the ball with one hand, setting it off course, and then ground Stabler into the sod. A yellow flag sailed into the air and Hamilton was penalized for roughing the passer. The intended receiver, Carl Garrett, meanwhile had been forcibly removed from the playing field by two New England defenders, but no official noted this, or the Raiders would have been given the ball on the four-yard line. Instead, they were given a first down on the thirteen-yard line with less than a minute to play. A pass and a run brought the ball to the two-yard line and then Stabler took it in himself with just ten seconds left.

The Patriot team, the entire bench, the assistant coaches, the small coterie of New England fans, and Coach Chuck Fairbanks very nearly brought a stop to the game with the vehemence of their protests against that penalty. "Why, I tipped the ball!" Hamilton yelled. "It *can't* be roughing the passer!" Alas, it could. It is the man attempting to block a kick who is held blameless for running into the kicker, if he manages to get a hand on the ball in the process. Hamilton's having tipped the ball only verified his guilt, for he had to know then that the ball was in the air and the passer was no longer fair game.

But there had been a good deal of flag-tossing in the game and the Patriots benefited from most of it, so the Oakland crew was not inclined to feel the least bit shy about accepting this benefice. Afterward the Patriots complained of "dirty play" and a great many spectators, among those who were not blinded by devotion to the Raiders, agreed that one play in particular, in which George Atkinson let New England receiver Russ Francis have a forearm in the face, breaking Russ's nose, seemed beyond the call of necessity.

(Atkinson, earlier in 1976, had separated Lynn Swann of Pittsburgh from his senses with a swinging forearm in a gesture that seemed to have very little connection with anything else that was happening on the field. Dark talk of "criminal elements" and counter threats of lawsuits ensued to add solemn overtones to the season.)

The Seventies' Super Bowls

Throughout the seventies there were those who held that the Super Bowl spectacle was growing duller and duller, until it seemed but a dreary sparring match between two heavyweights afraid of exposing themselves to a knockout punch. Yet the attendance, or at least the ticket sale never flagged. Indeed there always seemed to be a shortage of seats, even though, when the game began, there were empty patches in the stand where the no-shows left their seats unfilled. This no-show phenomenon was probably just a result of block-buying of seats by corporations that used such prizes as tax-deductible "entertainment," while some of the recipients of this largesse may have been folk who would rather go to the movies on a chilly afternoon. Tickets still sold in Super Bowl cities for multiples of their face value, and high-ticket restaurants in all the larger towns were barren of diners during the Super Bowl hours.

Yet it is true that there were relatively few moments of screaming excitement in any of the Super Bowls after 1972. The really memorable aspect of the 1972 game was the intrusion of the President of the United States into the game strategy. "I think," said ex-second stringer Richard Nixon to Coach Don Shula of Miami, "you can hit Warfield on a down-and-in pattern." All the world, including the coach of the opposing Dallas club, heard what he said. Miami had no "down-and-in" pattern. They did have a slant, which was probably what Nixon meant, for this was a play in which Paul Warfield — then deemed the best receiver in the game — had often taken the ball far downfield.

The Dallas club, however, secure in the faith that no man as honorable as the President of the United States would fake them out, practiced on ways to keep Warfield covered. And poor Paul never did get hold of a pass on that slant, for he never got far enough away from the attending enemy to get hold of the ball. (Paul complained afterward: "They made sure that under no circumstances would I be able to complete that pass.")

All the really successful passing was done by Dallas quarterback Roger Staubach, who was still getting used to having Coach Landry call the plays for him. ("I try to guess what the coach is sending in," Staubach observed. "And I'm always wrong.") The first touchdown of the game came almost at the end of the first half, when Staubach connected on a pass to Lance Alworth, deep in the corner, right on the goal line. Lance leaped to grab the ball before it went out of bounds and stepped right into the end zone.

The second half was mostly running by Dallas, who overwhelmed the Miami defense, shutting middle linebacker Nick Buoniconti practically out of the ballgame. The Cowboys set a new Super Bowl rushing record of 252 yards, with ninety-five yards contributed by their moody and often uncommunicative running back, Duane Thomas. After the Cowboys had taken the trophy, 24 to 3, Thomas was caught exhibiting some gladness in the locker room. "You look," said one newsman, "like a man landing on the moon." Thomas did not smile. "You been there, man?" he inquired.

The excitement of the next Super Bowl, played in January 1973, was overshadowed by the playoffs, in the game in which,

through a verifiable miracle, the Pittsburgh Steelers won the division title from the Oakland Raiders on the day before Christmas, 1972. This was the game that produced the "immaculate reception" by Franco Harris, who gathered in a pass that had already been broken up but had not yet touched the ground, and took it in for a touchdown that won the game. The play was so otherworldly that the referee stopped the game long enough to duck under the stands and verify his call with the help of the press-box TV.

The play had begun with what seemed a desperation pass by Terry Bradshaw. Oakland at the time was leading the Steelers 7 to 6. With only one minute and 13 seconds left, Ken Stabler had run 30 yards for the touchdown and Oakland needed only to keep the Steelers out of field goal range in order to win the game and their way into the Super Bowl.

Starting then on his own twenty-yard line, Bradshaw threw five passes in a row. Oakland defender Jack Tatum broke up two of them. The fifth pass, Terry's last hope to make a first down and keep their chances alive, had been planned as a pass to Barry Pearson. But Pearson met a lot of unfriendly people along the way who refused to make way for him, even strove to dissuade him from making the journey at all. Chased out of the pocket, robbed of his primary receiver, Bradshaw scampered out into the flat and looked for a pair of friendly hands. Frenchy Fuqua was well down field, hemmed in by the enemy. Franco Harris, seeing his quarterback in trouble, was somewhere in between, trying to break free and give Terry a target. But Terry chose to fling the ball in the general direction of Fuqua, and Frenchy made for it. "I thought I could catch the ball," he said later, "but somebody hit me." "Somebody" was Jack Tatum, who insisted afterward that he "touched the man but not the ball." The referee decided he had touched both so that made it legal for another offensive man to receive the ball. Harris, speeding toward the action, met the ball, which had bounced off somebody and zoomed back as if it had hit a backboard. Franco accepted this gift from the gods and continued on at top speed in the direction he was going. Fuqua, who had counted the pass dead and the game lost, saw Franco pound by and could not understand what had bitten him.

"What's going on here?" he asked himself.

Everybody else on the field knew what was going on: Franco was headed across the goal line, forty-two yards away. After he crossed it, Referee Swearingen called it a touchdown. Then, after apparently noting some dissenters among the other officials, and talking matters over with them, he called it nothing and took off for under the stands. Merry Steeler fans meanwhile poured onto the field to celebrate a victory

and players on both teams looked at each other in wild surmise.

Art McNally, league supervisor of umpires, had seen the play on the press-box TV. Swearingen called him on the phone.

"How do you call it?" McNally asked him.

"Touchdown," said Swearingen.

"That's right," said McNally.

So Swearingen ran back to the field, and after winning concurrence from the other men in striped shirts, he lifted both hands above his head and made the Steeler score official.

Afterward, Swearingen denied there had been any doubt in his mind. "I went under the stands to clear up some confusion," he said. Later he allowed that he "had to delay the touchdown call to restore order on the field." The touchdown call, however, prompted pure bedlam, not just on the field but in front of TV sets all over the land. Oakland fans and players wailed they had been gypped. Coach John Madden of Oak-

Sprinters run on their toes. But ball-carriers maintain balance by running with the whole foot in contact with the ground at each step. This is pro football's greatest runner of the '70's — O. J. Simpson of Buffalo, breaking loose, with a blocker at his side, in a game against Detroit in 1976.

Steve Riley, giant Minnesota tackle (six foot six and 258 pounds), keeps his quarterback, Fran Tarkenton, safe from all harm by torpedoing an enemy, Green Bay's defensive end, Alden Roche, amidships.

land never argued with the decision at all.

The Super Bowl that followed, in January 1973, featuring Miami (who beat the Steelers for the conference title) and the Redskins was naturally an anticlimax. But over 90,000 tickets were sold. (Only 82,000 seats were occupied.) And there were a few moments worth remembering. The incident that lived longest in most memories was the sight of little Gary Yepremian, the Miami field-goal kicker, trying to make like a football player when his field goal attempt was blocked and he found the ball back in his hands. Scurrying like an agitated duck, he had sense enough at least not to try to carry the ball over the goal line. He knew that you sometimes passed the ball if you couldn't run it, so he hauled off and flipped the ball feebly into the air, in the general direction of a Miami player who was not eligible to catch the ball. The Redskins' Mike Bass was eligible enough, however, and he took the ball instead, laughing off little Gary's feeble attempt to stop him, and running all the way

back to the Miami goal line for the only Redskin score. Miami was still ahead however; instead of winning 17 to 0 they won 14 to 7.

George Allen, the Redskin coach, had practically dedicated his life to getting his team into this game and now he was inconsolable.

"It doesn't do any good to get to the Super Bowl if you don't win," he mourned. "I can't get out of here fast enough."

He might better have let it go at that, but he was moved to offer excuses later, citing the "carnival atmosphere" and the "distractions" caused by the presence of wives and the countless TV interviews. Billy Kilmer, the losing quarterback, could not go along with his coach: "I wasn't distracted," he said. He was, however, intercepted once too often by Jake Scott, the Miami free safety, who took one of Kilmer's passes from the Miami end zone to the enemy forty-eight-yard line.

Super Bowl Number Eight, or VIII as it

was officially designated to assure its place in history, was decided in the first period when the Miami Dolphins gained 120 yards and scored twice against the Minnesota Vikings. The Vikings, featuring the Purple People Eaters, made one first down in that time. In the second period Miami kept the ball until they got to the Minnesota twenty-one-yard line. Then Yepremian, the wealthy necktie manufacturer, kicked a field goal to make the score 17–0. After that, there was just one moment when Minnesota hearts were lifted: John Gilliam took the second-half kick-off and ran it all the way to the Miami thirty-four-yard line. But he had no time to get adjusted to his surroundings. Someone had observed Viking tight end Stu Voigt in the act of clipping, so they took the ball away from Gilliam and set it down on Minnesota ten. The Vikings finally scored early in the final period when Fran Tarkenton scrambled in from the Miami four-yard line. That left Miami only 17 points ahead. A short kick-off worked exactly as it was supposed to for Minnesota, when Terry Brown, the Viking safety, trailing the free ball like a hound, fell on it at the Miami forty-eight. But Don Porter had been offside, so the play did not count.

The spell that had been cast over the Viking offense still hung over the field. With six and a half minutes left, Fran Tarkenton, in a final desperate effort to close the gap, let fly a beautiful long pass to Jim Lash, who had no one to keep him from going all the way home. But Jim, who may have been conditioned to Fran's cut-rate passes, or may simply have been bewitched, slowed down before he got to where the ball was headed, and Curtis Johnson, the Miami defender, helped himself to it. After that, for six mortal minutes, the Dolphins just clung to the football and ground out yardage enough to keep title to it.

Red Smith, *New York Times* sports columnist, who had been watching football since before any of the players were born, wrote a vivid two-word description of the game: "A disaster."

Super Bowl Number IX, played in the early days of 1975, between Pittsburgh and Minnesota, was not a disaster exactly. But Bud Grant, the Viking coach, who had been in on Number VIII and lost this one, too, looked back on it with controlled enthusiasm.

"It was not a very good game," he said. Pressed to expand his description, he characterized it thus: "A succession of errors by all *three* teams." The third team he referred to was the team of officials who made a number of calls that Bud disagreed with. Most notable was a "dead ball" call on what all the Vikings, some of the spectators, and probably a few of the Pittsburghers too, thought was a fumble. Larry Brown, the Steeler tight end, belted to the ground by the defenders as he tried to advance the football, lost his grip on the ball and saw it bound away. The nearest official ruled it a fumble, with Minnesota recovering on its own twenty-eight-yard line. But the referee, across the field, and behind the play, decided that Brown had hit the ground before the ball came loose and so still owned it.

But changing a few official decisions would not have been of much help to Minnesota. The New Orleans turf, well soaked by an early morning rain, proved wonderfully slippery, so that ball-carriers who tried to skirt the ends often found their feet flying out from under them before an enemy had even made contact. Even so the Minnesota offense was wonderfully inept. Terry Bradshaw, the Steelers' quick-footed quarterback, outgained the entire Minnesota team on the ground with twenty-four yards to their seventeen.

Bill Brown of Minnesota fumbled the second-half kick-off, pursued it a few yards and saw big Marv Kellum of Pittsburgh capture it on the Viking thirty-yard line. Franco Harris soon carried the ball to the Viking six and two plays later ran around left end for a touchdown.

Chuck Foreman, Minnesota's all-pro ball-carrier and receiver, fumbled on the Steeler five, with a touchdown in sight. Fran Tarkenton performed the weirdest play of the game, and perhaps the season, by "completing" a pass to himself. When he let the ball go, it was deflected by L. C. Greenwood, Pittsburgh's mile-high defensive end. The ball came right back to Fran, who ran off with it and let it fly forty yards downfield to John Gilliam. But the officials would not let John have it. It was illegal, they said, to pass the ball forward twice on the same play.

Poor Fran had actually scored the first points of the game, but he scored them for Pittsburgh when he attempted a pitch-out to running back Dave Osborn, lost his grip on the ball, and sent it rolling back into his own end zone. Fran scampered after the ball and recaptured it, but he was promptly dumped to the ground and scored a safety for the other side.

It was no wonder then that Bud Grant rated the game so low in interest. The Steelers thought it was a very good game indeed. They won it, 16 to 6. And this time there were no "distractions." Both coaches, Chuck Noll of Pittsburgh and Bud Grant of Minnesota, shut the wives out of the players' rooms the night before the game.

Super Bowl X, played in January, 1976, on the slightly played-out factory-made turf of the Orange Bowl in Miami, saw Pittsburgh back once more after the trophy. This time they faced the Dallas Cowboys who had been here twice before and had won in their last appearance, four years earlier. The Steelers looked about the same as they had the year before, with Terry Bradshaw running the offense and Rocky Bleier and Franco Harris pawing the ground in the backfield. Dallas no longer had Duane Thomas or Calvin Hill to carry the ball for them nor Lance Alworth to lope down the field after Staubach's bombs.

But Roger the Dodger was in top form, ready to use his shotgun formation (when the coach required it) and schooled not to try to run *too* much on his own. His new receiver was Preston Pearson, a running back out of Pittsburgh and Baltimore, who was still getting used to the complexities of Coach Tom Landry's attack.

"When I was in Baltimore," said Preston, "the quarterback's call was a sentence long. Here it's a whole paragraph!"

No one could have said that this Super Bowl was dull or disastrous. It was neck-and-neck the whole way, with plenty of passing, a quarterback knocked clean out of the game, frantic defenses, new records for sacking of the quarterback, another for catching passes, and only two penalties all afternoon. Besides, the movie makers were there to film crowd scenes for "Black Sunday" and kept everybody wondering if perhaps they were going to stage the killings too.

The Cowboys, who were destined to lose the game, led by three points in the last period and even at the end they were just thirty-eight yards away from victory, when Glen Edwards of Pittsburgh grabbed off a Staubach pass in the end zone. Pittsburgh in the final quarter scored fourteen points the hard way — with two field goals, a safety, and a touchdown. But Tom Landry, the Dallas coach, said the safety was what turned everything around.

This score came as a result of a kick, blocked by a second-string running back

Pro football's newest left-handed quarterback is Jim Zorn of the Seattle Seahawks. When he displayed his skills against the New York Giants at Giants stadium in 1976, the home fans began to chant: ''We want Zorn!'' Here he is getting ready to pass in a game against the Green Bay Packers.

named Reggie Harrison, and called Booby by his teammates because he did not always keep close track of what was going on around him. He blocked Mitch Hoopes's kick by charging right straight into the blocker and running over him. Once past the blocker, Harrison saw Hoopes all unguarded ahead, just taking his first step. Harrison got both hands up and told himself that that kick was not going to get off — NO way! It didn't. It smacked into Harrison and bounced clear back out of the end zone, to give Pittsburgh two points. Harrison never noticed that there was a

score. He pranced yelling and screaming to the bench, so overcome with happiness that he felt no pain.

''I thought I blocked the kick with my hands,'' he said. ''But my tongue is split right down the middle!'' When the Pittsburgh club scored on a field goal after that, and the scoreboard showed his club ahead 12 to 7, Harrison could not understand why they should get five points for a field goal. His teammates enjoyed explaining to him that he had scored two points himself.

The defensive feature of the game was

There were more thrills in the Oakland-New England playoff game that preceded Super Bowl XI than there were in the Super Bowl itself. Here Sam Hunt, New England linebacker, bats down a Stabler pass. Later in the game, in a play much like this, New England was called for roughing the passer — and they lost the game as a result.

the wholesale sacking of Roger Staubach, who was caught behind the line with the ball in his hands seven separate times. Assistant coach Woody Widenhofer of Pittsburgh explained that it was the shotgun formation that made this possible.

"There's no way you can run off the shotgun," he said, "so we could tee off on Staubach."

The offensive highlight was a hair-raising catch by little Lynn Swann, who is built more like a TV announcer than a wide receiver. Lynn plucked a Terry Bradshaw pass right off the ear of the man who was

covering him, Mark Washington. The pass had traveled fifty-nine yards in the air. Lynn traveled five more yards to make it worth six points. Meanwhile, back at the scrimmage line, a horde of enemy rushers had burst in upon Terry Bradshaw and separated him from his sense. He wobbled about a while, then gave the job over to understudy Terry Hanratty.

But everyone, even Bradshaw, and even the losers, enjoyed this game, which kept the crowd yelling from beginning to end. After it was over, Tom Landry vowed it had been a fine exhibition, all turning on that blocked kick, that cost them, in the end, five points. (The Steelers returned the free kick that followed the safety, right back almost within field goal range.) Mike Wagner, the Steeler who had completed his sixth year in the league, declared it had been a treat to see those marvelous sets and formations Tom Landry went in for. "Their game is so interesting, so calculated!" he exclaimed.

The season that followed was loaded with strange events and alive with bristling competition that proved what the cliché collectors had long propounded — that "any team in the league could beat any other team on any given Sunday." Even the New York Giants, whose quarterback, Craig Morton, became so engorged with rage and frustration one day that he stood up and threw a punch — not at an opponent or an official, but at the crowd! He missed by eighty yards — changed coaches in time to beat the Washington Redskins, a contending club. (The coach they let go, Bill Arnsparger, thought so little of his team's chances that he once refused a penalty that would have given his club third down and about eighteen yards to go instead of fourth down with twenty-three. Apparently he *knew* they could never complete a pass on third and long. The punt he had decided for was blocked.)

Early in the season the Baltimore Colts lost their coach, nearly lost their general manager, almost lost their entire team, got their coach back, lost their coach again, then got their coach, Ted Marchibroda, back for good. Ted, named Coach of the Year in 1975, had quit rather than put up with verbal abuse from the ownership for losing *exhibition games!* The management accepted Marchibroda's resignation twice. The team growled about boycotting practice. Quarterback Bert Jones, after allowing that someone might have been drinking too

much and that he was on the coach's side, walked into the office of General Manager Joe Thomas and talked Thomas into making peace. Marchibroda came back and very nearly brought his team into the playoff finals.

The club that threw a halter on the Colts in the playoffs was the Pittsburgh Steelers, who saved no one knows how many lives in that game by beating the Colts by so wide a margin that the stands were nearly emptied before the game was over. A good thing, too, for a light airplane chose the final moments of the game to buzz the field where the contest was held — Memorial Stadium in Baltimore. Fifteen minutes after the game was over, when the seats might still have been partially filled with fans edging toward the gates, the plane settled like an Alfred Hitchcock butterfly into the upper deck of the stadium. The stands being almost barren of human life, no one was hurt except for three policemen, two of whom were overcome by gasoline fumes and one of whom was cut when a piece of the plane's wing sheared off and struck him. The pilot, to the satisfaction of many who saw the crash, was knocked unconscious. Nobody wanted him killed. But a good hard bump on the head — well, that might have put some sense back into him.

The Buffalo Bills, who were never in contention for a playoff spot, still managed to help O. J. Simpson to the biggest days of his career — his football career that is, for O.J. had two more careers, one as a movie star and another as a star in TV commercials where he limbered up by leaping over airport ticket counters. On November 25, O.J. gained 273 yards while the Bills were losing to the Detroit Lions. That was the most he had ever gained in one game and it was the fifth game in which he had gained over 200 yards. And *that* was a league record too. Even the enemy crowd rejoiced with him, standing en masse to chant "Juice! Juice!" in his honor.

Late in the season it was whispered that George Allen was finished as the coach of the Redskins, inasmuch as his club, having lost to the Giants, seemed shut out of even the "wildcard" spot in the playoffs. But George, who was too wily a man to surrender while he still had a shot in his locker, remembered that there was a player on the loose who was skilled at blocking punts — and that a blocked punt could save a season sometimes. So he called up Bill Malinchak, who had been cut from the squad more than a year before, and talked him into playing football again. Bill rejoined the team and promptly blocked a punt that enabled the Redskins to beat the favored Dallas Cowboys and earn a spot in the playoffs. And George, who had never known a losing season since he became a head coach, had another one.

The teams that got into the Super Bowl, however, were the Minnesota Vikings, who had been there three times before, and the Oakland Raiders who had been there only in the dim past, and then had fallen victim to Vince Lombardi's Green Bay Packers, who were beating everybody in sight anyway. This time the Raiders, having made it right to the threshold of the Super Bowl more times than they wanted to talk about, were perhaps the most wildly motivated club — except for the New York Jets in 1969 — who had ever played in this game.

Never before had there been a more vivid demonstration of the value of emotion in football. Facing what was supposed to have been the toughest defense in the league — including Alan Page, Carl Eller, and Jim Marshall, who ate quarterbacks and ball-carriers alive—the Raiders picked out the weak spot and just walloped it until they got what they wanted. Even Page, who was not a heavy man but agile and fast as a catamount, seemed "easy" to the aroused Oakland offense. Arthur Shell, the monstrous offensive tackle for the Raiders, who was said to strip at about fifteen pounds less than three hundred, acted as if he had never heard of the prowess of old Jim Marshall, nearing his fortieth birthday and giving away almost seventy pounds, who played opposite Shell at defensive end. The "people eaters" this time had lost some of their appetite, having sat down at the table a few too many times.

The game was played in the Rose Bowl — up to then inviolate from professional athletics. But this year, all was different. The local excitement was three points above fever heat. The local big spenders were hauling in "business associates" by the jet-plane-load. Twenty-dollar tickets could be had for $100 outside the gate and there were none for sale at the ticket offices, even though the Rose Bowl seats over 103,000. There was a zoom camera aboard the Goodyear blimp, in order to provide still another far-out view of the action to the TV audience. The image of the game was broadcast throughout the world to a scattering of watchers estimated at five million. The worst snowstorm of the year had so paralyzed most of the nation that there was no place to go but the TV set anyway, so the national audience was probably the greatest ever. It was also the biggest betting event of the season. (At least a billion dollars wagered, said the man from Las Vegas.)

The game was not the greatest, except from the point of view of the Oakland fans. Actually the playoff game against the Patriots that had earned this game for the Raiders was far more exciting, far more closely contested, far more "physical," and much longer argued over.

But the Super Bowl was a good game,

without the usual timid sparring and shadow boxing that had spoiled some other Super Bowls as too-cautious coaches waited for the other guy to make a mistake. This time excitable John Madden (he could not swallow his breakfast) who coached Oakland, and cool, cool Bud Grant (he never raised his voice or cracked a smile) who coached the Vikings, were both out to win from the first kick-off. Both quarterbacks were individually motivated — Ken Stabler because his skills had never been properly honored and Fran Tarkenton because of the "loser" tag that clung to him season after season as he "failed to win the big ones."

The Oakland plan right from the start was to run to the left where that great big tackle named Shell was counted on to blast open holes for them or keep Jim Marshall on his own side of the scrimmage line. So Ken Stabler aimed his attack that way and really overwhelmed the enemy. At half-time they were ahead 16 to 0, for the new three-four defense Oakland had adopted shut off those short passes Tarkenton had always made so much hay with, and choked off the Viking running attack as well. (A good part of the Minnesota "running" attack had included short flips to Chuck Foreman, who specialized in carrying the ball a long way after he caught it.)

In the third quarter the Vikings did seem to get some traction under their wheels and they drew as close as they were ever going to get — seven points to nineteen. But then two men named Willie — Willie Hall and Willie Brown — took turns stealing passes from Fran Tarkenton and the Minnesota attack dropped dead. Fran had been passing on every down and had moved the ball fifty-eight yards in twelve plays before spinning the ball to Sammy White for a touchdown. But when he got the ball back and started passing again, Willie Hall

moved in front of one and carried it to midfield. Stabler immediately fired the ball to Fred Biletnikoff, his free-thinking receiver (Fred liked to slit his uniform pants down the back of each leg to give him "freedom") and Fred set it on the two-yard line, whence Pete Banascak transported it into the Viking end-zone.

Once more Fran Tarkenton came out throwing. This time Willie Brown interrupted the proceedings with a grab and run that carried him seventy-five yards for still another Oakland touchdown. That was the longest run with an interception that had ever been seen in a Super Bowl.

Poor Fran Tarkenton, a man who had never missed a game because of injury in all the seventeen seasons he had been playing the game, was taken out in the final quarter and watched glumly from the sideline as back-up quarterback Bob Lee passed to tight end Stu Voigt for a touchdown that was not nearly enough to do any good. The final score was Oakland 32, Minnesota 14. The Raiders had gained 429 yards altogether, more than the Vikings used to give up in three or four games. This was another Super Bowl record. There was also a record of some sort between the halves, when Boy Scouts managed to distribute 125,000 varicolored "flash cards" so the spectators might participate in forming some spectacular designs, on signal, to amaze the TV audience. (About ninety percent of the spectators cooperated in this performance.)

The Raiders had done about everything to the Vikings. In addition to intercepting the crucial passes, they blocked a punt by Ray Guy — the first he had ever had blocked in four seasons. Linebacker Phil Villapiano had stripped Viking running back Brent McLanahan (who *never* fumbled) of the football at the line of scrimmage, inside the Viking five-yard line. And punt-returner Neal Colzie had made two spectacular punt returns that led quickly to scores. Ken Stabler completed ten passes out of fifteen, six of them in a row. But one thing the Raiders could not manage. When they paraded, rejoicing, from the field, they tried to put big John Madden, the happy coach, on their shoulders to lead the procession. When they got him shoulder high, they lost their grip and dropped him. And far away, at San Clemente, a famous football fan celebrated his sixty-fourth birthday, sitting alone before the TV. Nobody at the game remembered to wish ex-President Nixon Many Happy Returns.

There were no spectacular innovations in the play that day — nothing like Hank Stram's tight-end I formation and "Kansas City stack" defense that had highlighted the 1970 Super Bowl. The Minnesota Vikings, who had lost that one too, were still concentrating on old-fashioned football and about all the Oakland Raiders displayed that was new for the seventies was their three-four defense, that had been in use all over the league. But the game was still the same. It still required men to have at each other with unbridled ferocity, either to clear a way for the ball-carrier or to bring him down to stay. It was still a spectacle of mass violence, not always controlled (George Atkinson, whom some coaches rated as a sort of hired hit-man, still provided pass coverage for the Raiders). But it really was not a means of treating blood-thirsty spectators to visions of mayhem and the letting of gore. It was *victory* the fans truly desired, and they would accept it just as gladly at the hands of a bumbling official. To triumph over some enemy or obstacle, and to do so in common with one's kind — that is what sports fans thirst for endlessly, seeking it season after season, as long as the sun keeps coming up.

The best running quarterback in the game, according to New England fans, is young Steve Grogan of the Patriots. Here Steve, his eyes closed against the sun, tries in vain to sprint out of the grasp of Jim Merlo, New Orleans linebacker.

INDEX